Human–Computer Interaction Series

The Human–Computer Interaction Series, launched in 2004, publishes books that advance the science and technology of developing systems which are effective and satisfying for people in a wide variety of contexts. Titles focus on theoretical perspectives (such as formal approaches drawn from a variety of behavioural sciences), practical approaches (such as techniques for effectively integrating user needs in system development), and social issues (such as the determinants of utility, usability and acceptability).

HCI is a multidisciplinary field and focuses on the human aspects in the development of computer technology. As technology becomes increasingly more pervasive the need to take a human-centred approach in the design and development of computer-based systems becomes ever more important.

Titles published within the Human–Computer Interaction Series are included in Thomson Reuters' Book Citation Index, The DBLP Computer Science Bibliography and The HCI Bibliography.

More information about this series at http://www.springer.com/series/6033

Tracy Hammond · Manoj Prasad ·
Anna Stepanova
Editors

Inspiring Students with Digital Ink

Impact of Pen and Touch on Education

Springer

Editors
Tracy Hammond
Sketch Recognition Lab, Department of
Computer Science and Engineering
Texas A&M University
College Station, TX, USA

Manoj Prasad
Customer Experience, Universal Store
Microsoft United States
Redmond, WA, USA

Anna Stepanova
Sketch Recognition Lab, Department of
Computer Science and Engineering
Texas A&M University
College Station, TX, USA

ISSN 1571-5035 ISSN 2524-4477 (electronic)
Human–Computer Interaction Series
ISBN 978-3-030-17397-5 ISBN 978-3-030-17398-2 (eBook)
https://doi.org/10.1007/978-3-030-17398-2

This Springer imprint is published by the registered company Springer Nature Switzerland AG
The registered company address is: Gewerbestrasse 11, 6330 Cham, Switzerland

Preface

Ken Forbus, Ph.D., 2017 Conference on Pen and Touch Technology (CPTTE) conference chair, is one of the founding researchers of the field of pen-and-touch research. He has had a long and continuous impact on the work of many. Ken's work on spatial and qualitative reasoning has impacted my work in sketch recognition. I remember my first discussions with Ken at the weekly CSAIL/AI MIT Friday GSB (Girl Scout Benefit), these discussions occurred while I was a graduate student, and he was already a full professor at Northwestern, visiting us from time-to-time. Thank you, Ken, for hosting the fruitful 2017 conference, upon which we have based this manuscript.

The 2017th CPTTE conference marks the 11th annual iteration of this conference. The meeting began as a workshop, and this marks the second year as a conference. This manuscript also marks the fourth CPTTE manuscript as part of Springer's Human–Computer Interaction series. The first CPTTE book in the series entitled "The Impact of Pen and Touch Technology on Education," reported the contents of 2 years of the workshop, 2013 and 2014 (Hammond et al. 2015), focusing mainly on the accepted paper presentations. The second book entitled "Revolutionizing Education with Digital Ink" (Hammond et al. 2016), reported on the workshop in 2015, including results from a high school contest directing high school students to come up with creative new pen-and-touch education solutions for the future. The third book entitled "Frontiers of Pen and Touch," reported on the results of now-termed "conference" in 2016 (Hammond et al. 2017) and encompassed not only papers but also keynote talks and panel transcriptions. This book, "Inspiring Students through Digital Ink," covers the results of the 2017 conference chaired by Ken Forbus, including two insightful keynote reports as well as the updated accepted papers.

While I enjoyed editing all of the manuscripts, this manuscript was particularly enjoyable. I appreciated reviewing the two keynotes who described excellent work close to my own heart and inspirational to my work in haptics (Prasad et al. 2014a, b, c, d; Cummings et al. 2012) and sketching forensics (Polsley et al. 2016;

Hammond 2017). Of special meaning to me is that Tom Stahovich, keynote speaker, and I shared a dissertation adviser, Dr. Randy Davis, at MIT CSAIL/AI Lab.

All accepted papers in this manuscript (and the three books prior) were complete and peer-reviewed before being accepted for presentation at the conference. The authors were invited to do minor edits before publication based on feedback during the sessions. Some of the talks highlighted previously published work. In such works, to be included here, the authors wrote a uniquely new (again peer-reviewed) paper. The keynote speakers edited their transcribed talks, which were then peer-reviewed after completion. Each manuscript took a long time to collect, prepare, and edit, with each one taking over a year to complete.

One testament to the quality of these works is the total number of reads and references to these still newly published works, with "The Impact of Pen and Touch Technology on Education" having 40,233 downloads between 2015 and 2018, "Revolutionizing Education with Digital Ink" having 17,256 between 2016 and 2018, and "Frontiers in Pen and Touch" having 4277 between 2017 and 2018.

I continue to re-reference and re-read these books, and I continue to be surprised at the breadth and depth of the work described in these four books. The conference has involved many movers and shakers of the educational technology community, with the ideas continuing to impact forward-thinking.

Several technologies have continued to support this work over the years, with Microsoft (Windows, OneNote, Surface, and Research) at the front of the pack, and also Wacom, Dyknow, Fujitsu, Samsung, PDF Annotator, and HP being top supporters. We also recognize the efforts of Ken Forbus, Andy van Dam, Jonathan Grudin, Mark Payton, Eric Hamilton, and Kimberle Koile. Those members chaired recent conferences or participated in almost all of the eleven meetings. Thank you also to the paper chairs and co-editors of these many volumes, including Anna Stepanova, Manoj Prasad, Aaron Adler, Mark Payton, and Stephanie Valentine. Thank you to Beverly Ford, our initial Springer contact, for helping us with this book series. Thank you to David Hoeft for videotaping the sessions. Thank you also to the Sketch Recognition Lab for your endless dedication. Thank you to my husband, Dan, and my parents for continuous support during the countless editing hours. Thank you to my newborn, Roxy, and toddler, Ziggy, for smiles while playing under my feet.

I first entered the field of pen-and-touch in August of 2000, and I gave my first academic presentation in 2002. I remember the struggle to convince colleagues that the tablet-PC would be a part of the future. The death of the Apple Newton was close in their minds, and the world was now obsessed with the circular dial of the newly invented iPod. We are finally at the cusp of change, where pen-and-touch laptops are no longer a niche product, but now standard fare within the classroom. As such, we are now starting to see a plethora of research papers dominating the other conferences at lightning pace. Researchers, educators, and students are responding to the educational benefits provided by pen-and-touch computers, and change is occurring. I am excited to be part of this new world we are currently changing as well as the future we are creating.

Most of all, thank you to the pen-and-touch community for the impact you have made on the world thus far.

College Station, USA Prof. Dr. Tracy Hammond

References

Hammond T, Valentine S, Adler A et al (2015) The impact of pen and touch technology on education, 1 edn. Human–computer interaction series. Springer, Switzerland. ISBN: 978-3-319-15593-7, http://dx.doi.org/10.1007/978-3-319-15594-4

Hammond T, Valentine S, Adler A (2016) Revolutionizing education with digital ink: the impact of pen and touch technology on education, 1 edn. Human–computer interaction series. Springer, Switzerland. ISBN: 978-3319311913, http://dx.doi.org/10.1007/978-3-319-31193-7

Hammond T, Adler A, Prasad M (2017) Frontiers of pen and touch: impact of pen and touch technology on education, 1 edn. Human–computer interaction series. Springer, Switzerland. ISBN: 978-3-319-64238-3, https://doi.org/10.1007/978-3-319-64239-0

Prasad M, Russell M, Hammond T (2014) Designing vibrotactile codes to communicate verb phrases. ACM Trans Multimedia Comput Commun Appl (TOMM) 11(1):11.1–11.21. ISSN: 1551-6857, http://doi.acm.org/10.1145/2637289

Prasad M, Russell M, Hammond T (2014) A user centric model to design tactile codes with shapes and waveforms. In: Haptics symposium (HAPTICS), pp 597–602. IEEE, Houston, TX, USA. ISBN: 978-1-4799-3131-6

Prasad M, Taele P, Goldberg D, et al (2014) Turn-by-turn haptic route guidance interface for motorcyclists. In: Proceedings of the 32nd annual ACM conference on human factors in computing systems (CHI), pp 3597–3606. ACM, Toronto, Canada, Canada. ISBN: 978-1-4503-2473-1

Prasad M, Taele P, Olubeku A et al (2014) Haptigo: a navigational 'tap on the shoulder'. In: Haptics symposium (HAPTICS), pp 339–345. IEEE, Houston, TX, USA. ISBN: 978-1-4799-3131-6

Cummings D, Lucchese G, Prasad M et al (2012) Haptic and ar interface for paratrooper coordination. In: Proceedings of the 13th international conference of the NZ chapter of the ACM's special interest group on human-computer interaction (CHINZ), pp 52–55. ACM, Dunedin, New Zealand, New Zealand. ISBN: 978-1-4503-1474-9

Polsley S, Ray J, Nelligan T et al (2016) Leveraging trends in student interaction to enhance the effectiveness of sketch-based educational software. In: Hammond T, Valentine S (eds) Revolutionizing education with digital ink: the impact of pen and touch technology on education, Human–computer interaction series, Chap. 7, pp 103–114. Springer, Switzerland. ISBN: 978-3-319-31193-7, http://dx.doi.org/10.1007/978-3-319-31193-7_7

Hammond T (2017) Learning through the lens of sketch. In: Hammond T, Prasad M (eds) Frontiers in pen and touch: impact of pen and touch technology on education, Human–computer interaction series, Chap. 21, pp 301–341. Springer, Switzerland. ISBN: 978-3-319-64239-0, https://doi.org/10.1007/978-3-319-64239-0_21

Contents

Editors and Contributors

About the Editors

Prof. Dr. Tracy Hammond was the chair of the 2014 Workshop on the Impact of Pen and Touch Technology in Education as well as an editor of the manuscripts produced from the outcomes of the five conferences since 2013. Director of the Sketch Recognition Lab and Professor in the Department of Computer Science and Engineering at Texas A&M University, Dr. Hammond is an international leader in sketch recognition and human–computer interaction research. Her sketch recognition research has been funded by NSF, DARPA, Google, Microsoft, and many others, totaling over 9 million dollars in peer-reviewed funding. She holds a Ph.D. in Computer Science and FTO (Finance Technology Option) from M.I.T., and four degrees from Columbia University: an M.S. in Anthropology, an M.S. in Computer Science, a B.A. in Mathematics, and a B.S. in Applied Mathematics. Prior to joining the TAMU CSE faculty in 2006, Dr. Hammond taught for 5 years at Columbia University and was a telecom analyst for 4 years at Goldman Sachs. Dr. Hammond is the 2011–2012 recipient of the Charles H. Barclay, Jr. '45 Faculty Fellow Award. The Barclay Award is given to professors and associate professors who have been nominated for their overall contributions to the Engineering Program through classroom instruction, scholarly activities, and professional service.

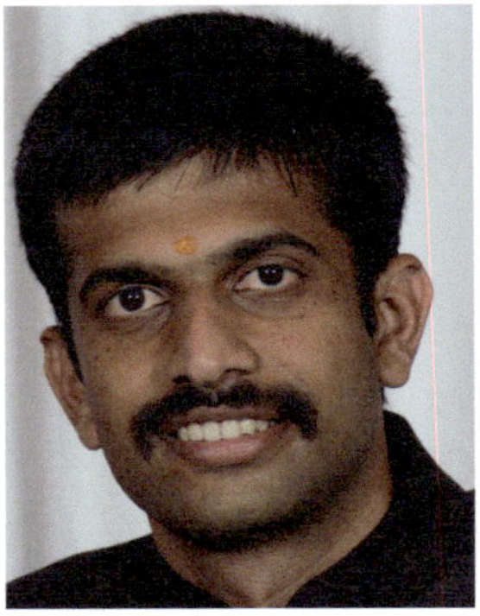

Dr. Manoj Prasad is a software developer in MSEG Customer Experiences R&D, Microsoft and researcher collaborating with Dr. Tracy Hammond, Sketch Recognition Lab. He holds a Ph.D. in Computer Science from Texas A&M University and a Bachelor's degree in Computer Science from Birla Institute of Technology and Science. His research interests include haptic user interfaces and sketch recognition. His dissertation involved creation of a haptic jacket for motorcyclists navigation (HaptiMoto) and pedestrian navigation (HaptiGo). This work was published in ACM CHI, a renowned conference in Interaction space. He is currently working on a sketching interface for an application in Windows. This application will let support agents remote into customer's box and annotate on the customer's screen to guide them to their support issue.

Dr. Anna Stepanova is a researcher at the Sketch Recognition Lab at Texas A&M University. She holds a Ph.D. in Geology from the Paleontological Institute of the Russian Academy of Sciences, as well as a Master's and a Bachelor's degrees in geology from Moscow State University. Anna's research interests are in geosciences and education. Anna has worked on various projects as an editor, including editing the previous volumes of the Impact of Pen and Touch Technology on Education series. She published more than 10 papers as a first author, including a monograph, in peer-reviewed international journals.

Contributors

Alexander Berman Department of Computer Science and Engineering, Texas A&M University, College Station, TX, USA

Josiah Coad Department of Computer Science and Engineering, Texas A&M University, College Station, TX, USA

J. Edward Colgate Northwestern University, Evanston, IL, USA

Elizabeth Cowan eGrove Education, San Diego, CA, USA

Nathan Delson UCSD, La Jolla, CA, USA

Sheelabhadra Dey Department of Computer Science and Engineering, Texas A&M University, College Station, TX, USA

Leela Krishna Chaitanya Gottumukkala Department of Computer Science and Engineering, Texas A&M University, College Station, TX, USA

Eric Hamilton Pepperdine University, Malibu, CA, USA

Tracy Hammond Sketch Recognition Lab, Department of Computer Science and Engineering, Texas A&M University, College Station, TX, USA

Jorge Iván Herrera-Cámara Sketch Recognition Lab, Department of Computer Science and Engineering, Texas A&M University, College Station, TX, USA

Ethan Hilton College of Engineering and Science, Louisiana Tech University, Ruston, LA, USA

Zepeng Huo Department of Computer Science and Engineering, Texas A&M University, College Station, TX, USA

Prateek Jukalkar South Fayette School District, McDonald, PA, USA

Loide Kapenda Ministry of Education, Arts, and Culture, Windhoek, Namibia

Wayne Li School of Industrial Design, Georgia Institute of Technology, Atlanta, GA, USA

Julie Linsey George W. Woodruff School of Mechanical Engineering, Georgia Institute of Technology, Atlanta, GA, USA

Wayne T. Marko Engineering, Math & Physical Sciences Division, College of Lake County, Grayslake, IL, USA

Bob Mihelich McHenry County College, Crystal Lake, IL, USA

Helena Miranda University of Namibia, Windhoek, Namibia

Savinay Narendra Department of Computer Science and Engineering, Texas A&M University, College Station, TX, USA

Chitra Nayak Tuskegee University, Tuskegee, AL, USA

Elizabeth Ngololo University of Namibia, Windhoek, Namibia

Aileen Owens South Fayette School District, McDonald, PA, USA

Seth Polsley Sketch Recognition Lab, Department of Computer Science and Engineering, Texas A&M University, College Station, TX, USA

Manoj Prasad Microsoft, Redmond, WA, USA

Francis Quek Department of Visualization, Texas A&M University, College Station, TX, USA

Samantha Ray Sketch Recognition Lab, Department of Computer Science and Engineering, Texas A&M University, College Station, TX, USA

Matthew Runyon Sketch Recognition Lab, Department of Computer Science and Engineering, Texas A&M University, College Station, TX, USA

Parv Shrivastava South Fayette School District, McDonald, PA, USA

John Solomon Tuskegee University, Tuskegee, AL, USA

Thomas Stahovich University of California, Riverside, USA

Anna Stepanova Sketch Recognition Lab, Department of Computer Science and Engineering, Texas A&M University, College Station, TX, USA

Lelli Van Den Einde UCSD, La Jolla, CA, USA

Blake Williford Sketch Recognition Lab, Department of Computer Science and Engineering, Texas A&M University, College Station, TX, USA

Part I
Introductions and Welcome

Chapter 1
Inspiring Students Through Digital Ink: An Introduction

Anna Stepanova, Manoj Prasad and Tracy Hammond

Abstract Derived from contributions to the Conference on Pen and Touch Technology in Education (CPTTE) in 2017, this edited volume highlights recent developments for pen and tablet research within the domains of computer science, education, and outreach. This book will be of great interest for researchers and educators at every level. The book includes seven sections and explores topics on sketching forensics in education, sketch recognition and teaching STEM through sketch, teaching sketching skills, creating your learning environment with sketching, and forward directions with haptics. In this book, you will find new ideas and future perspectives in digital learning.

1.1 Introduction

This monograph represents a collection of papers from 2017 Conference on the Impact of Pen and Touch Technology on Education (CPTTE) held from October 12 through October 14, 2017, at Northwestern University Campus in Evanston, Illinois. The conference was chaired by Dr. Kenneth Forbus, Walter P. Murphy Professor of Computer Science and Professor of Education at Northwestern University. The paper chairs were Dr. Aaron Adler, Scientist at BBN Technologies and Dr. Manoj Prasad, Software Engineer, Microsoft Research Collaborator.

The 2017 CPTTE was the last of the eleven annual instantiations of the conference organized first as a workshop in 2006. The conference was held in a different location each year and highlighted research and applications of ink-based computing, contin-

A. Stepanova · T. Hammond (✉)
Sketch Recognition Lab, Department of Computer Science and Engineering, Texas A&M University, College Station, TX, USA
e-mail: hammond@tamu.edu

A. Stepanova
e-mail: anna_stepanova@tamu.edu

M. Prasad
Microsoft, 14820 NE 36th Street, Building 99, Redmond, WA 98052, USA
e-mail: dasarpjonam@gmail.com

T. Hammond et al. (eds.), *Inspiring Students with Digital Ink*, Human–Computer Interaction Series, https://doi.org/10.1007/978-3-030-17398-2_1

uing to demonstrate that pen-based computing holds several significant advantages over traditional keyboard/mouse interfaces for promoting student learning and effective educational practice. These applications motivate a new landscape, in which such interfaces will alter the use of technology and enable more effective collaboration and learning experiences. The conference and this resulting manuscript defines how pen and touch computing are positively impacting the whole of education.

1.2 CPTTE 2017 Venue

CPTTE 2017 was held at Northwestern University in Evanston, Illinois. Northwestern University is a private institution that was founded in 1851. It was ranked #11 in the National Universities category in the 2018 edition of Best Colleges. Northwestern is one of the leading research universities with a comprehensive doctoral program and one of the most selective undergraduate programs in the United States. It is famous for its vibrant campus life and beautiful views of Lake Michigan, highlighting its rich historic and cultural setting.

1.3 CPTTE 2017 Keynotes

In 2017, the conference had two keynote speakers. Dr. Thomas Stahovich gave a keynote talk on Thursday morning, the first day of the conference. Dr. Edward Colgate's keynote was on Friday.

Dr. Thomas Stahovich opened the conference with his keynote "The Quantified Student: Using Smartpens and Data Mining to Understand Student Learning and Achievement." He talked about his research approach to using data as an engineer and as a computer scientist. Dr. Stahovich spoke about the effects of study skills on academic achievement, stating that no consistent relationship between the two has been found. He explained that this is due, in part, to the use of research methods that rely on surveys and students' self-reports of study habits. Dr. Stahovich showed his approach to overcome these limitations by using smartpens and an instrumented document viewer to objectively measure studying that enables the use of data mining to examine the relationship between studying and achievement. In his talk he presented novel data mining techniques, as well as the results of several studies that reveal new insights about the relationship between traditional learning activities, completing homework, taking lecture notes, and reading and performance in introductory engineering courses. Finally, Dr. Stahovich discussed the interventions that are based on these insights and are designed to improve student engagement and increase academic achievement.

Dr. Stahovich received a B.S. in Mechanical Engineering from UC Berkeley in 1988. He received an M.S. and Ph.D. in Mechanical Engineering from MIT in 1990 and 1995, respectively. He conducted his doctoral research on computational sketch understanding techniques at the MIT Artificial Intelligence Lab. After serving as an Assistant and Associate Professor of Mechanical Engineering at Carnegie Mellon University in Pittsburgh, PA, Dr. Stahovich joined the Mechanical Engineering Department at UC Riverside in 2003. He also holds cooperative appointments in the Computer Science and Engineering Department and the Electrical Engineering Department at UC Riverside.

Dr. Edward Colgate gave a talk entitled "Touching with Feeling: Bringing Haptics to the Surface" in which he talked about haptics and their vital role in everyday life. He explained, that on the contrary, haptics are decidedly less important when interfacing to the digital world. He showed how our touchscreens treat the finger as a pointer and more-or-less ignore the thousands of mechanoreceptors within, not to mention the somatosensory cortex. Dr. Colgate explained that part of the reason is technological: how do you go beyond simple vibrations and create versatile, programmable haptic experiences? Over the last decade Dr. Edward Colgate and his team focused on solving this question and thinking about how to harness friction to send information back to the finger, harnessing coefficient of friction, normal force, and relative velocity. He described some incipient efforts his research team has made and offered some thoughts for the future.

Dr. Colgate received a S.B. in Physics, S.M. in Mechanical Engineering and a Ph.D. in Mechanical Engineering from MIT. Dr. Colgate is the Allen K. and Johnnie Cordell Breed Senior Professor in Design. Professor Colgate's principal research interest is human-robot interaction. He has worked extensively in the areas of haptic (touch) interface, remote manipulation, and advanced prosthetics. In recent years, Professor Colgate's research has focused on bringing haptic feedback to touch-based interfaces such as touch screens and touch pads.

1.4 CPTTE 2017: You-Try-Its

One of the main benefits of CPTTE conferences is the availability of hands-on learning experiences. Researchers and practitioners present interactive demo sessions where the users can interact with various hardware and software solutions to see how they can apply them in their own classrooms or research. These sessions include both, elements of workshops and courses to facilitate the hands-on learning.

Microsoft supplied tablets for the various demo experiences with all of the sample software preloaded so that every participant could take part in real time no matter what their own personal device was.

You-Try-It: Sketch Worksheets (Ken Forbus and Madeline Usher). Sketch worksheets are a new kind of sketch-based education software designed to facilitate spatial learning. Each worksheet represents a particular exercise, which the student does on a computer. Students get feedback, based on automatic comparison of their sketch with a hidden solution sketch. A software gradebook, which uses scoring rubrics in the solution sketch, is intended to help instructors in grading. Sketch worksheets have been used in classroom experiments with college students and with middle school students. They are domain-independent, requiring only that the exercise involves visual distinctions that the software can understand. This session will provide hands-on experience with sketch worksheets, and with the authoring environment that is used to make them. Participants will be guided through making a simple sketch worksheet themselves, using the authoring environment built into CogSketch, the underlying software. (CogSketch has been developed by the NSF-sponsored Spatial Intelligence and Learning Center, and is freely available online.)

You-Try-It: Pen-Based Video Making with Screen Capture (Eric Hamilton). Eric Hamilton provided an introduction to creating short educational videos, with an emphasis on pen input and video editing, which contribute to rapid video production and high learner engagement. In the limited time provided, participants experienced video making through the screen capturing, pen input, and also through editing multiple video/audio tracks. The activities were heavily scaffolded using premade project templates, where much of the initial learning curve is suspended in order to experience the more creative and engaging aspects of educational media making. Various software were utilized, and alternatives, including free options that were demonstrated and/or displayed. This short session has proven popular in numerous conferences in the US and overseas. The overall effort is connected to a Fulbright research fellowship in sub-Saharan Africa and to a National Science Foundation Cyberlearning project in California and in Nevada. The workshop gave a meaningful initial experience of video making/editing, however, further resources will be provided so that willing participants can master other skills in their own time.

You-Try-It: SketchTivity: Putting the "A" in STEAM Education (Marie Isokpunwu, Randy Brooks, Eric Mott, Blake Williford, Matthew Runyon, and Tracy Hammond). In the era of STEAM education, learning artistic skills, and particularly how to sketch and communicate visually, is increasingly valuable. SketchTivity is a pen-based educational application used at Georgia Tech to teach engineers to draw in 2D-perspective. The system is web-based and can be used on a variety of devices with an internet connection. It guides the user through interactive sketching lessons on the basic fundamentals. It provides sketching challenges as well to encourage creative application of those skills. Lastly, SketchTivity includes a novel sketch-based game called ZenSketch that uses gameplay to encourage quality freehand line work. This application gives students immediate feedback on their sketching by providing relative scores for precision, smoothness, and speed. The use of SketchTivity makes students more comfortable and confident with sketching as well as improve their sketching ability overall. We believe that students can become more expressive communicators and better problem solvers by using this system.

1.5 CPTTE 2017: Socialization

One of the main benefits of the conference is the networking opportunities that encourage university and high school pen and touch researchers to intermingle. CPTTE is unique in that it blends perspectives from a wide variety of researchers, including high school teachers, technology administrators, college deans, university professors, and others interested in pen and touch technology and its impact on education.

The conference provided one socialization session. The first evening of the conference (Thursday) started off with a Reception and Poster Session at Hilton Garden Inn (Evanston, IL). The evening agenda provided networking opportunities for all the participants, from schoolteachers to college deans and professors. About sixty researchers and educators with various backgrounds were discussing innovative technologies for the classroom.

1.6 Monograph Organization

CPTTE 2017 included two keynotes, eight long papers, and three short papers describing new technology in development, practical application of pen and touch technology in education, describing research experiments in the classroom, three You-Try-It sessions, and three highlights of previously published research at other peer reviewed conferences. All paper submissions were peer reviewed by 3–5 expert researchers in the field. Dr. Kenneth Forbus, Dr. Aaron Adler (BBN technology), and Dr. Manoj Prasad (Microsoft) were the Program cochairs of the conference and handled the assignment of the paper reviews. Accepted papers were invited for resubmission as a chapter in this edited volume. Those papers are organized as follows:

Section 1: Introduction. Chapter 1: Inspiring Students through Digital Ink This introductory chapter provides a detailed overview of CPTTE 2017 conference and this book.

Section 2: Sketching Forensics in Education: What we can learn from how you sketch? This section contains an insightful keynote from Tom Stahovich looking at what other information we can gain from pen-based education.

Chapter 2: Keynote. "The Quantified Student: Using Smartpens and Data Mining to Understand Student Learning and Achievement" by Tom Stahovich. In his talk, Tom Stahovich showed novel data mining techniques, as well as the results of several studies that reveal new insights about the relationship between traditional learning activities, such as completing homework, taking lecture notes, reading, and performance in introductory engineering courses. Tom Stahovich pointed out the limitations of research methods that rely on surveys and students' self-reports of study habits. In his work, he overcomes this problem by using smartpens and an instrumented document viewer to objectively measure studying.

Section 3: Teaching STEM through Sketch. This section includes two chapters on various educational tools and applications in higher education classes. In the chapter by John Solomon, Eric Hamilton, and Chitra Nayak, the authors discuss their work on developing a protocol assisting in the preparation of undergraduate students for higher level engineering courses. In the chapter by Eric Hamilton, Loide Kapenda, Helena Miranda, and Elizabeth Ngololo, the authors describe five pen-based media making workshops for teachers and students in Namibia aimed at introducing them to the process of creating and editing instructional videos that incorporate mathematics and science school subject matter.

Chapter 3: "Repairing Misconceptions and Inadequate Preparation in Upper-level Undergraduate Engineering: the KACIE Model and Pen-Based Computing" by John Solomon, Eric Hamilton, and Chitra Nayak. The authors report on an NSF-funded initiative to develop a protocol assisting in the preparation of undergraduate students for higher level engineering courses. They use a number of strategies, referred to as protocols that entail a labor-intensive, methodical, and stepwise approach to working with upper-level students with less course preparation than they should have. The overall approach is referred to as "Knowledge and Curriculum Integration Ecosystem (KACIE) 1 protocol." The paper shows statistically significant learning achievement gains by participants as revealed by pre- and post-testing with a comparison group.

Chapter 4: "Sub-Saharan Teacher STEM Professional Development with Digital Ink: Follow-up" by Eric Hamilton, Loide Kapenda, Helena Miranda, and Elizabeth Ngololo. The authors report on research activities since 2015 WIPTTE conference. The authors received additional funding from the Namibian Ministry of Education, Arts and Culture, the US State Department's Fulbright Program, and new, multiyear funding from NSF. The paper describes the evolution of the project and five themes emerging from it, in addition to describing a new four-year effort related to the original paper. The 2015 paper focused on activities in Kenya, Ghana, Uganda, and Namibia. The present paper centers on follow-up activities in Namibia.

Section 4: Sketch Recognition in STEM. This section includes two chapters on using sketch recognition to develop tools for teaching STEM subjects to undergraduate students. The chapter by Marko Wayne describes Cogsketch—an open domain sketch understanding system to tutor students in the geosciences. In the chapter by Samantha Ray, Jorge Iván Herrera-Cámara, Matthew Runyon, and Tracy Hammond, the authors propose a novel smartphone application Flow2Code that allows users to draw flowchart, take a photo of it, interpret it, generate code, and execute the generated code. In the last chapter of this section the authors Savinay Narendra, Sheelabhadra Dey, Josiah Coad, Seth Polsley, and Tracy Hammond describe an interactive tool Freestyle that allows drawing sketches of web-based HTML elements to transform the sketch into an interface.

Chapter 5: "Qualitative Assessment of CogSketch Worksheets in Introductory Geoscience Laboratory Courses" by Marko Wayne. This chapter reports on the mixed-use of paper-based exercises and tablet PCs equipped with CogSketch—an open domain sketch understanding system to tutor students in the geosciences. The study revealed potential benefits of using CogSketch worksheets that include increased group focus and reduced barriers to starting laboratory exercises without a decrease in grading efficiency. The author suggests that increasing the proportion of CogSketch worksheets used during lab sessions will improve grading efficiency and amplify benefits in classroom social dynamics and teaching efficiency that may lead to learning gains.

Chapter 6: "Flow2Code: Transforming Handdrawn Flowcharts into Executable Code to Enhance Learning" by Samantha Ray, Jorge Iván Herrera-

Cámara, Matthew Runyon, and Tracy Hammond. This work describes a novel smartphone application Flow2Code aimed at assisting in understanding flowcharts when learning to program by depicting algorithms, thus making them easier to read and understand. The authors propose a system that allows users to draw their flowcharts directly on paper, photograph it, and the system interprets it, generates code, and executes the generated code. Flow2Code uses off-line sketch recognition and computer vision algorithms to recognize flowcharts drawn on paper.

Chapter 7: "FreeStyle: A Sketch-based Wireframing Tool" by Savinay Narendra, Sheelabhadra Dey, Josiah Coad, Seth Polsley, and Tracy Hammond. The authors describe a novel wireframing tool Freestyle to design interfaces. The authors believe that sketching the initial design will make the process more intuitive, thus going beyond traditional methods of website interface designing. FreeStyle is an interactive tool that allows designers the ability to quickly sketch a web-based interface electronically and transform it into an interface.

Section 5: Teaching Sketching Skills This section includes two chapters on teaching, sketching, and developing new educational tools with personalized feedback for undergraduate students. Elizabeth Cowan, Nathan Delson, Bob Mihelich, and Lelli Van Den Einde describe an app used in a spatial visualization course at the University of San Diego where students took pre- and post-spatial visualization assessment tests. In the chapter by Ethan Hilton, Blake Williford, Wayne Li, Tracy Hammond, and Julie Linsey the authors report their results on their project SketchTivity—a web-based intelligent tutoring system that utilizes pen and tablet technology to teach students sketching through a series of sketching exercises with feedback.

Chapter 8: "Improvement in Freehand Sketching Application for Spatial Visualization Training" by Elizabeth Cowan, Nathan Delson, Bob Mihelich, and Lelli Van Den Einde. The authors discuss the importance of spatial visualization training and the new application for spatial visualization training application in which students freehand sketch on a touchscreen and receive automatic immediate feedback. In spring 2014, the app was used with iPads in a one unit spatial visualization course where students took pre- and post-spatial visualization assessment tests. In 2014, 46% of the students who scored low on the pre-assessment had a significant improvement of 10% or more on the post-assessment. This chapter describes how the app was modified to increase student gains: the user interface and assignments were modified, taking advantage of color and cues that are not present in traditional paper-based sketching assignments. The spatial visualization course was taught at the University of San Diego with the newly modified app in 2017, during which 82% of incoming students with low spatial skills showed significant improvement. The increase from 46 to 82% is attributed to the capability of pen and touch technology to be adapted effectively for educational purposes.

Chapter 9: "Teaching Engineering Students Freehand Sketching with an Intelligent Tutoring System" by Ethan Hilton, Blake Williford, Wayne Li, Tracy Hammond, and Julie Linsey. The authors discuss the effect of supplementing instructor taught sketching with an online sketching tutor that utilizes artificial intelligence to provide humanlike feedback to user sketches. The authors measured the impact by using pre- and post-course spatial visualization evaluations and sketching quizzes on students who used the online tutor against students who only completed paper-based sketching homework. Significant improvement was recorded for students using the online tutor.

Section 6: Creating your Learning Environment with Sketching This section includes two chapters on using sketching to create a learning environment in K-12 education. In the chapter by Parv Shrivastava, Prateek Jukalkar, and Aileen Owens, the authors describe the personalizing student learning application MyEduDecks deployed in the Spanish language seventh grade classroom. In the chapter by Alexander Berman, Leela Krishna Chaitanya Gottumukkala, Zepeng Huo, Seth Polsley, Francis Quek, and Tracy Hammond, the authors introduce a novel system that allows users to generate customized cartoon avatars through a sketching interface.

Chapter 10: "Personalizing Student Learning and Enhancing Peer-to-Peer Networks through the Pen-Based MyEduDecks Application" by Parv Shrivastava, Prateek Jukalkar, Aileen Owens. The authors present an updated pen-based digital flashcards application that has been in development since 2013 at South Fayette High School. The first iteration of the application was extended to meet the user needs at South Fayette by personalizing student learning and building collaborative networks in the classroom by leveraging pen-based technologies and their benefits. MyEduDecks application uses the Microsoft Ink API to integrate digital ink into the app and encourages the user to use a stylus to input questions and answers in an electronic flashcard format. The paper reported on the progress that has been done on the app development and evaluated its impact on a K-12 learning.

Chapter 11: "iCanTrace: Avatar Personalization through Selfie Sketches" by Alexander Berman, Leela Krishna Chaitanya Gottumukkala, Zepeng Huo, Seth Polsley, Francis Quek, and Tracy Hammond. The authors describe a novel system that allows users to generate customized cartoon avatars through a sketching interface. The authors demonstrated a sketch-guided avatar customization system and its potential to simplify the avatar creation process.

Section 7: Forward Directions with Haptics. One of the main reasons for the increased adoption of Tablet PCs has been the improvement of the feel of the digital pen. Early tablet PCs faced significant complaints that the digital pen and tablet did not have the same touch and feel of natural pen and paper. Haptics is the study of touch. Ed Colgate provides us with an insightful talk about the current state of the art of haptics, describing advancements that go beyond just realistic pen and paper, and describing how our paper can come alive, acting like other materials as well.

Chapter 12: Keynote. "Touching with Feeling: Bringing Haptics to the Surface" by Edward Colgate. Ed Colgate spoke about haptics and their vital role in everyday life. In his talk, he explained the rapidly expanding capabilities of "surface haptic" technologies. Ed Colgate showed how to use haptics to create great experiences for education, entertainment, or elsewhere. He described some incipient efforts and offered some thoughts for the future.

1.7 Conclusion

The 2017 Conference on Pen and Touch Technology in Education brought together a diverse audience of researchers interested in new educational tools and pen and touch technology.

This collection of papers highlights research performed by users, researchers, developers, decision makers, students, and teachers. Scientists shared their experiences on using the pen and touch interfaces across various education settings.

We thank you, the reader, for your growing interest that motivates research and helps us learn and generate new ideas for future directions.

Thank you to Beverly Ford, our initial Springer contact, for helping us with this book series. Thank you, Ken Forbus, for hosting the conference. Thank you to David Hoeft for videotaping the sessions. Thank you to Mark Payton, Jonathan Grudin, and the Sketch Recognition Lab their continued support through the years.

Your editors,
Tracy, Manoj, & Anna

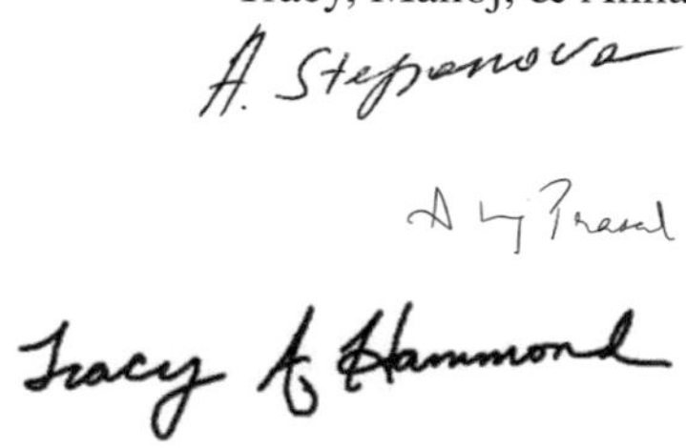

Part II
Sketching Forensics in Education: What We Can Learn from How You Sketch

Chapter 2
The Quantified Student: Using Smartpens and Data Mining to Understand Student Learning and Achievement

Thomas Stahovich

Abstract Dr. Thomas Stahovich gave a keynote in the morning of the first day of the conference. He showed how researchers have long sought to understand the effects of study skills on academic achievement but found no consistent relationship between them. Dr. Stahovich explained that this is due, in part, to the use of research methods that rely on surveys and students' self-reports of study habits. In his work, he overcomes this limitation by using smartpens and an instrumented document viewer to objectively measure studying. This combination of technology provides a fine-grained view of the learning process not available with conventional assessment methods and enables the use of data mining to examine the relationship between studying and achievement. In his talk he presented novel data mining techniques, as well as the results of several studies that reveal new insights about the relationship between traditional learning activities—completing homework, taking lecture notes, and reading—and performance in introductory engineering courses. Finally, Dr. Stahovich discussed interventions that are based on these insights and are designed to improve student engagement and increase academic achievement. This chapter provides an edited transcription of that keynote. Thank you to David Hoeft for videotaping the sessions.

2.1 Keynote Transcript

Dr. Thomas Stahovich: I'm very honored to be here and to have this opportunity to present some of our research examining the relationship between students' study habits and academic achievement. My approach to research is grounded in my background as both a mechanical engineer and a computer scientist. I enjoy solving problems and sifting through data to find the solutions.

Here is an example of a small problem that I recently faced. This is an image of Folsom Lake in California in 2011 (Fig. 2.1). This is the same lake in 2014 during a severe drought in California. The drought had a direct effect on me in the form of my

T. Stahovich (✉)
University of California, Riverside 92521, USA
e-mail: stahov@engr.ucr.edu

T. Hammond et al. (eds.), *Inspiring Students with Digital Ink*, Human–Computer Interaction Series, https://doi.org/10.1007/978-3-030-17398-2_2

Fig. 2.1 Folsom Lake, California in 2011 and 2014. Note the effects of the drought. Image from California department of water resources

Fig. 2.2 Dr. Tom Stahovich showing the Raspberry Pi device he created to measure the water usage at his house

water bill. Because of the drought, Californians were given strict water budgets each month, and exceeding the budget was expensive. I dreaded reading my monthly water bills to see how much water I used, and how much it would cost. After receiving one particularly costly bill, I decided I needed real-time water usage data. I constructed a sensor system, connected it to a Raspberry Pi computer, and installed it next my water meter in the sidewalk in front of my house (see Fig. 2.2). I also obtained evaporation data from the state's weather database allowing me to compute my allowed daily water budget before I received my water bill. That was my last big water bill.

Here is a second example of a much more important problem that data enabled me to solve. I have a family member with Type One Diabetes, the autoimmune disease that cannot be fixed with diet and exercise. For about a week, she was unable to control her blood glucose levels. She tried all of the usual remedies including increasing insulin doses, but nothing worked. She suspected that the insulin had gone bad, but had no data with which to determine this. If insulin gets too warm or too cold, the potency can be greatly diminished. It turned out that a new bottle of insulin did fix the problem. To prevent future problems, and to eliminate uncertainty

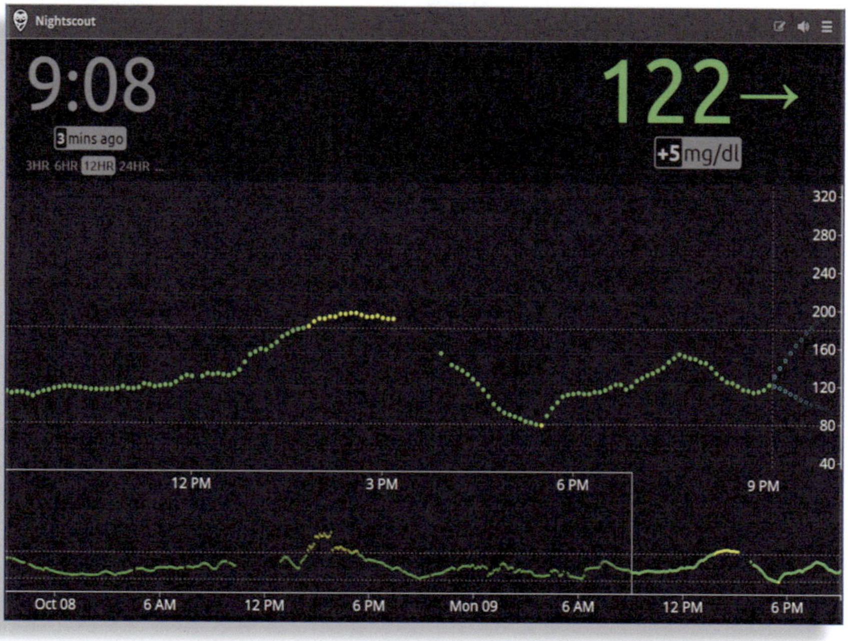

Fig. 2.3 Real-time blood glucose data from a person with type one diabetes

in treatment decisions, I developed a web-enabled temperature controller for a small refrigerator which is now used to store the insulin. The temperature is controlled within about a three-degree temperature range, the temperature data is logged, and the controller sends text and email messages if there are malfunctions.

Having access to data allowed me to fix problems with two devices, my water meter and a refrigerator. Real-time data is now becoming an important part of how we manage our health. For example, Type One diabetics can now wear continuous glucose monitors that provide blood glucose measurements every 5 min (Fig. 2.3). When the blood glucose levels are out of range, the monitor provides an audible alarm enabling one to take corrective action. This is a particularly welcome feature when blood glucose levels fall while one is asleep at night. This notion of data-driven healthcare is expanding are there are commercial efforts to create medical devices that provide live feeds of clinical data to help in monitoring and treating various diseases.

Monitoring of physiological signals has become popular. Many people now use gadgets to track their sleep, exercise, and diet. The "Quantified Self" movement is focused on turning one's life into a set of numbers, enabling one to understand and improve one's health. Athletes now use various kinds of technology including heart rate monitors, accelerometers, power meters, and so on to optimize their performance. *If devices are now widely used to understand our body, why can't we use a similar approach to understand what goes on in our head?*

In my work, I have been developing data-driven approaches to understand how students learn. I am pursuing the notion of the *Quantified Student*. Rather than accelerometers and heart rate monitors, I use digital pens that record what students write when they study, do homework, and take tests. I use an instrumented document viewer that quantifies how students use course documents including the textbook. While the Quantified Self movement is focused on capturing data to optimize health and athletic performance, my goal is to capture data to optimize student learning and academic achievement.

When I came up with the title for this talk, I was excited because I thought I might have coined a new term. Then I Googled it. Unfortunately, somebody beat me to it. A company called Portfolium, announced that 2016 was the year of the quantified student (Inc 2019). Their notion of the quantified student is based on an electronic portfolio containing copies of student work—the product of learning. I'm interested not in the product of learning, but rather the process. Athletes optimize their performance by monitoring their training and performance during an event, not just the final outcome.

A recent study at Dartmouth provides a step toward the Quantified Student (Harari et al. 2017). The study included 48 students including 38 undergraduates and 10 graduate students. The students' had software on their smartphones that used the microphone to record ambient sound levels, the accelerometer to sense motion, and the GPS unit and WiFi radio to determine location. Location data was used to determine if students were in the library, the gym, or a nightclub, for example. Likewise, sound levels were examined to determine if a student was in an environment conducive to studying. The measurements from the smartphone software enabled researchers to make fairly accurate predictions of students' GPA.

Two of the graphs from the website for the project at Dartmouth (Wang 2019) show when students party and when they study. One interesting thing here is that Wednesday appears to be the party night, and Tuesday appears to be the study night. This seems to be balanced, equal amounts party time and study time. However, more careful examination of the figures reveals that the scales are uneven; the scale for studying is stretched compared to that for partying. On a typical Wednesday, the 48 students have 220 hours of partying, and on a typical Tuesday, they have 30 hours of studying. This is a little troubling.

I want to use ubiquitous sensing of students' learning activities to understand how they learn. We want to obtain data about a wide variety of learning activities (Fig. 2.4). For example, we use an instrumented document viewer that we have developed to examine how do students read the course materials. Do they use the textbook? Do they actually look at the feedback they receive on their graded homework? In my classes, I make my lecture slides available after lecture. Do students actually look at them? Not just do they download them, which is what Moodle or Blackboard can tell you, but do they actually look at them? How long do they spend on each page? When do they do this? We also provide students with digital pens to capture their writing on coursework including lecture notes, homework assignments, quizzes, and exams. These devices enable us to know what students write and when they do so.

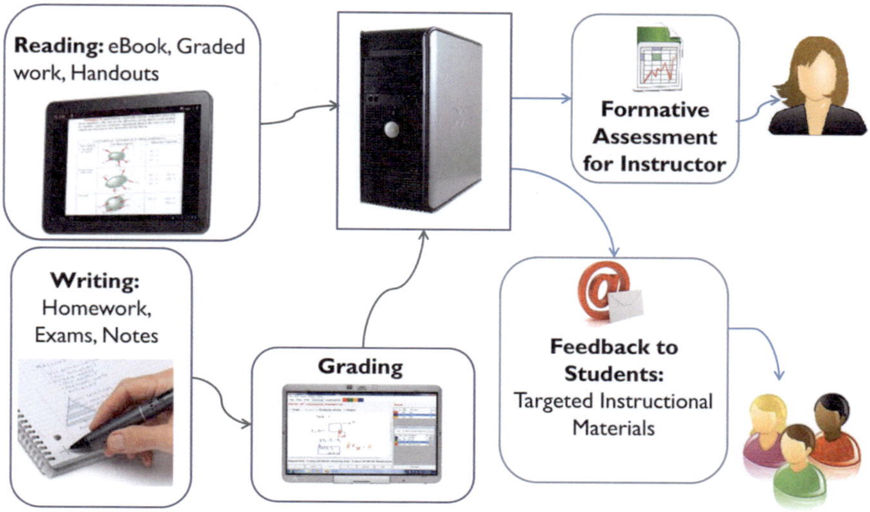

Fig. 2.4 System for using smartpen and instrumented document viewer for fine-grained formative assessment of student learning

Our document viewer continuously streams reading data to a cloud server. Students submit their written work by docking their digital pen using a USB cable. We grade their work electronically, which produces another data stream. All of this results in a large data set suitable for data mining. One goal of the data mining is to provide the instructor with formative assessment, enabling him or her to tune the instruction to the students' needs. Another goal is to provide targeted feedback to students—individualized messages to specific students about what they need to do to improve their performance.

Here is an example of the kind of data we collect (Fig. 2.5). This is a video of a student solving a problem. This video, which is sped up, was constructed from the time-stamped pen stroke data recorded by a digital pen. You might not be able to tell it from the back of the room, but the ink starts as blue and ends up here as red. We added this color code after the fact, to show the progression of writing. It looks like the student got the problem right. However, after a delay, they crossed out the answer and did more writing. You can see the new writing, which is red, in various places. The student realized he made a mistake. Long after he first solved the problem, he went back and crossed things out and fixed them. If you're looking only at the ink on the submitted page, you miss all of that process. We capture the process with the digital pens we're using. Our analysis of student work is able to examine how students construct and revise their work.

We are able to get the process of learning not just the product. We have data about what students are reading, when they're reading it, what they're writing, and when they're writing it. With this data, we wanted to understand if homework is a useful thing. Those of us who teach assign homework in our courses, but have you

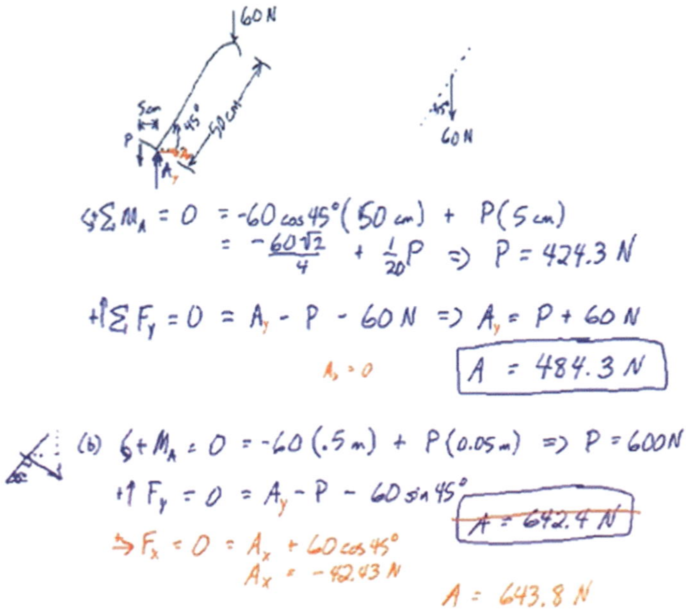

Fig. 2.5 Ink from a student's handwritten solution to a statics problem

ever seen any evidence that it's useful? Have you ever seen a study that shows that homework is useful? We all believe it is, but is it? This is a very old question. The first study I found is almost a century old. It was done by Jones and Ruch (1928). They examined the relationship between study time and first-semester GPA. They did find a statistically significant correlation between the amount of time spent on homework and GPA. Unfortunately, the correlation was negative.

[laughter]

Dr. Thomas Stahovich: The students who did the most homework performed the worst. That's a frightening thought. Is it possible that homework is not only not useful, but also harmful? There have been a series of studies over the last century examining this. For example, Schuman et al. did a study in 1985 that found no relationship, or very little relationship, between doing homework and success (Schuman et al. 1985). They attributed this to "the possible invalidity of student reports of their own studying." How do we know that what students are telling us is accurate? In 1997, Blumner and Richards made that point a little more explicitly (Blumner and Richards 1997). They concluded that: "It will be necessary to directly observe students in the act of studying. Only in this manner can it be determined that students actually do what they say in response to such an inventory." Unfortunately, much of the research on the effects of homework have relied on students' self-reports of effort.

We conducted a study to measure the effect of homework (Rawson et al. 2017). We did the study in a sophomore-level engineering course called statics, which is a physics-based course. It's required for mechanical engineering majors. We looked

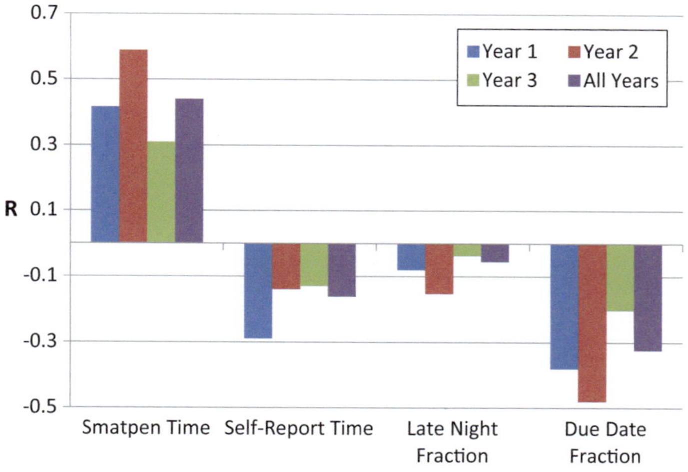

Fig. 2.6 Correlation between homework effort and final course grade for three offerings of a statics course considered individually and combined. "Smartpen Time" is objectively measured with a digital pen; "Self-Report Time" is students' self-reported homework effort; "Late Night Fraction" is the amount of homework done between midnight and 4 a.m.; "Due Date Fraction" is the fraction of homework done in the last 24 hours before the due date

at three course offerings of this course with a total 328 students. It's a very large sample size. We collected writing data for the homework, quizzes, and exams. We collected every pen stroke that students wrote on nearly all of the deliverables. This comprised about 6.6 million pen strokes, which is a very large dataset.

We also conducted an end-of-class survey in which we asked students, "How much time did you spend on homework?" We found a statistically significant correlation between self-reported homework and grade, but again, it was negative (Fig. 2.6). Those students who reported doing the most homework actually performed the worst. However, we had digital pens and we objectively measured how much time students spent writing on their homework. From this data, we found a much stronger correlation between actual homework effort and grading. Fortunately, this time it was positive. The problem here is that students cannot accurately report what they do. It could be that they don't want to say what they actually do, but it's more likely that they just don't have awareness of what they're actually doing.

We have lots of measures. We know not only how much time they're spending on their homework, but also when they're doing it. For example, we looked to see if it makes a difference if they're doing their homework at two or three in the morning. It turns out that there was a small negative correlation between the amount of homework done in the wee hours and grade, but it's not statistically significant. Students can stay up all night long and do homework if they want.

This is the one that's interesting. We examined the fraction of the homework done in the 24 hours just prior to the due date of a homework assignment. We found that this fraction has a significant negative correlation with course grade. For example,

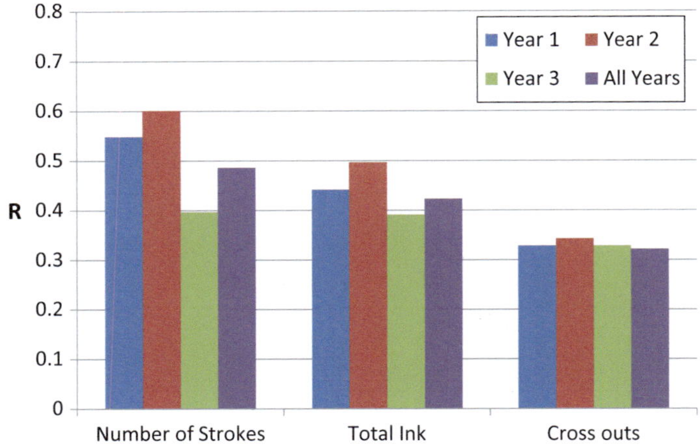

Fig. 2.7 Correlation between amount of writing on homework and final course grade for three offerings of a statics course considered individually and combined. "Number of strokes" is the number of pen strokes written with a digital pen; "Total Ink" is the total distance the pen tip moved on the paper measured in inches; "Cross Outs" is the number of pen strokes used to cross out undesired writing

for the second year of our study, the correlation coefficient was almost $r = -0.5$. This is a very strong correlation, and it is negative. When considering all 328 students from the three years of the study combined, the correlation between the fraction of homework done in the last 24 hours and grade had a correlation of about $r = -0.3$. Doing homework at the last minute is a very bad thing.

We now know that students don't accurately report how much work they're doing. We know that the amount of work that they actually do is important, and when they do it is important. Waiting until the last minute is bad.

We also considered some other measures. For example, we looked at the number of pen strokes that students wrote (Fig. 2.7). That turns out to be our best predictor of course grade. If you look just at the number of pen strokes, for all 328 students combined, the correlation is about $r = 0.5$. That means that about 25% of the variance in final course grade can be explained by one variable: the number of pen strokes written. That's a pretty significant predictor.

The total amount of ink on the page, measured in units of inches, is also a good predictor of grade. It is not quite as good as the number of pen strokes because some students have large writing, while others have small writing. The number of pen strokes is independent of that.

The digital pens use ink, thus the only way to fix a mistake is by crossing it out. We decided to look at how many cross outs students make. In this solution, these black parts are places where the student has crossed out the ink because he or she made a mistake (Fig. 2.19). We examined the frequency of cross outs and found a positive correlation with grade. We haven't dug into the reasons for this. It is entirely possible that those students who were making errors and crossing them out were

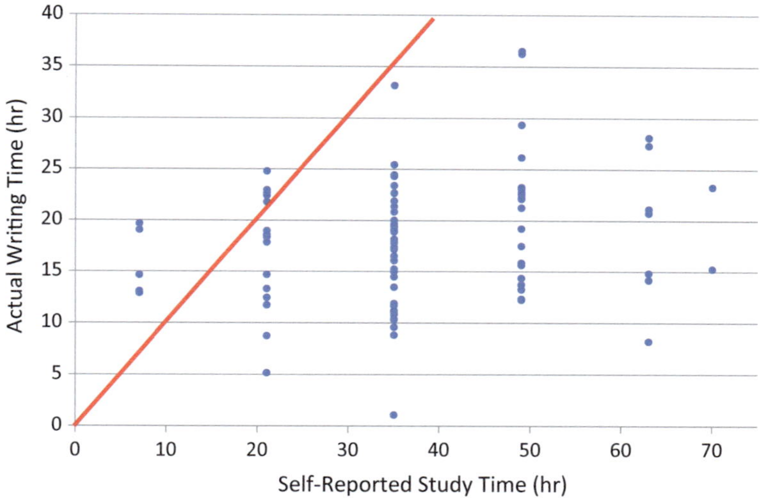

Fig. 2.8 Self-reported time spent on homework versus actual time measured with a smartpen

really engaged with the homework. It is possible that the students who were not making cross outs were copying their work, for example.

Let's go back to the accuracy of students' self-reports of studying (Fig. 2.8). On this axis (the abscissa) is the number of hours of self-reported homework effort. This axis (the ordinate) is the objective measure. In the survey, students selected among a set of discrete options to specify how much time they spent on homework. This is why the plot is stratified. The interesting thing is that 90% of the students overreported the amount of time they spent on homework. Almost everyone reported that they did much more than they actually did. Here is a student, for example, claiming that they spent 65 hours over the quarter on homework, when objectively they spent about seven. The student may not have wanted to accurately report their study time, or perhaps they did not have accurate perceptions of their study time.

All right, we looked at homework. Does homework help? We found that it does. The more effort a student puts into their homework, the better. We also found that students' reports of their effort were inaccurate. Next, we wanted to see what students read. This effort quickly switched from "what do students read?" to "do students read?"

[laughter]

Dr. Thomas Stahovich: This is the document viewer (Fig. 2.9) that we created for this study (Gyllen et al. 2018). It runs on Windows tablets and Windows PCs. It is a PDF viewer that is configured to read specially encrypted PDFs. We encrypt all of the course documents so that they can be read only with our software. Students can't use Adobe Acrobat®[1] or other software to read the documents. We designed

[1]https://www.adobe.com.

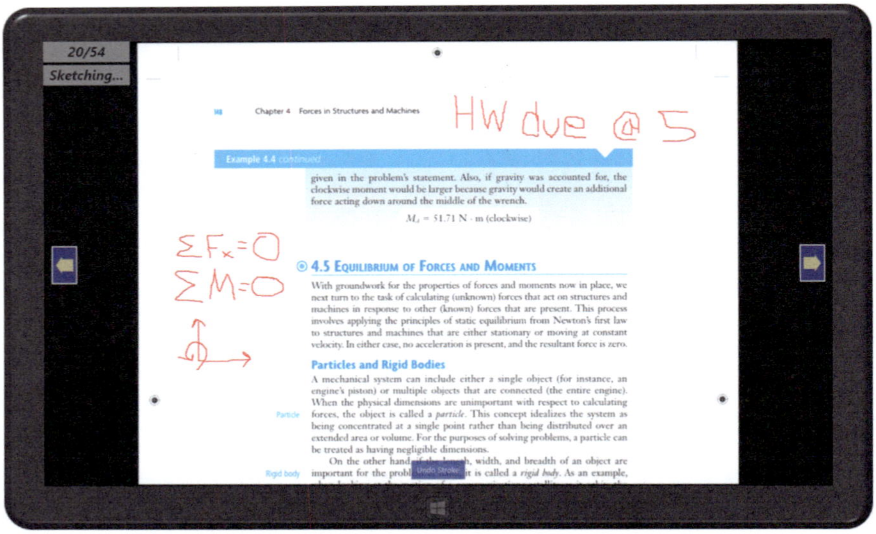

Fig. 2.9 Instrumented document viewing software

the system this way to ensure that we get accurate measurements of reading. We also made the screen turn off after 2 minutes of inactivity, so that if a student opens a page and does nothing, this will not be recorded as a long episode of reading time. The student must interact with the screen every 2 minutes to keep the display awake. We tried to make the system very user-friendly, with lots of features to entice students. We have a "pinning" feature. When students are working with multiple pages in the textbook—solving a problem and looking at an example, for instance—they can pin those pages at the bottom of the screen and can then tap the pins to switch between them. The software also enables students to highlight text and write notes. We tried to make it very useful to encourage students to use it. We also designed it so that we could get accurate measurements.

We did this study in a very challenging sophomore-level course. This is a 10-week course that has a reasonably high failure rate. Students who don't get at least a C-in this course cannot move on in the mechanical engineering major. So, this is a gateway course. How many hours over the 10-week quarter do you think students spent reading the textbook? Anyone want to guess.

Audience Member 1: Three.

Dr. Thomas Stahovich: Wow, all right. Any other guesses? It's a 10-week long.

Audience Member 2: 10.

Dr. Thomas Stahovich: 10, all right. Three.

[laughter]

Dr. Thomas Stahovich: 3 hours! They spent 3.3 h on average reading the textbook over the entire 10-week quarter (Fig. 2.10). Actually, it's an 11-week course if you count finals week. Students spent 22 hours looking at the pages at the end of each

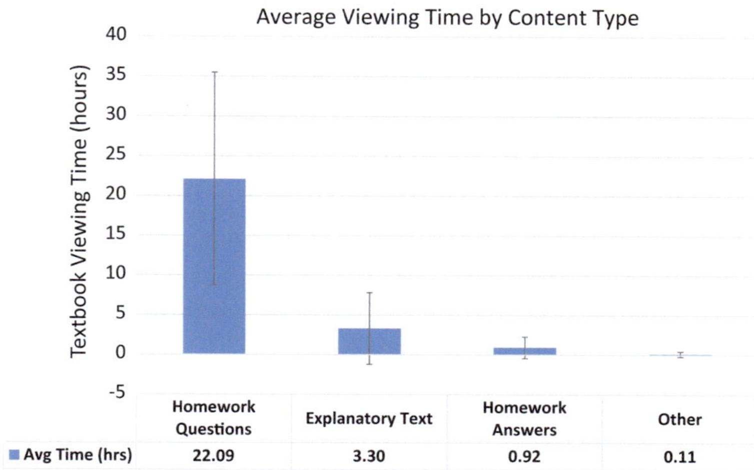

Fig. 2.10 Average amount of time students spent reading various types of content in the course e-textbook during a 10-week course in statics

chapter containing the homework problems. Thus, we knew they were using the electronic textbook to read the homework questions. With 10 assignments this would mean 2.2 hours per assignment on average. That is a reasonable time to be viewing the questions. Students were using the book to read the questions, they just weren't using it for anything else.

The final answers to the problems are in the back of the book. Students spent almost an hour on average looking at the answers. They spent 3.3 hours reading the text in the textbook and an hour reading the numerical answers listed in the back of the book. So, they don't read. We measured not only the time that they spent on pages, but also how many times they viewed each page, and it's a similar story. They view homework question pages 205 unique times on average, but the explanatory text pages they viewed only 76 times on average. This is the text that explains what they're supposed to know! It's very interesting and I was actually fairly shocked by these statistics. When I was an undergraduate, I read my books, and my classmates read their books. This is no longer the case.

My daughter is in high school and I'm finding out that high school students are often not asked or encouraged to read textbooks. Many students make it through high school without reading, and are successful there. They don't read in high school and then try to carry those habits on to the university.

Students read, on average, about 75% of the pages at the end of the chapters that contained problems that were assigned for homework. It is interesting to consider how they were able to answer all of the questions without reading all of the assigned problems. Perhaps they worked in groups. Students read, on average, only about 25% of the assigned pages with explanatory text. It appears that students use the textbook primarily as a source for homework problems, rather than as a source for information.

We tried to determine if there was any correlation between reading and achievement in the course, and we found very little correlation. This is not surprising because if students don't read, there can be little correlation between reading and achievement. Nevertheless, the amount of reading, measured both by the total viewing time and the number of unique page views, did correlate significantly and positively with grades on homework and quizzes. This makes sense, as those are short-term measures. Students do their homework, and then the day it is submitted, they take a quiz. These measures of effort include time spent reading the homework questions. It is not surprising then that time spent with the homework questions is related to good performance on the homework and on the related quizzes. The total amount of reading effort is not correlated significantly with either exam grades or final course grades.

Another way to consider reading effort is in terms of the fraction of the effort spent on each type of content. For this analysis, we've broken down the explanatory text into the actual text and the worked examples. We found that both of those fractions had a statistically significant negative correlation with grade. Students read very little of the explanatory text, but those who read more of it tended to do worse in the course. I don't think this means that reading the textbook is detrimental. I suspect that students who were otherwise struggling in the course chose to read the textbook to get additional help. I like to believe this explanation of the results because it would be very bad to find that reading was detrimental to academic performance!

Audience Member 3: Did you ask them, "Did you ever look at a paper textbook? Did you ever–?"

Dr. Thomas Stahovich: Yes. Most of the students said that they did the bulk of their reading with the tools that we gave them. According to the self-surveys that we gave them, they reported using our tools, however …

[laughter]

Dr. Thomas Stahovich: …who knows what that means. The survey results may not be meaningful. However, the amount of time that students spent viewing homework questions is what we would expect. This makes us somewhat confident that the electronic textbook we were measuring was the book they were using. I wouldn't think that they would use the e-textbook to read questions for homework and then use some other textbook to read the explanatory material. It's possible, but I think it is unlikely.

We found that the fraction of the effort spent on homework questions correlated positively and significantly with course performance. We similarly found that the fraction of the effort spent on the homework answer portion of the book correlated positively with performance. However, for the answers, the correlations were not as significant. These two results are consistent with our study of homework effort and provide further evidence that time spent on homework leads to high achievement.

In another study we examined the difference between the amount of time students claim they read versus the time they actually read. We considered reading effort on a variety of course materials: the textbook, the instructor's solutions to the homework assignments, feedback on graded assignments, and lecture slides. Here again, students vastly overestimate the amount of time they spent reading. Depending on the type of course content, between 76% and 92% of the students overreported the reading. To determine if errors in students' judgments of study time are related to course performance, we looked at the correlation between the error in the reported reading time and grade. For example, if a student said they spent 3 hours and they spent only one, the error was 2 hours.

We found that the error in self-reported reading time does correlate with final course grade. Errors in judgments of study time could be suggestive of a lack of meta-cognitive skills. A large error means that students simply aren't aware of how much time they're spending and the students who have the poorest awareness of that tend to do worse in the class. This measurement could be a way of getting at a student's meta-cognitive skills.

So far we have talked about homework—effort matters. We also looked at reading; unfortunately, students don't read. The next question we consider is: is it useful to take lecture notes? We all think that taking lecture notes is useful. We expect our students to take lecture notes.

We did a study in which students took lecture notes with smartpens. To incentivize students to submit their notes, we gave a small amount of course credit for doing so. We gave credit only if the bulk of the notes were written during the lecture period—the pens have clocks. We found that some students were copying classmate's lecture notes after class and submitting them, but no credit was given for this.

The correlation between lecture attendance and course grade was significant. The correlation was a little larger than $r = 0.3$. Apparently, attending lecture does relate to success in the class. We also looked at a variety of properties of students notes, such as the size of the writing. We found some evidence that larger writing was associated with poorer performance in the course. However, we're not really sure what that means yet. We also looked at cross outs. We found that the more places the student crossed out their work, the poorer they did in the course.

This is my favorite measure (Fig. 2.11). It is a histogram. It is essentially, the instantaneous pen speed over the lecture. We computed the graph by computing the number of inches of ink written in each 30-second time slice during the lecture. There is about 10-min at the beginning with no writing because class doesn't actually start then. We have a 10-min passing period, there may be a few announcements, and then writing start. Lots of writing. This is the average writing pace of all of the students in the class during a particular lecture. We compare the writing pace of each individual student to the class average. In the figure, the black trace is the average pace of the class. The dashed line represents the pace of a particular student. Where this is red, this student is writing less per unit time than the class average. Where it is green, the student is writing more.

This representation enables us to examine the extent to which a student is engaged in the lecture. We consider the average pace to be a measure of how much needs to be written at each point in the lecture. Surprisingly, we found that there was a statistically significant correlation between a student's deviation from the average pace and grade.

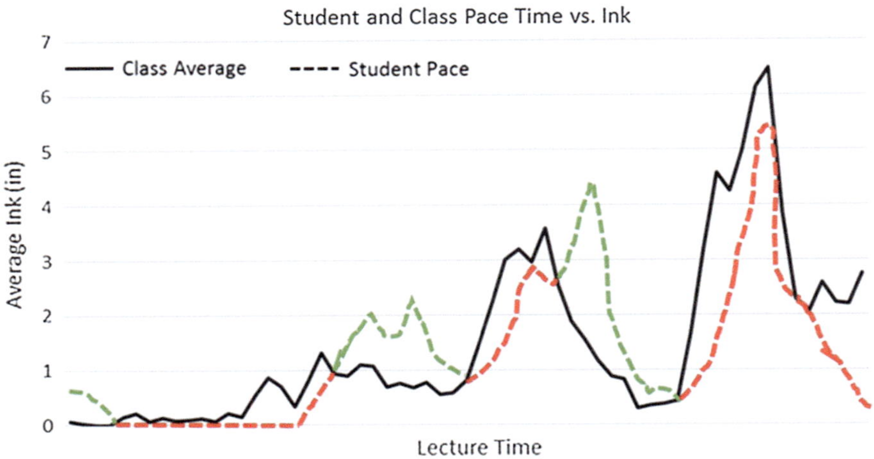

Fig. 2.11 Comparison of a student's writing pace to the class average while taking lecture notes

The students that deviated the most from the average pace did the worst in the course. We measure the deviation as the root mean square (RMS) difference between the student's pace and the average. We thought, "Okay, that reinforces the notion that students who are not taking thorough notes don't do well." But then we looked at the red parts separately from the green parts. We call this red stuff the "behind-pace writing" and the green stuff is "ahead-of-pace." We found that students with a lot of ahead-of-pace writing—students who write more than the class average—tend to do worse in the class. Conversely, the students with a lot of behind-pace writing—students who write less than the class average—tend to do better. This may suggest that the students who try to write down every word they hear in the lecture—without any interpretation, without processing it, without deciding what's important and what's unimportant—are the students that don't do as well in the course. However, these results are preliminary and our continued investigation of writing pace has produced mixed evidence. Thus, we can't make any conclusions about this yet.

About the time we were doing this analysis, we saw a paper that had been published saying that doodling on your notes during a meeting keeps your mind engaged and you actually walk away from the meeting with more (Andrade 2010). We tested this. We had some under graduates go through all the notes and find all the doodles. There was absolutely no correlation between doodling and achieving high marks. At least for undergraduates in our class, doodling seems to have no effect.

We looked at the number of lectures students attended, the amount of ahead-of-pace and behind-pace writing, the size of the writing, and so on. Using a total of 15 different features characterizing lecture notes, we were able to explain 51% of the variances, final course grade. This is a large amount of variance. The correlation coefficient is the square root of that, which is about $r = 0.71$. That's a fairly strong correlation. It appears that the behaviors students exhibit during note-taking are revealing of how well they will perform in a course.

For decades, education researchers have examined the "time-on-task" hypothesis which holds that "the amount of time a student spends engaged in an academic task is related to achievement" (van Gog 2013). Our studies give additional insight on the time-on-task hypothesis. We found that the amount of time that students spent studying—time actually spent studying, not self-reported study time—does correlate very strongly with achievement in a course. We also found that effortful engagement is a strong predictor of achievement. The amount of writing, which is a measure of effortful engagement, is a stronger predictor of achievement than the amount of time spent. Also, the quality of the time matters. Trying to do homework in the last few minutes before the assignment is due is not quality studying.

Although I haven't presented the data here, we have preliminary evidence to suggest that dividing a homework assignment into multiple separate episodes is beneficial. We have found that number of distinct homework episodes during the week correlates positively with achievement. This is the notion of distributed practice. Trying to learn everything in one sitting is not as effective as breaking the task into multiple sessions.

This work has some interesting methodological implications. The first is that self-reports are extremely inaccurate. The bulk of research examining the relationship between study habits and achievement has relied on student self-reports. We have also found that the inaccuracy of student self-reports may be an indicator of meta-cognitive skills. This suggests a new way to investigate meta-cognitive skills.

There are some practical implications of this as well. Students overestimate the amount of work they do and they don't read. I'm amazed; engineering textbooks are $200 apiece. We tell students to buy them, and then they don't read them. Also, students tend to leave homework to the last minute, which turns out to be a very bad strategy. Understanding all of this, what can we do to improve student achievement? We're working on building automated coaching systems and early warning systems.

Here is one of our first attempts at building an early warning system (Fig. 2.12). Our goal was to identify data available early in the course that could predict final course grade in a 10-week statics course. This graph represents the correlation between a variety of measures and course grade for three offerings of a statics course. The first set of columns represent the correlation between a concept inventory score (CI), which was given as a pretest at the beginning of the course, and course grade. For the first 2 years of the study, we used the Statics Concept Inventory (Steif and Dantzler 2005) as the pretest. However, this was not predictive of grade. It is likely that, prior to taking the course, the students had insufficient knowledge of statics concepts for the Statics Concept Inventory to be useful. For the third year, we used the Force Concept Inventory (Hestenes et al. 1992) as the pretest. This is a more appropriate test as students are expected to have a knowledge of forces prior to taking statics, and forces are the primary focus of statics. The Force Concept Inventory explained about 21% of the variance in final course grade ($r^2 = 0.21$).

We also examined students' scores on the third homework assignment and the third quiz (HQ) as predictors of course grade. These scores, which are based on work form the first three or four weeks of the course, explain about 30% of the variance in final course grade ($r^2 = 0.3$).

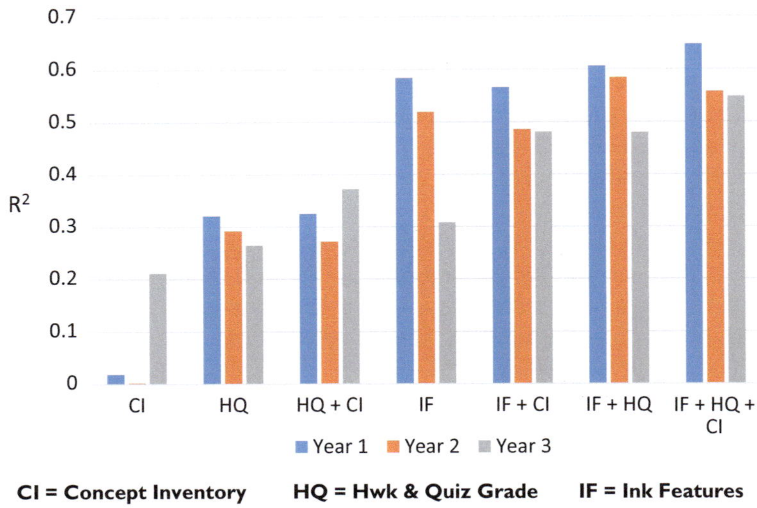

Fig. 2.12 Early predictors of student performance in an introductory statics course

The concept inventory score and homework and quiz scores are traditional assessments. We use these as a benchmark for predictions afforded by our digital pen approach. We computed a variety of features from students' writing on the third homework assignment. The features include things like the total amount of ink written, the number of pen strokes, and the amount of time spent writing. These features explain between 30% and nearly 60% of the variance in course grade. The features are better predictors of course performance than homework, quiz, and concept inventory. Combining all of these things together—concept inventory score, score on the third homework, score on the third quiz, and the ink features—produces a very strong early prediction of course grade.

The predictive power of the ink features reveals that homework habits at the beginning of the course are highly predictive of how students will ultimately perform. Based on this, and knowing that students' self-reports of study time are highly inaccurate, we did an experiment to see if we could help students to improve their performance. Each week we gave students a grade report. It said, "Here's how you've performed to date. Here's what you did and here's what you should do to perform better in the course." We gave students written documents with individualized feedback explaining what they needed to do to be successful in the course. Guess what? They didn't read it.

[laughter]

Dr. Thomas Stahovich: This is an overstatement, but there's perhaps a little truth there. We found that this feedback resulted in no changes in student behavior or outcomes. Our next iteration was to make it so that there was no way that they could avoid seeing the individualized feedback. We built our own course management system. We replaced Blackboard with our own dashboard. Our dashboard provides students with measures of their effort on homework and reading assignments. The system also provides suggestions for how to improve performance. To ensure that students saw the feedback, we used our system to distribute the homework assignments. Students had to use the system at least once a week to get their homework.

The feedback from the system included things like: "You completed only 80% of homework 2. Try to do all of the next assignment." "Good job taking notes during lecture 5." "You didn't complete the reading assignment before lecture 8. Try completing the next reading assignment before the next lecture." The system also gave students a predicted final grade by simply extrapolating from the currently graded work. "Okay, if you continue working like you are now, this is the grade you're going to get at the end of the quarter."

With our system, students have everything they need to know. They know how much work they're actually doing. They know what grade they are heading toward. They know what they're supposed to do to improve their performance. In essence, our system is like a "Fitbit"®[2] for the brain. With a traditional fitbit, people monitor things like: "How many hours of sleep did I get? How many steps did I walk? How many miles did I run?" We provide analogous measures for the brain. "How much studying did I do? What is my level of performance? What do I need to improve on?"

What we found unfortunately was that the fitbit model doesn't work for learning. There were no measurable changes in student behavior or learning outcomes. This is very surprising. We can show students what they need to do and how it's going to affect their grades, but they don't alter their study habits.

We haven't given up on this, though. We're doing another round of experiments, this time with extrinsic motivation built into the system. I suspect that students don't believe the feedback. For example, students don't feel the need to read despite what the system says. I think this is an important problem and one that needs to be studied on a larger scale. When I teach our introductory freshmen engineering course, I ask the students, "How many of you did homework in high school?" Almost none of them raise their hands. They're in engineering, so they were "A" students in high school. We now have students who get A's in high school without doing large amounts of homework and they try to carry that into a university environment. I'm quite interested in knowing how universal this is.

I'm going to change the focus a little. So far I have been talking about using data-driven approaches to understand how students learn. Now I am going to about our work in automatically grading student work. The analyzes that I have talked about so far don't look at the content of the writing in any great depth. They simply look at things like elapsed time and the distance the pen travels on the page. What can we get by looking deeper into the content?

Here is the research question: What properties of a student's writing on an exam problem indicate how well the student performed on that exam problem? This is an example of an exam question from my statics class (Fig. 2.13). It's a little bit of a Rube Goldberg machine. There is a linkage with a cable going over a pulley. There's

---

[2]https://www.fitbit.com.

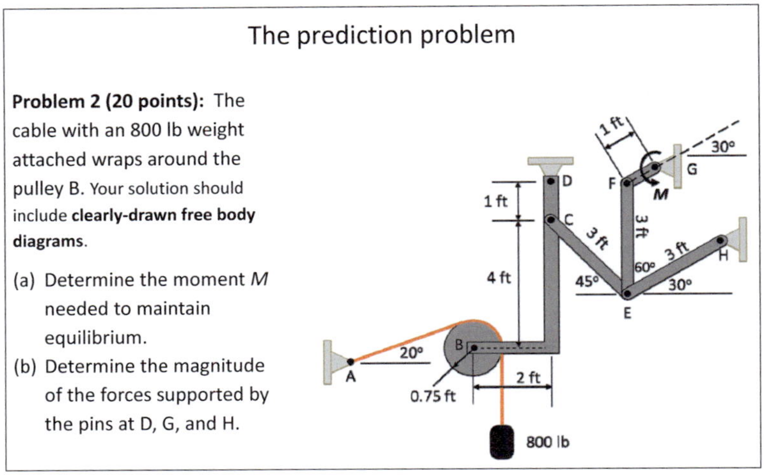

Fig. 2.13 An exam problem from a statics course

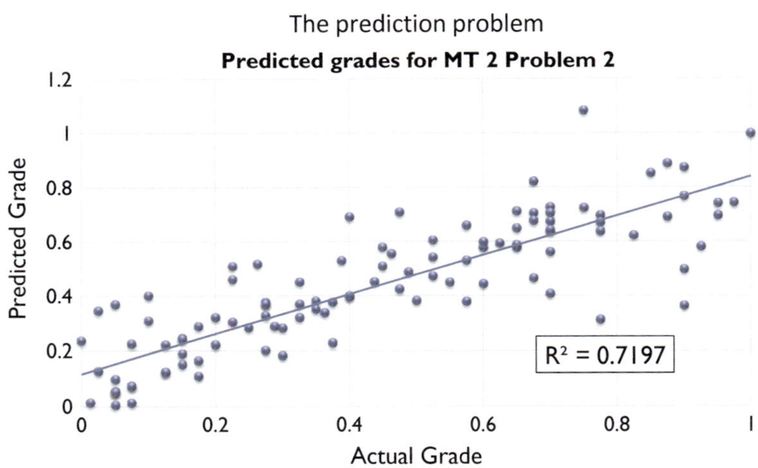

Fig. 2.14 Results of automatically grading students' solutions to the problem in Fig. 2.13

a moment, or a torque if you prefer, applied to link FG. The question is how big does that moment have to be in order to hold that 800-lb weight?

We extract features of the students writing—from the digital ink—on a problem like this, and use those features to train a model to predict the score the student received on the problem (Van Arsdale and Stahovich 2012). Here is an example of the performance of one such model (Fig. 2.14). The abscissa is the grade assigned by a human grader, and the ordinate is the grade predicted by the model. This is a very high correlation. I suspect that if you took two teaching assistants and have them both grade the same problem that you might not get that high of a correlation.

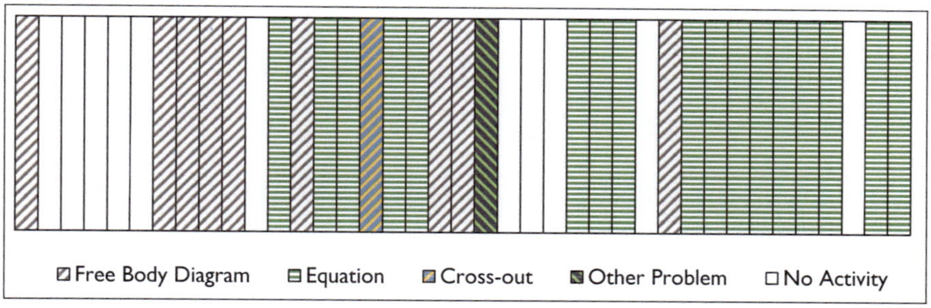

Fig. 2.15 A portion of a typical discretized activity sequence describing a student's effort while solving an exam

Our models employ a variety of features. Some of them capture the behavior I showed you earlier in the video in which the student writes a solution and then goes back and crosses things out and makes changes. Our hypothesis is that a student who can go from the top of the page to bottom without doing that might understand the material better than a student who keeps going back and changing their earlier work.

We created a variety features that characterize how students organize their work in time and space. This representation (Fig. 2.15) is one of the ways that we do this. We call this the DNA sequence. We take the time a student spends solving a problem and divide it into 400 times slices. We then label each time slice according to the predominate activity. For example, in some time slices the student might be primarily writing equations, while in others the student might be primarily drawing diagrams. Time slices with no shading represent intervals of time when no writing occurred. Perhaps the student was thinking about what to do then. Some time slices represent digressions, intervals of time when the student interrupts the work on the present problem to work on another. From this sequence, we compute measures that describe the organization of the work. For example, we compute the entropy of the sequence, which gives a measure of how balanced the effort is on each of the tasks.

My favorite feature is a measure of the complexity. We represent the sequence as a string, with each type of activity represented by a specific character. For example, time slices for equations might be labeled with an "e." We then use a data compression algorithm to compress the string. The smaller we can compress the string, the simpler the students' solution process was. If the student first draws all of the diagrams and then writes all of the equations, the string will compress to almost nothing—the complexity will be low. This is, in fact, how students are taught to solve the problem. Diagrams are drawn to represent the problem and then equations are constructed based on the diagrams. Low complexity would be an indicator that the student is following this model.

We also developed some measures of how students go back and change earlier work. We construct a sliding window (Fig. 2.16). The timestamp for the window is set based on the time that the ink was first written in the window. If the student comes back and adds ink after the window has passed, that ink is now considered out

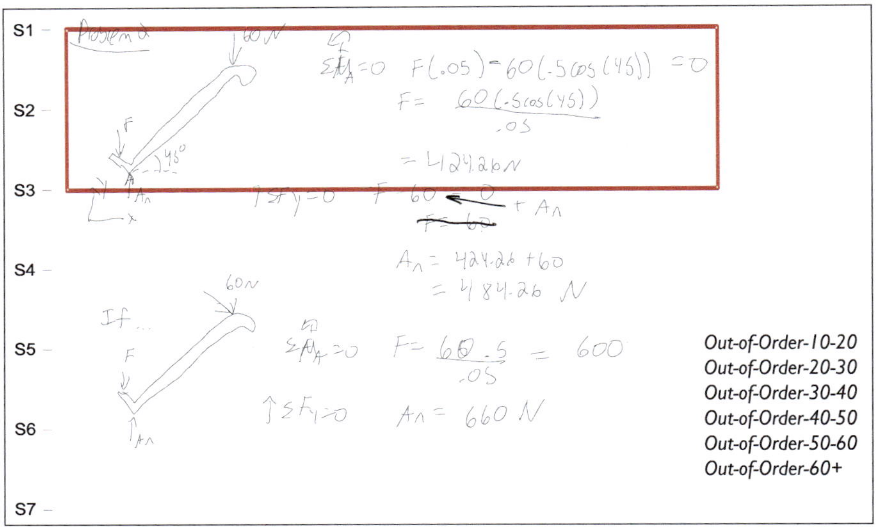

Fig. 2.16 A sliding window used to identify out-of-order work

of order—it is delayed writing. We measure how much out-of-order writing there is, and the extent to which it is out of order. For example, if a student spends 10 min on a problem, and 9.5 min later—or 95% of the time later—they go back and change something, that writing is considered 95% out of order. One set of features counts the amount of writing in various ranges of out-of-order-ness. For example, one range might be stroked that are between 50% and 60% out of order. We also measure out-of-order-ness using local analysis. We examine the neighborhood of each stroke and find the biggest time delay between the stroke and its neighbors.

When you look at a student's solution to a statics problem, it may appear to be organized into regions containing only diagrams or only equations. Some of our features extract properties of these regions, which we call "clusters." One of my graduate students came up with a clever way to identify the clusters. We imagine an exponential force field from each data point on each pen stroke (Fig. 2.17). If the data point is from a diagram the force field is positive, and if it's from an equation the force field is negative. We sum up the force fields to get a three-dimensional surface. We then construct level surfaces to identify regions of the surface that correspond to diagrams (positive regions) and to equations (negative regions). The result of this process is a set of clusters (Fig. 2.18). We compute various features to characterize the clusters, such as how frequently the student revisits them to make changes.

Another set of features concerns the number of cross-out gestures that are used to cross out undesired ink (Fig. 2.19). We consider various kinds of cross outs. For example, a typo cross out is one in which the student wrote something and then immediately crossed it out, as if fixing a typo. By contrast, a problem-solving cross out is one in which the fix happens a few minutes later, as if the student later realized

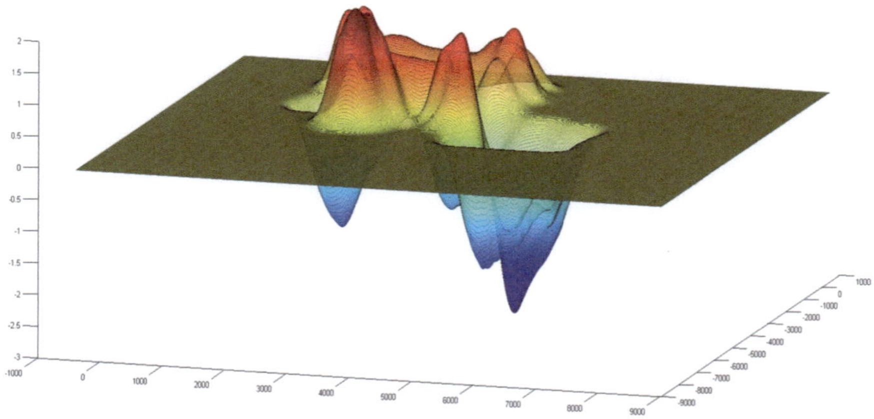

Fig. 2.17 A force field computation for identifying clusters of diagram strokes and equation strokes

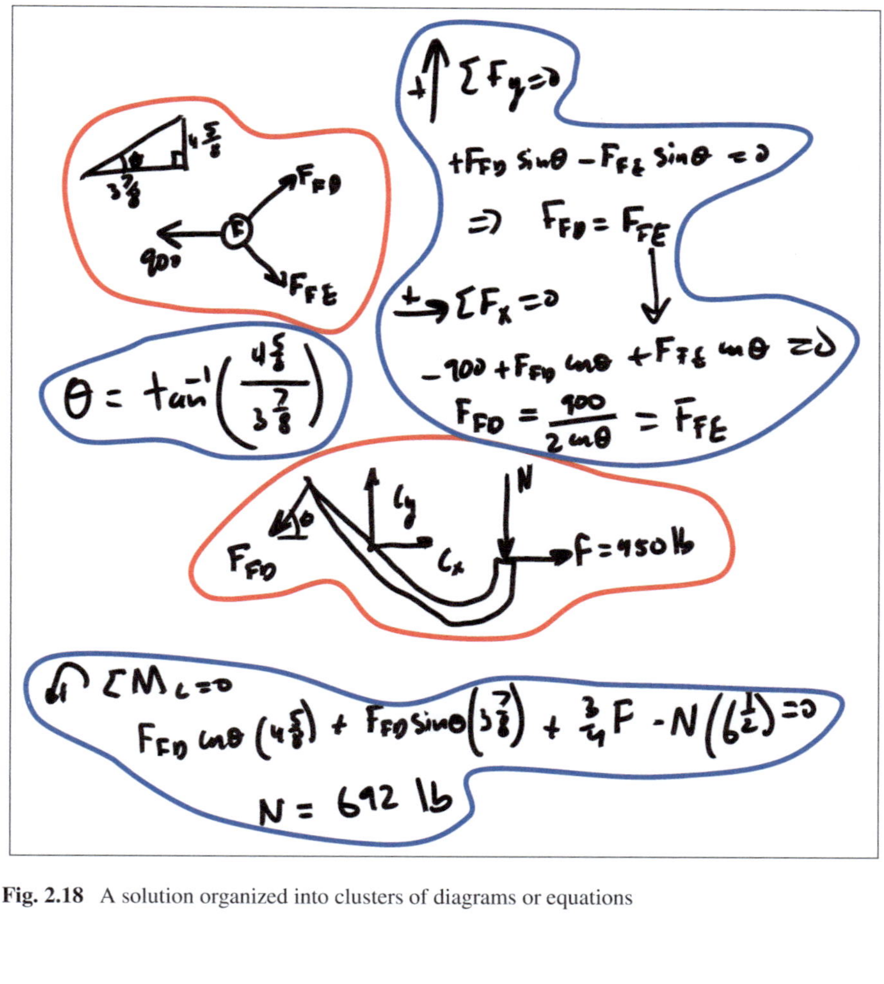

Fig. 2.18 A solution organized into clusters of diagrams or equations

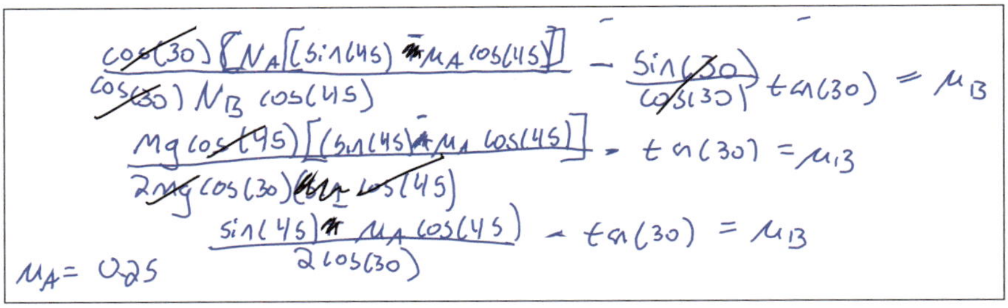

Fig. 2.19 Examples of cross outs (black ink) used to mark undesired writing

"Oops, I made a mistake." Finally, big cross outs are gestures that cross out big parts of the solution.

Using this set of features we are able to build regression models that predict the correctness of a student's work—the score assigned by the instructor. For the problem in Fig. 2.13, these models explained 72% of the variance in the score. Our models were not this successful for all of the exam problems we considered. We wanted to understand why this was. We compared the accuracy of the models to the mean scores of the exam problems. We found that for problems that turned out to be easy—the ones most students got right—our models were poor at predicting grade variations. However, for the difficult problems—the ones which separated high and low performing students—our models did very well at identifying the correctness of the work. What this means is that for easy problems, this approach is limited in its ability to identify student competence, but for challenging problems, it is quite effective.

Let me just wrap up with a couple of thoughts. The first is that capturing ink data with smartpens and reading data with an instrumented document viewer allows us to use data mining techniques to understand students' learning. I believe that great advances in our understanding of student learning will come from a fitbit-like approach of ubiquitous sensing of student's everyday learning activities. In fact, a recent discussion of this work Strauss (2016) suggests that much of the existing work examining the relationship between homework and achievement needs to be reconsidered in light of our findings that are based on objective measurements of student effort.

Our work has resulted in some interesting findings. For example, we found that students' self-reports of study effort are very unreliable. We also found that we can predict student grade in a course based on measures of effort—how much time students spend on homework, how much writing they do, and when they do their work. We can even make useful predictions of final course grades based on work in the first three weeks of the term. Something that I find very interesting is that we can get a good sense of the correctness of a student's work simply by looking at the process by which the ink went on the page. We don't actually have to look at the answers to determine this! If any of you have graded students' work and felt that you could guess the grade just by looking at it—you can.

Finally, I think this is perhaps this is the biggest takeaway for educators. I have spent many years trying to come up with methods to improve student learning. I have created intelligent tutoring systems (e.g., Lee et al. 2008) and explored innovative ways of teaching my class, but these efforts all seem to achieve little. I now realize that the problem is not with the teaching methods, it is with student engagement. For example, students rarely read, and they often do their homework at the last minute. Lack of engagement is the biggest problem. Rather than working to develop better lectures, better instructional materials, better projects, and so on, we need to find ways to foster student engagement. That's a tough problem.

This work was generously funded by the National Science Foundation through Grants 0935239, 1432820 and 1612511. My collaborator on this work is Rich Mayer, a Professor of Psychology at UC Santa Barbara. I also owe great thanks to the team of talented graduate students in my lab at UC Riverside that has done this work over the last almost 10 years.

Thank you.

[applause]

Ken Forbus: We have time for questions.

Jonathan Grudin: This may reflect the fact that I am also data driven, but this is one of the most interesting talks I have heard in a long time. It was a really, really nice talk. I hope that you're writing a book that will encompass this and anything else you're doing. I think part of it is, of course, as you're aware, because so much of this is correlational, there are a lot of other possible explanations to explore. In addition, there's also a lot of dependency on the specific tasks involved.

For instance, the engagement and pen activity doesn't work in lecture, in taking lecture notes, because the assumption is there's actually some sort of engagement going on that's not reflected in the ink. It's just a very complex space to explore. I think even a course—you should have a course just on this particular phenomenon. I would like to be a virtual member of that course if you do all that. It's very nice and I think we could spend a week exploring some of the different points in here so…

Tom: Yes. I think the next thing is going to have be eye tracking and the little headset to measure brain waves.

[laughter]

Jonathan Grudin: Very nice. Thank you.

Tracy Hammond: Yes, awesome talk. I'm curious about your fitbit-like interventions not working. Do you have any ideas of other interventions—like students working in pairs, so that the other one would go and knock on your door and say, "Hey! I can see that you haven't opened your textbook yet." Do you have other intervention ideas in the works?

Tom: What we're actually doing in the winter quarter, so in another two and a half months, is to add gamification to the dashboard.

Tracy Hammond: So can they see other people's achievements—how they compare to everybody else?

Tom: Actually, it turns out that we're not comparing them to others because apparently, there is some research suggesting that this can be discouraging, so what we're doing is providing games and levels to achieve. It's surprising that those kinds of measures are very effective. I have a graduate student in my lab who decided that he needed to drink more water and so he had this app on his phone where every time he drinks water, he logs it on his phone so at the end of the day, he can get a virtual reward, which is just a picture, but he does it for drinking water.

It turns out that these badges and levels and things—students are very engaged by them. That's our next topic. We've heard some criticism that extrinsic motivation won't last. We might get them to study in this class, but in the following class, they won't. Our hope is that if we show them that, "Wait a minute, I did this in one class and now I got an A instead of C," they might remember that for the next quarter. I don't think they fully appreciate the relationship between the required effort and grades.

Audience Member 4: This is fascinating, the idea that the early warning system and the dashboard does not have any impact. You touched on this a little bit—whether some of these predictors are actually showing that they have lower metacognitive skills, less of an ability to plan. I'm wondering if maybe one thing that even the extrinsic motivators might be missing—even if you know you shouldn't be doing your assignment at the last minute, but you're not able to plan ahead, maybe there's actually a missing skill there. I'm just wondering if you have thought at all about that.

Tom: I have. I think that that is a really good question because essentially what we have to do is to teach students to learn. That's probably going to be the fourth number on that list. Yes. That is something that I am planning on doing because I was very shocked when I discovered in the data this lack of engagement and this lack of ability to do things in a timely fashion is really hurting students. I think that's an excellent idea.

Audience Member 5: Sorry if I missed it, but do you require students to basically self-report or do all their notes for homework that were separate from the book onto your software? Because I remember I had to take 3 years of physics which I struggled with because it wasn't necessary for my major. I would desperately find Khan Academy or YouTube videos to write down and follow the problems through video. Did you require them to do that?

Tom: No, we were just looking at the lecture notes. They used the digital pens to write the notes during class. We haven't looked at the use of YouTube videos or other things. I think that would be useful too. In some of our course offering we have given students surface tablets. I have 150 of them that I passed out to all of the students. It would be nice to actually monitor what they're looking at on the web. On the other hand, I don't know that I want to know.

[laughter]

Tom: That would be interesting to be able track.

Audience Member 5: Or maybe just their notes when they're following along and redoing the problems. Maybe that would be less privacy invading. You can see how much extra writing they do that's still physics.

Tom: My real fear is that there isn't any extra writing.

Audience Member 5: I think from my anecdotal experience, that there would be a lot because it is the replacement for the book work. They're just desperately trying to get that material, but I don't know that for sure.

Tom: That's interesting. We could give sort of an extra credit opportunity for students to turn in notes on material they took outside of class. We would be able to capture that. That is an interesting idea.

Audience Member 5: Then I don't know if your school has TA office hours, but that's another source that people are probably writing notes and doing problems. I don't know, maybe that's another extra credit thing. They go to those hours and do it, maybe.

Tom: That's true. Right now we require them to turn in the ink for specific deliverables. We could expand that to basically any time the pen moves during the quarter.

Audience Member 3: Were there any behavioral changes when the students were confronted with some of the information? I know you anecdotally said "Not so much," but some students must have responded by looking at the dashboard and responded in different ways.

Tom: We did measure it. Students were looking at the dashboard daily. So we measured when they went there, what things they clicked on. We have detailed click-through logs of use of the dashboard, but when we looked at two of the big measures—which are how much reading they did and how much of their homework did they do in the last 24 hours—those two metrics seem to be unchanged. Now it's possible that there are other kinds of behavior that change that we haven't looked at. I guess I shouldn't write this off yet. We just did this experiment. Our initial analysis of the behavior suggests that there were no big differences, but there may still be.

Audience Member 6: Were there any direct faculty interventions or TA interventions with the students that were designated as being lower achievers?

Tom: No. That was actually by design. Because of our human subjects protocol, I was not allowed to see any of the data from the system until after I assigned the final course grades. The students got all of their feedback in a way that was completely invisible to me and the teaching assistants.

Audience Member 6: I was just going to say because that has worked for us on occasion. Of course, we're not doing this kind of research, but if students are not following up on what they need to do and this is pointed out to the faculty member and the faculty member directly confronts the student, that often helps with the change in behavior.

Tom: I agree with that and I think that when we transition from our research studies to just using it for real classroom use, I think then it will be completely legitimate for us to take the assessment data and talk to students. I do agree. It's just that right now, students can opt in or opt out, and so because of that, we've had to make it in a way where there's absolutely no risk for them to participate.

Ken Forbus: I'm stunned that you can actually get this much data. That is, that you can actually enforce that there are going to do all this. So you've actually made it smooth enough that there's no complaints, no whining, no why do we have to use this machine for this—?

Tom: We get some of that, but it's always balanced by students who are very happy that we are doing this and actually like participating. Some of the things I do in lecture, I point out, "by the way, students who took this 5 years ago were the ones who revealed this problem with student learning and now we're fixing it in lecture so that you don't have this problem." They see that and I think that helps them appreciate that they are a part of a system that keeps contributing to each other's improvement.

Jonathan Grudin: Just as examples of how this opens up the space for thinking about these things: There are a couple of other things going on in students' lives. One is that you've got one course—and I kind of believe the last minute finding—but students also have multiple courses that they're taking at a time. That's one way—that's a technique for time management. You also have this overall pattern that they have to worry about. At an even higher level, there's their career and it could well be that spending more time on homework would decrease their effectiveness at partying. And if their ultimate job depends more on their social network than on their grade in the course, then they maybe—there's just a lot of things going on in that space that are fascinating.

Tom: It would actually be interesting to combine sort of what we're doing with what Dartmouth is doing, and do that for four years.

Ken Forbus: With that, it's time for our break. Thank you again.

[applause]

Ken Forbus: We'll be back here at 11:00 for the next topic.

Acknowledgements This work was conducted at the University of California Riverside. This material is based upon work supported by the National Science Foundation under Grant Numbers 0935239, 1432820, and 1612511. Thank you to David Hoeft for videotaping the sessions.

References

Andrade J (2010) What does doodling do? Appl Cogn Psychol Off J Soc Appl Res Mem Cogn 24(1):100–106

Blumner HN, Richards HC (1997) Study habits and academic achievement of engineering students. J Eng Educ 86:125–132

Gyllen J, Stahovich T, Mayer R (2018) How students read an e-textbook in an engineering course. J Comput Assist Learn 34(6):701–712

Harari GM, Gosling SD, Wang R, Chen F, Chen Z, Campbell AT (2017) Patterns of behavior change in students over an academic term: a preliminary study of activity and sociability behaviors using smartphone sensing methods. Comput Hum Behav 67:129–138

Hestenes D, Wells M, Swackhamer G (1992) Force concept inventory. Phys Teacher 30(3):141–158

Inc P (2019) Portfolium. https://portfolium.com/. Accessed 23 Feb 23, 2019

Jones L, Ruch GM (1928) The twenty-seventh yearbook of the national society for the study of education: nature and nurture, part II-their influence upon achievement. In: Whipple GM (ed) Achievement as affected by amount of time spent in study. Public School Publishing Co, Bloomington, IL, pp 131–134

Lee W, de Silva R, Peterson EJ, Calfee RC, Stahovich TF (2008) Newton's pen: a pen-based tutoring system for statics. Comput Graph 32(5):511–524. https://doi.org/10.1016/j.cag.2008.05.009

Rawson K, Stahovich TF, Mayer RE (2017) Homework and achievement: using smartpen technology to find the connection. J Educ Psychol 109(2):208

Schuman H, Walsh E, Olson C, Etheridge B (1985) Effort and reward: the assumption that college grades are affected by quantity of study. Soc Forces 63(4):945–966

Steif PS, Dantzler JA (2005) A statics concept inventory: development and psychometric analysis. J Eng Edu 94(4):363–371

Strauss V (2016) A new wrinkle in the research about the real value of homework. https://wapo.st/29kXIEr?tid=ss_mail&utm_term=.4beadca49de8

Van Arsdale T, Stahovich T (2012) Does neatness count? What the organization of student work says about understanding. In: Proceedings of the 2012 American society for engineering education annual conference and exposition

van Gog T (2013) Time on task. In: Hattie J, Anderman EM (eds) Educational psychology handbook series. International guide to student achievement. Routledge/Taylor & Francis Group, New York, pp 423–433

Wang R (2019) Student life study. http://studentlife.cs.dartmouth.edu/. Accessed 23 Feb 2019

Thomas Stahovich received a B.S. in Mechanical Engineering from UC Berkeley in 1988. He received an M.S. and Ph.D. in Mechanical Engineering from MIT in 1990 and 1995 respectively. He conducted his doctoral research on computational sketch understanding techniques at the MIT Artificial Intelligence Lab. After serving as an Assistant and Associate Professor of Mechanical Engineering at Carnegie Mellon University in Pittsburgh, PA, Dr. Stahovich joined the Mechanical Engineering Department at UC Riverside in 2003. He also holds a cooperative appointment in the Computer Science and Engineering Department at UC Riverside.

Part III
Teaching STEM Through Sketch

Chapter 3
Repairing Misconceptions and Inadequate Preparation in Upper-Level Undergraduate Engineering: The KACIE Model and Pen-Based Computing

John Solomon, Eric Hamilton and Chitra Nayak

Abstract Engineering educators frequently discover that students coming into upper-level courses lack the foundational knowledge necessary for course success, and frequently entertain misconceptions common to entry-level engineering students. This chapter reports on an NSF-funded initiative that approaches this difficulty with a comprehensive portfolio of research-based strategies for students to acquire, manipulate, express, and revise conceptual systems around engineering. These strategies referred to as protocols, entail a labor-intensive, methodical, and stepwise approach to working with upper-level students with less course preparation than they should have. The overall approach is referred to as "Knowledge and Curriculum Integration Ecosystem (KACIE)" protocol, formerly known as "Tailored Instruction and Engineered Delivery Using Protocols (TIDE UP)". One aspect of the strategy portfolio involves the use of pen-based computing. The chapter reviews statistically significant results from this approach as a prelude to ongoing research to assess the efficacy of the digital ink component of the project (Hamilton et al. Inspiring students through digital ink: impact of pen and touch technology on education. Springer, 2019).

3.1 Introduction

A sizable research literature indicates that student engagement in classrooms correlate strongly to academic and professional success (Crawley et al. 2014; Froyd et al. 2012; Graham 2012). Student engagement in engineering classrooms is a challenge for several reasons, including inadequate course preparation, low self-efficacy, socioeconomic factors, and ineffective course delivery methods (Duncan

J. Solomon · C. Nayak
Tuskegee University, Tuskegee, AL, USA
e-mail: jsolomon@mytu.tuskegee.edu

C. Nayak
e-mail: cnayak@mytu.tuskegee.edu

E. Hamilton (✉)
Pepperdine University, Malibu, CA 90263, USA
e-mail: eric.hamilton@pepperdine.edu

T. Hammond et al. (eds.), *Inspiring Students with Digital Ink*, Human–Computer Interaction Series, https://doi.org/10.1007/978-3-030-17398-2_3

and Hmelo-Silver 2009; Schunk 1990; Shulman 2002). The main goal of this project is to test a research-based approach designed to improve engagement and success of third and fourth year engineering students in classroom settings.

This short chapter describes the overall project approach and the role of the digital ink and pen-based computing component of it, as the project enters its third year of activity.

Engineering courses require continuous development of strong mathematical skills throughout the curriculum. Moreover, learning complex engineering concepts in higher level classes requires minimum prerequisite knowledge. Prerequisite knowledge deficits can lead to attention problems, aversion to the course, and to overall poor course performance. While these issues are partly addressed by the curriculum rules on mandatory prerequisite courses, a major fraction of students can enroll in higher level courses with a minimum grade in these prerequisite courses. Since their understanding of this prerequisite information is weak, they may face significant difficulties in understanding the advanced courses and may eventually drop out or change their engineering major.

3.2 Major Goals

While this issue is prominent in all engineering programs, it is more critical and pervasive in Historically Black Colleges and Universities (HBCUs) (Nave et al. 2016). In this project, we look specifically at this problem in an HBCU context and aim to understand the challenges and then to provide a pair. The goal of this project is to develop an effective teaching-learning model to address these issues. We approached model development by seeking with a microgenetic approach, seeking to identify and repair conceptual shortcomings immediately and at the level of small increments, customized to each learner, using approaches established in learning sciences literature and taking advantage of findings in cognitive neuroscience. In this model, referred to as "Knowledge and Curriculum Integration Ecosystem (KACIE)" protocol (Solomon 2015), course topics are presented as connected concept modules. The modular representation is intended to inform the students that a complex engineering concept is connected to several subconcepts and that a student's lack of understanding of pre-connected concepts, including math, will hinder their learning ability. The model provides an opportunity for students to review and reconnect to these basics and prerequisite knowledge before they attempt to learn and understand the higher level engineering concepts. Each of these concepts is linked to short, animated video lectures, student activities, and quizzes that are developed based on a number of mandatory learning principles established in the learnings sciences and cognitive neuroscience literature. We call the steps based on these mandatory learning principles steps as KACIE protocols, or just protocols. These principles are expected to help students to learn such prerequisites independently. As an example, Protocol 1, or P1, reminds faculty to deliver prerequisites before introducing higher level concepts

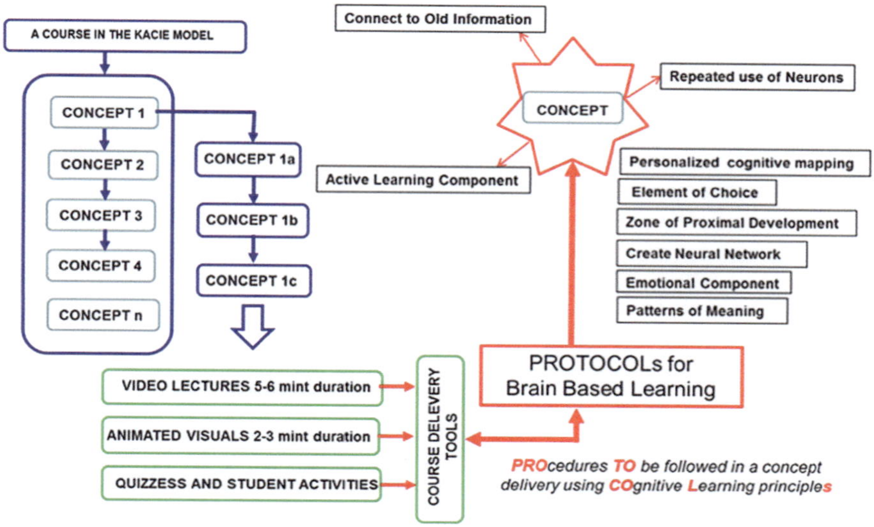

Fig. 3.1 Schematic representing knowledge and curriculum integration ecosystem (KACIE)

in order to connect to old information. This is one of the several learning protocols we introduce in the KACIE model. Elements of the KACIE model and its protocols appear in (Fig. 3.1).

3.3 Tablet Computing and Digital Ink Component

In addition to the tailored content media, each class employs a system of shared screen interaction over ink-enabled tablet computing devices (Csikszentmihalyi 1997). The use of shared screens, by which the instructor can see both groups thumbnails of student problem-solving and fullscreen views of an individual student's work in real time classroom activity has been shown to promote significantly higher engagement in subject matter content (Roschelle 1996; Rittle-Johnson and Koedinger 2005). The intention behind this ensemble of protocols, or content-rich, media rich, and feedback-rich strategies is straightforward. This effort seeks to facilitate more immediate, precise, and successful interaction between each individual student, the engineering knowledge and skills they are acquiring, and the classroom instructor who is facilitating that knowledge and skill acquisition. The combination of pen input and shared screens facilitates embodied cognition via active manipulation of mathematical symbolism and sketching while the instructor can view and provide rapid feedback to this manipulation. The system allows the instructor more immediate or ready access to the student work because of the combination of the digital ink affordance and remote view of the work provided to the instructor. An instructor view of student screens appears in (Fig. 3.2). The strategy is carried out with tablet comput-

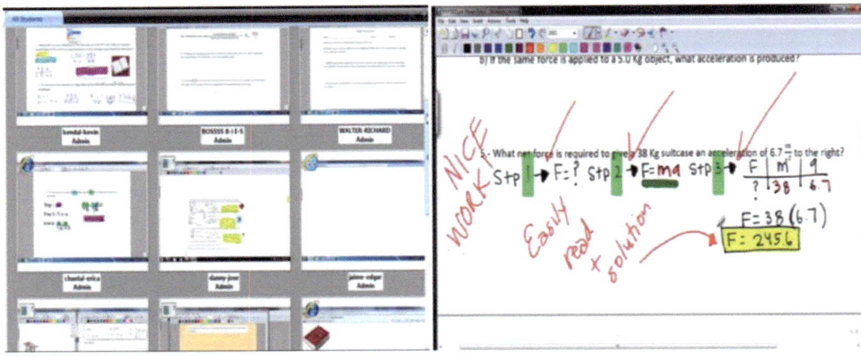

Fig. 3.2 Sample teacher view when applying zone of proximal development (ZPD) protocol

ers, as noted below, with students working in pairs. This component of the ensemble of protocols is called the Zone of Proximal Development (ZPD) protocol, referring to the social learning theory of Lev Vygotsky (1964, 1978). This theory emphasizes the importance of scaffolding learning at the outer edges of an individual's learning "zone," between trivial tasks (boredom) and tasks that are not manageable (learning to frustration).

Csikszentmihalyi (1992, 1997) relied heavily on the ZPD framework in his work on studies of flow consciousness, or states of profound immersion, and engagement. The ZPD protocol finds application in this project through pen-based computing in the following way. Because digital ink in this type of collaborative workspace permits the instructor to "see" the student cognition, and because it permits the instructor to give immediate feedback, the instructor is able to help maintain the delicate equilibrium of task difficulty at the outer edges of a student's ability, thus sustaining student engagement in the classroom and even promoting flow like learning experiences in upper-level engineering. The ensemble of protocols, with its focus on methodically introducing, reinforcing, and furnishing tailored feedback to a student's conceptual development, includes the ZPD protocol as the primary avenue for real time, highly informed feedback to the student.

3.4 Student Attitudes Towards Pen-Based Computing

Each protocol is an important part of the stepwise effort to bring student success in the upper-level courses. One current task involves unpacking not only the theoretical role but the perceived value for each protocol. The survey reported in Table 3.1 is an opening part of that process. Using a 5-point Likert scale (5 = strongly agree, 1 = strongly disagree), students were asked whether their use of the digital ink affordances in the ZPD protocol boosted their learning. This scale was only administered to the treatment of students, but will be used for forthcoming research and comparisons

Table 3.1 Student attitudes toward using pen-based computers in ZPD component of program ($n = 14$)

Mode	Mean	Question
4	4.071	During these sessions, my partner or I actively used the pens for the problems we were asked to solve
4	3.667	The pens felt pretty natural so that writing with them on the computer screen was reasonably similar to writing with a pen on paper
3	2.429	The use of the pen significantly improved the effectiveness of in class communication of ideas to the instructor
3	3.071	The use of the pen made it easier for my partner and I to communicate engineering ideas to each other
4	3.643	The use of the pen made it easier for us to solve problems on the computer in class
4	3.929	It was usually easier for us to solve problems on paper and then write down a solution for the teacher
4	2.929	Sometimes the instructor could use software that enabled them to see your display as you were typing or writing on it. The ability of the instructor to see our work significantly changed how the class could function
4	4.071	I think it would be valuable to have this type of pen-based tool in other science, engineering, or mathematics classes
4	4.143	I would use a computer that had pen capabilities for other courses
4	4.143	Having a partner in class made it a better experience than if I was using the computer alone
4	3.714	The touch capability of the screen was just as important to my experience as the pen capability
4	3.572	I used the touch capability on the computer more than I used the mouse for navigating the device

in the project. Likert scale analysis should treat means based on interval data as limited in value, reporting primarily on mode. These results suggest a strong but not intense affinity for the use of digital ink in helping to maintain student learning in the proximal development zone. Informal feedback from instructors and students alike reinforce a need common to all technology based interventions, namely consistency in usage in combination with attention to technical support requirements.

3.5 KACIE Material Development and Intervention in Fluid mechanics (2016 Fall semester)

As noted in the first page, this effort, funded by the National Science Foundation IUSE Program is entering its third year (Solomon 2015). The major activity of year two was instructional material development for KACIE course fluid mechanics. For each of 55 concepts in this course, a scripted, animated short video lecture was developed using various protocols along with a KACIE sheet for formative assessment. These movies, designed to leverage the maximum attention span, are 2–6 min in duration and are available to students through a YouTube channel (Solomon 2019).

3.6 Protocol Examples

The ZPD protocol discussed above is one of several in the project. Various other pedagogical protocols used are explained with respect to concept one "density." The first protocol involves the principle of connecting new concepts to prior knowledge (Rittle-Johnson and Koedinger 2005) and thus reviews prerequisites that can be connected to the density concept. The video starts by reviewing the basics of physical units and unit conversion, as the concept requires them as its prerequisites. After introducing and reviewing prerequisites, the actual concept is methodically repeated with examples and slight variations to strengthen neural connections (Harel 2013). In this example, the definition of density as mass per unit volume is introduced with a few examples. An active learning component (Taraban et al. 2007; Freeman et al. 2014) is introduced via creating an imaginary situation where students are asked to solve practical examples where they can calculate the density of a fluid. The protocol associated with attention to affect or emotion also comes into play. The famous "eureka" story of Archimedes is related to the concept of density and a revisit of this story then reinforces this concept. Several other protocols involving conceptual variation, abstracting a higher level perspective or generalization of the concepts of interest (Roschelle 1996), and development of a concept map round out a suite of eight strategies or protocols that each student experiences strategies in this and each of the other 54 topics in the course.

3.7 Preliminary Results

This is admittedly a highly intensive and methodical approach to repairing inadequate preparation for upper-level courses. Pre and post testing with a comparison group suggests strong and usually statistically significant learning achievement gains by participants, reported in Solomon et al. (2018).

Acknowledgements The authors wish to acknowledge the sponsorship of the US National Science Foundation in supporting this research.

References

Crawley EF, Malmqvist J, Östlund S, Brodeur DR, Edström K (2014) Historical accounts of engineering education. In: Rethinking engineering education. Springer, pp 231–255

Csikszentmihalyi M (1997) Flow and the psychology of discovery and invention, vol 39. HarperPerennial, New York

Csikszentmihalyi M, Csikszentmihalyi IS (1992) Optimal experience: psychological studies of flow in consciousness. Cambridge University Press

Duncan RG, Hmelo-Silver CE (2009) Learning progressions: aligning curriculum, instruction, and assessment. J Res Sci Teach 46(6):606–609

Freeman S, Eddy SL, McDonough M, Smith MK, Okoroafor N, Jordt H, Wenderoth MP (2014) Active learning increases student performance in science, engineering, and mathematics. Proc Natl Acad Sci 111(23):8410–8415

Froyd JE, Wankat PC, Smith KA (2012) Five major shifts in 100 years of engineering education. Proc IEEE 100:1344–1360 (Special Centennial Issue)

Graham RH (2012) Achieving excellence in engineering education: the ingredients of successful change. Royal Academy of Engineering, London

Hamilton E, Kapenda L, Miranda H, Ngololo E (2019) Sub-saharan teacher stem professional development with digital ink: follow-up (sub-saharan pen-based computing follow-up). In: Hammond T, Prasad M, Stepanova A (eds) Inspiring students through digital ink: impact of pen and touch technology on education. Springer (in press)

Harel G (2013) The Kaputian program and its relation to DNR-based instruction: a common commitment to the development of mathematics with meaning. In: The SimCalc vision and contributions. Springer, pp 437–448

Nave FM, Bonner FA, Lewis CW, Frizell S, Parker A, McFrazier M, Robinson PA (2016) African American students' academic achievement in stem at HBCUs. Advancing Educational Outcomes in Science, Technology, Engineering, and Mathematics at Historically Black Colleges and Universities, p 119

Rittle-Johnson B, Koedinger KR (2005) Designing knowledge scaffolds to support mathematical problem solving. Cogn Instr 23(3):313–349

Roschelle J (1996) Designing for cognitive communication: epistemic fidelity or mediating collaborating inquiry. Comput Commun Ment Model 13:25

Schunk DH (1990) Introduction to the special section on motivation and efficacy. J Educ Psychol 82(1):3

Shulman LS (2002) Making differences: a table of learning. Chang Mag High Learn **34**(6), 36–44 (2002)

Solomon J (2015) Collaborative research: tailored instructions and engineered delivery using protocols (KACIE). NSF Award #1504692 to Tuskegee University

Solomon J (2019) Youtube channel. URL http://bit.ly/tuskegee-tiedup

Solomon JT, Hamilton E, Viswanathan V, Nayak C, Akasheh F (2018) A protocol-based blended model for fluid mechanics instruction. ASEE-22514

Taraban R, Anderson EE, DeFinis A, Brown AG, Weigold A, Sharma M (2007) First steps in understanding engineering students' growth of conceptual and procedural knowledge in an interactive learning context. J Eng Educ 96(1):57–68

Vygotsky LS (1964) Thought and language. Ann Dyslexia 14(1):97–98

Vygotsky LS (1978) Mind in society. Harvard University Press, Cambridge, MA

Chapter 4
Sub-Saharan Teacher STEM Professional Development with Digital Ink: Follow-Up (Sub-Saharan Pen-Based Computing Follow-Up)

Eric Hamilton, Loide Kapenda, Helena Miranda and Elizabeth Ngololo

Abstract This chapter reports on research activities originally reported at the 2015 WIPTTE conference, the last one held prior to the conference name change. The chapter, entitled "A Model and Research Agenda for Teacher and Student Collaboration Using Tablets in Digital Media Making: Results from Sub-Saharan Workshops" reported on a series of science, technology, engineering, and mathematics (STEM) projects funded by the Kenyan Ministry of Education, Microsoft Research, and the National Science Foundation. The research has continued since then, with additional support from the Namibian Ministry of Education, Arts and Culture, the US State Department's Fulbright Program, and new, multiyear funding from NSF. The chapter describes the evolution of the project and five themes emerging from it, in addition to describing a new four-year effort related to the original paper. The original paper focused on activities in Kenya, Ghana, Uganda, and Namibia. This chapter centers on follow-up activities in Namibia.

4.1 Introduction

This chapter reports on research activities originally reported at the 2015 WIPTTE conference, the last one held prior to the conference name change. The chapter, entitled "A Model and Research Agenda for Teacher and Student Collaboration Using Tablets in Digital Media Making: Results from Sub-Saharan Workshops"

E. Hamilton (✉)
Pepperdine University, Malibu, CA 90263, USA
e-mail: eric.hamilton@pepperdine.edu

L. Kapenda
Ministry of Education, Arts, and Culture, Windhoek, Namibia
e-mail: loidekapenda@yahoo.com

H. Miranda · E. Ngololo
University of Namibia, Windhoek, Namibia
e-mail: hmiranda@unam.na

E. Ngololo
e-mail: engololo@unam.na

T. Hammond et al. (eds.), *Inspiring Students with Digital Ink*, Human–Computer Interaction Series, https://doi.org/10.1007/978-3-030-17398-2_4

Hamilton et al. (2016) reported on a series of STEM-related projects funded by the Kenyan Ministry of Education, Microsoft Research, and the National Science Foundation. The research has continued since then, with additional support from the Namibian Ministry of Education, Arts and Culture, the US State Department's Fulbright Program in Namibia (Hamilton 2014), and new, multiyear funding from NSF (Hamilton and Culp 2014).

The 2016 CPTTE conference included a paper on pen-based computing interfaces as entrée into learner flow in mathematics (Hamilton 2016). This chapter argued that keyboards are the haptic tools that enable embodied cognition in writing. That is, cognitive and affective processes underlying narrative or prose creation and manipulation are converted into text through the keyboard typing, and that conversion then provisions those processes with the digital tools associated with word-processing or other automation and file management affordances. It was not until the advent of digital inking tools that a similar form of embodied cognition was available for the cognitive and affective processes underlying mathematical or scientific symbol manipulation. While sophisticated software for representing mathematical or scientific notation has greatly simplified publishing in those fields, such software follows and formalizes cognition, rather than facilitating it in real-time.

The ability for school teachers to engage in such embodied cognition in doing mathematics facilitates induction into high engagement, and often flow states, while doing mathematical and scientific operations. Such engagement and flow states are possible without the digital resource of a pen-based computer, of course, but in our research, we have discovered that digitizing such processes provides access to greater collaborative resources and a broader landscape of intellectually challenging activities (Hamilton et al. 2010). In particular, using digital ink interfaces to produce videos that explain or illustrate scientific or mathematical ideas repeatedly has proven profoundly immersive to students and teachers alike. Under a conjecture that growth of mathematical and scientific competencies unfold in an optimal way if individuals are fully absorbed, undistracted, and in full concentration, digital inking in mathematics and science becomes a critical enabler or link behind such growth.

The 2015 paper highlighted challenges facing teachers in low-income nation settings. Teaching is complex and challenging in the US and other wealthy countries. That complexity and difficulty is profoundly intensified in low income nation settings. Some of the most salient limitations might be expected. These include limitations on curriculum materials, especially as low-income countries transition from colonial era curriculum models to independent curricula that reflect context, culture, and customs. Related to this are dynamics associated with language, dynamics that profoundly complicate the challenges low-income countries with multiple dialect and linguistic profiles face. The countries discussed in the earlier paper (Uganda, Namibia, Kenya, and Ghana) each mandate English as the official language of instruction. There is a general consensus in these countries that English proficiency in educational settings are necessary for full entrée into global economics and society. Secondary and often upper primary school instruction typically takes place only in English. Yet recent research confirms that preventing the use of the language of origin in formal learning settings results in lost complex cognition and diminished complex reasoning for many students in comparison to peers in multilingual settings that include the language of origin (Yarzebinski et al. 2015).

One of the overarching principles of the work reported here is an understanding that local culture, context, and language is the starting place for education reform initiatives. Digital media-making of the kind that appear in this work is designed to permit code-switching and subtitling in media to scaffold learning and reasoning within a student's language of origin. One way to view this is that pen-based computing opens up new avenues for embodied STEM cognition. The digital inking affordance thus plays a crucial role in connecting formal learning in STEM contexts to flow experiences and to the embedding of digitally-mediated learning in local culture, context, and language.

4.2 Original Research Method

When first reported at WIPTTE, the project was taking the form of a hybrid design experiment and phenomenological study, under a three year research grant from the US State Department's Fulbright program (Hamilton 2014). The design iterations were organized around the analysis of three primary data sources. The first involves the artifacts that teachers produced in workshops that engaged teacher participants in pen-based video-making. The second involves structured interviews and reflections with each participant. The third involves debriefing with university and Ministry of Education officials who helped facilitate each workshop. It should be noted that while this three-step design study allows for significant alteration, or macro-redesign, between phases, important "micro-redesign" adjustments took place between each of the workshops that form the basis for this chapter.

4.2.1 Research Venue: Teacher Workshops with Tablet Computers

The Ministry of Education and different departments of the University of Namibia organized release time and logistics for five workshops, each held in a region in the northern half of the country along with one in the Omaheke region in east central Namibia (Fig. 4.1). Table 4.1 depicts the attendance at each workshop. The final workshop was held for year three students in secondary mathematics education registered at the Hifikepunye Pohamba Campus of the University of Namibia. The first four workshops were attended primarily by secondary mathematics educators and administrators in their respective regions. The numbers of participants varied in each workshop, from approximately twelve participants to over thirty. The workshops took place over an eight-week period in 2015. Structured interviews and written reflection tools were administered to all participants after the first workshop.

Fig. 4.1 Pen-based media making workshops for teachers in Namibia

Table 4.1 Phase 1 workshop population and data collection

Workshop	1	2	3	4	5
Teacher attendees/interviews/reflection tools (53)	11/0/0	12/12/12	9/9/9	11/11/11	0
Administrator attendees (7)	2	3/0/1	1/0/0	1/0/0	0
Student (UNAM) attendees (23)	0	0	0	0	23/0/0
Learner attendees (5)	5/0/0	0	0	0	0
Total	15/0/0	15/12/13	10/9/9	12/11/11	23/0/0

All participants signed informed consent forms permitting the use of their data and images for research reports. The first workshop included one afternoon by which secondary learners participated with teachers. The workshop duration was site-specific, dependent on local arrangements and attendance and averaging 2.5–3.5 days, with one workshop lasting only for two days.

These workshops were designed to introduce teachers to begin the process of creating and editing instructional videos that incorporate mathematics and science school subject matter. The technology took several forms. For hardware, teachers were provided with pen-based computers (such as Windows-based devices from Fujitsu, Microsoft or Hewlett Packard), Surface Pro devices, or else pen-based writing boards that connect to notebook computers or computers in a classroom lab, (such as Wacom Intuos or Bamboo boards). The writing boards are nearly as functional as the tablet computers at about 5% of the computer price. Working with both provided opportunity to compare the interface usability.

On the software side, teachers were provided with two types of tools. The first was the freely available GeoGebra mathematics visualization software, enabling teachers to prepare powerful, precise, and highly interactive representations of mathematical structures. The second software tool is a suite of programs that allow teachers to record screens into editable and sharable videos. These tools include the Microsoft Journal system, OneNote, and TechSmith's Camtasia. All of the teachers were also provided with sound files, video clips, and a repository of photos that they could use to supplement videos that they designed. With this software, teachers were in a position to produce video-lessons directly on their computers as if they were on a chalkboard or whiteboard, recording and then editing their productions.

Workshops typically began with an introduction to the computer hardware and software, and opportunities for participants to work independently with each. As discussed earlier, one of the most important aspects of working in a pen-based computing environment is an adaptation to the haptic feedback associated with digitizing pen input to computers (Hamilton 2016). For virtually every participant, the workshop represented their first exposure to this interface. The process is not only of adapting to the use of a digitizing pen but connecting the affordance of that interface to their daily instructional practices. In simplified terms, step one is to adapt to the technology, and step two is to use the technology to express one's imagination or content knowledge. Participants were often asked to use the pen to write a short life story that they could share with others.

Next, teachers learned the basic elements of screen-recording. Expressing mathematical or scientific thought on a digital tablet permitted the participants to prepare and record a lesson, using a digital writing tableau such as Windows Journal or OneNote as a digital chalkboard or whiteboard. It is important to understand that this process tacitly obligates countless interactions with the technology and implicitly and explicitly leads teachers to build many new ICT and digital ink competencies.

The process of translating a lesson from a physical whiteboard or chalkboard to a digital ink mode opens an expansive set of affordances to help teachers express their ideas coherently. Teachers report that this is because the process of making a video requires them to treat prepared lessons not as one-off experiences that have no life beyond one class, but rather as reusable artifacts (Hamilton et al. 2010). There is more at stake in expressing the content clearly and concisely. And, every step of the lesson is editable until finalized. In practice, missteps or vague or incorrect explanations in a difficult class lesson usually remain unrepaired—the class ends, and everyone moves on. The editability of a video—mediated by digital ink—means not only that a teacher can give the science or mathematics lesson electronically, but can take the time to make the lesson that as strong and clear as possible. And, as mentioned above, those tools multiply the ways that ideas can be expressed, giving teachers more flexibility in using their imagination to clarify underlying conceptual structures with drawing and scientific and mathematical symbols. Media-making with freehand, digital notation and writing nurtures not only scientific and mathematical coherence but also creativity.

The workshops thus comprised a mixture of starting from a zero baseline of editing skills to building those skills while implementing them using to express mathematical or scientific concepts using the freehand symbol systems that represent those concepts. This puts upward pressure on each participant to increase their skill base, which in turn gave more flexibility in shaping content for learners. All teachers produced videos of mathematical content, but in the 2–3 day period of instruction, the results were generally quite rudimentary. Additionally, the workshop duration generally did not leave sufficient time for practice in converting the final products into sharable mp4 formats.

4.2.2 Tablet Computer and Media-Making Workshop Pedagogical Rationale, Continued

Elsewhere, the rationale for implementing the "media-making" approach has been outlined at some length (Hamilton et al. 2010). An important and distinguishing feature of this effort is that the originating driver or motivation for the workshops is not ICT or pen-based computing, but mathematics (and science) learning. This contrasts with workshops devoted to introducing content-independent ICT tools, such as word processing or spreadsheets. In this case, though, disciplinary content holds priority, over and above the ICT. Yet it turns out that in content-dependent ICT competencies, and pen-based competencies, in particular, that media-making leverages are at least as rich and useful as those that are fostered in more generic ICT exposure.

Our aim in ICT competence is not only to promote technical skills, but for teachers to reflect deeply about content and pedagogy in ways that can advance mathematics and science learning of those they teach. In this regard, teachers consistently report greater attention to mathematical coherence when they plan and create a lesson that will last more than a single class (i.e., have a persistent life as a video); they anticipate students' misconceptions more thoughtfully; they enjoy the deeply creative and imaginative aspects of mixing and remixing media to produce a finished product; and they enter into a deeply absorbed state or flow condition when they are allowed to produce video media (Hamilton 2013, 2017). The digital video editing technology itself, in providing immediate, highly visual, and colorful feedback, affects all of these factors and perhaps most importantly the first—coherence. These findings, outlined below, have also appeared in the US versions of the research. Lack of mathematical coherence has been documented as the most glaring deficiency in mathematics education in the US (Schmidt et al. 2002, 2007). Although there are no known studies focusing directly on the coherence construct in mathematics education in Sub-Saharan Africa, there is no evidence to suggest the situation differs in Namibia. Students acquire skills in manipulating symbols, often with some understanding, but fundamental idea sets remain unconnected, and individual lessons leave students confused with negative feelings directed both at themselves ("I can't do this") and mathematics ("this is not useful or understandable") when the cause for misunderstanding may have been a deficient presentation or inadequately prepared teacher—leaving the mathematics symbols unusable for problem solving or operations at what should be the learner's next level of understanding. The process of editing a video benignly coerces coherence, in that the media-maker must think and re-think how each frame connects with the previous frame and with the next frame. This not only induces coherence, but it also deepens the teacher's command of the subject matter. This form of meaningful repetition with a slight variation aligns tightly with the "R" or Repetition principle of Harel's Dualism-Repetition-Need (DNR) framework for deep mathematical reasoning (Harel 2013).

It is in a context of building coherent digital media that this effort sought not simply to integrate pen-based computing and ICT into the classroom, but to do so in a manner that promotes deep thinking and understanding. There are many layers of ICT skills that our learners must acquire for successful participation in an economically growing society. Many of these skills are rudimentary but foundational to more advanced competencies. This particular research focuses on developing the more advanced competencies of helping teachers build digital resources that can help them convey deeper understandings of mathematics and science concepts. These factors led to the original funding proposals to hold these workshops, and the section below furnishes some data that supports this approach.

4.3 Themes from Research Findings

This follow-up chapter briefly overviews five critical themes that have emerged from the research. Teachers in this study did indeed perceive pen-based media-making as a potentially powerful tool for more effective teaching. Five important themes recurrently emerged in interviews and written reflections to support their analyses. The concern over a positivity bias is mitigated by the fact that teachers proved able to express these themes differently and with sophistication. They see the pen-based video-making activity as professionally and personally integrative.

Theme 1: More access to technology desired.
The first theme was mentioned by every teacher and was a factor expected from the outset. It entailed a desire for greater access to hardware and software, and especially tablet computers, such as that employed in the professional development workshops. Many teachers reported an intention to buy costly notebook or tablet computers themselves for continuing to develop and use media-making software tools. All expressed a desire for educational authorities to furnish more technology resources in schools. Resource constraints that face education authorities worldwide are certainly present in Namibia.

Theme 2: Mathematical representation affordances. Teachers routinely were in awe of the digital inking capabilities of their devices and reported in different ways that digital ink permitted them to express mathematical concepts. **A recurrent**

theme in teacher interviews involved the usefulness of a media tool that allowed them to represent mathematical ideas quickly and accurately.

- *Media making gives me maximum confidence to teach troublesome concepts like transformations. I will be able to draw all required graphs and learners will be able to hear and see what is happening using media. The best way media making can help me to teach a troublesome topic is by drawing pictures and diagrams while learners are there. I can tell that the workshop left me with enough skills to use media in my class and to share these skills with other teachers at my workplace.*

Theme 3: Broader sense of professional well-being. The ability to represent mathematical structure is consistently viewed as a critical factor in making mathematics more accessible. More broadly, the representational affordances of video-making software are viewed **means to promote teachers' creativity, autonomy, and sense of personal empowerment, as shown in the reflections below**:

- *Digital media has expanded my creativity in a way that I have positive ways of teaching some of the topics that I use to struggle with, to make my explanations self-explanatory.*
- *This project aroused my eagerness to use tech to improve my students' results. It is even very easy to prepare the lesson the way I want it and leave work behind when I am away. This activity expanded my creativity in a way that now I can create my own videos.*
- *The (pen-based video-making) expands my creativity a lot and I am able to do much work on my own which will attract learner's interest in the lesson.*
- *Teaching in itself is an art… I think creating these videos expands creativity.*
- *Producing materials have altered my sense of personal creativity… (now) I have positive ways of teaching some of the topics that I use to struggle with.*
- *(I am)… more empowered with the knowledge to produce my own video.*
- *The instruction to me as a teacher gives me the courage to do my work as an individual and I am ready to support my learners and confident in eradicate the myths of learners who say mathematics is a difficult subject.*
- *I would have loved this time to be extended just for maybe three months or so…*

Theme 4: Teacher-learner collaboration (participatory teaching) potential. In our meetings with the participants, we often observed commentary about the impact of media-rich instructional materials for learners. One topic, though, was of special note here. One relates, in part, to the question of time. What do you think, we asked the teachers, of the idea of learners helping their teachers create videos for peers? Responses from teachers were unanimously positive. Many of them related to the question of youngsters respecting and appreciating one another's perspectives and ways of looking at mathematical ideas. This teacher voiced several important sentiments, expressing intrigue in drawing learners into using media to teach other learners. This teacher's first observation is that learners may, in at least some contexts, comprehend material more readily when provided by others. At the same time, the process of learners helping others is itself an intrinsic learning process—and one that presents content in a way that differs in form from teacher instruction.

- *That (learners helping make videos to benefit other learners) is going to be very interesting. We are saying that if learners are explaining matters to the other learners, then they (will) comprehend easier than teacher teachings, so this is going to be very good. Involving learners in our activities lets them do the work, so, say if the other one is doing this then also the learning process is going to be going up… Others will be listening to them. The way they are talking to each other is not the same way we experience them or how we interact. It is also different.*

Another teacher shared similar reflections, stressing the different ways that learners acquire new understandings—and that they can use technology more readily than their teachers:

- *I think the learners would be happy (to help teachers make videos). Because they are also involved, they would be able to come up with their own videos also. It would just be easier for them in answering questions on the exam.*

4.3.1 New Project on Participatory Teaching

It is important to note that Themes 3 and 4 are not overtly related to the digital ink affordances that teachers experienced in their workshops, but those affordances are implicated in the themes. Digital ink gives real-time "voice"—that is, representational functionality to mathematics and teachers (Ellington et al. 2011) that helped forge the sense of professional self-respect and well-being and the potential for participatory teaching.

One of the most important challenges facing teachers in contemporary Namibia is common across most cultures and societies: teachers do not have sufficient time to delve deeply into forming new competencies or adopting novel pedagogies. Time for reflective practice is generally considered a prerequisite to the development of new pedagogies. Yet teachers are hard-pressed to engage in such reflection, let alone devote quality time, and often personal resources to such development. The positive sentiment that teachers across the project expressed in support of collaborating with learners in the media-making process may prove to address the time challenge. Drawing learners into participating in teaching in this way—we call it participatory teaching, a construct substantially larger than peer tutoring or reciprocal teaching—is at the heart of a new project that involves Namibians and counterparts in Kenya, Finland, and the US. Supported by the US National Science Foundation, the project entitled "Research on an International Network for STEM Media Making and Student-led Participatory Teaching" (Hamilton and Culp 2014) builds on the experiences of teachers reported here and will operate over 2017–2020 time frame, exploring how teachers and learners collaborate in media production.

Theme 5: Code-switching as potential strategy. A final theme that emerged in these interviews was the positive sentiments that Namibian participants expressed towards the increasingly strategic area of media-making that involves code-switching or multilingual expression. One of the most significant, under-appreciated problems is the policy adopted across many multi-dialect countries, like Namibia, to adopt English as a language of formal education. The policy is pragmatic: educating the next generation in a language that has limited or non-existent use outside of that generation's region or country is a dead-end for full engagement in a broader global society. Recent studies have demonstrated significantly adverse effects of English-only school environments for English language learners. English language learners who are not allowed to use their home language in problem-solving produce solutions that fall short of those from peers permitted to move between their original language and English (Finkelstein et al. 2013; Yarzebinski et al. 2015). Essentially, preventing the use of the language of origin informal learning settings results for many students in lost complex cognition and diminished complex reasoning in comparison to peers in multilingual settings that include the language of origin (Webb and Webb 2008). These findings have important implications. They may be even more significant in countries for which development of materials in multiple dialects are commercially infeasible but manageable if carried out locally.

In other words, English-only practices leave important cognition behind. Additionally, in countries that adopt English as an official language but where only a tiny fraction of the teaching population knows English as a first language, the quality of English instruction is suspect. Our interest is in determining teacher attitudes towards producing policy-compliant English language video artifacts with first language captioning and/or oral scaffolds. Every teacher was interviewed except one supported code-switching in their videos.

- *You know um… I think for my side, English is the second language for the kid. It is not their first language, and if somebody tells you a story in your own mother tongue you will remember better than if somebody told your story in English. It happens because… if the learner wouldn't understand one word then it is out of their whole system, he will not understand anything.*
- *Yeah I think (dual language in making videos) would help tremendously. Of course, even if sometimes concepts are very difficult for learners to understand, we as teachers can also take the concepts and explain them in our own languages.*

The general sense shared by teacher practitioners reinforces the research findings cited earlier, that important cognition can often only be expressed through a student's original language. The one dissenting participant out of 53 argued that reliance on a student's original language came at the expense of acquiring advanced competencies in English.

This research relates to the implementation of pen-based computing. The use of handwritten input in an intervention that yielded encouragement to incorporate code-switching may seem counterintuitive. Yet enabling code-switching and enabling pen-based input for learning share an epistemic provenance. They both means by which meaning can be represented, shared, and manipulated to solve problems and to produce new knowledge. Permission to speak in one's original language when expressing scientific or mathematical cognition promotes intellectual agency.

Provision of tools to digitally represent scientific and mathematical symbolism similarly promotes intellectual agency, while also developing technological competences.

4.3.2 *Reflection on Themes of Future Learning Environments*

The future of pen-based computing will depend in part on the degree to which it effectively facilitates progress in emerging visions of the formal and informal educational experience. Since the start of this work reported in the pen-based computing community, the project has adopted the macro-competence framework developed by the Institute for Basic Education at UNESCO (Marope 2017b). The framework is connected to a broader vision of the future of curriculum across the life cycle (Marope 2017a), and identifies seven competences that should be integrated and normative in future learning environments. These include lifelong learning, self-agency, interactively using diverse tools and resources, interacting with others, interacting in and with the world, trans-disciplinarity, and multi-literateness. This chapter does not permit treatment of each of these, but this Sub-Saharan digital ink initiative intersects at least five of them in important ways. In the initiative this chapter reports, pen-based computing proved a catalyst for promoting important dimensions of personal, academic and system growth. It has offered opportunities for much greater intellectual agency. The communication approach enables collaboration, and eventually led a current research effort by which students from multiple countries were able to work together, in an effort supporting computational thinking and personalized learning (Hamilton and Owens 2018).

Acknowledgements This work was carried out under the sponsorship of the Republic of Namibia's Ministry of Education, Art, and Culture, the US National Science Foundation's Cyberlearning, National STEM Digital Library, and Advancing Informal Science Learning Programs, Pepperdine University, and the US State Department's Fulbright Research Program. Their financial sponsorship is gratefully acknowledged.

References

Ellington AJ, Wilson JH, Nugent JS (2011) Use of tablet pcs to enhance instruction and promote group collaboration in a course to prepare future mathematics specialists. Math Comput Educ 45(2):92

Finkelstein S, Yarzebinski E, Vaughn C, Ogan A, Cassell J (2013) The effects of culturally congruent educational technologies on student achievement. In: International conference on artificial intelligence in education. Springer, pp 493–502

Hamilton ER (2013) Finding creativity and flow in a high-stakes assessment context. Ir Educ Stud 32(1):109–117

Hamilton E (2014) Theoretical and evidentiary foundation for high performance learning in African schools. Namibia, Fulbright Sub-Saharan research fellowship (#48140035). http://bit.ly/fulbright-work-proposal-2015-2017. Accessed 10 May 2018
Hamilton E (2016) Digitizing mathematical symbolism through pen and touch technology: a beginning taxonomy of affordances for learner flow in mathematics. In: Conference on pen and touch technology in education, Brown University. 31 March–2 April 2016
Hamilton E (2017) Digitizing mathematical symbolism through pen and touch technology: a beginning taxonomy of affordances for learner flow in mathematics. In: Frontiers in pen and touch. Springer, pp 83–92
Hamilton E, Culp K (2014) Research on an international network for stem media making and student-led participatory teaching. National Science Foundation Award DRL-161284 (Advancing Informal STEM Learning (AISL) Program)
Hamilton E, Harding N, Berque D, Reed R (2010) Tablet computing, creativity and teachers as applied microgenetic analysts: a paradigm shift in math teacher professional development. Impact of pen-based technology on education, pp 47–56
Hamilton E, Kapenda L, Mbasu Z, Miranda H, Ngololo E, Ogwel JC, Sarmonpal S, Stern D (2016) A model and research agenda for teacher and student collaboration using pen-based tablets in digital media making in Sub-Saharan Africa. In: Revolutionizing education with digital ink. Springer, pp 223–230
Hamilton E, Owens AM (2018) Computational thinking and participatory teaching as pathways to personalized learning. In: Digital technologies and instructional design for personalized learning. IGI Global, pp 212–228
Harel G (2013) The Kaputian program and its relation to DNR-based instruction: a common commitment to the development of mathematics with meaning. In: The SimCalc vision and contributions. Springer, pp 437–448
Marope M (2017a) Future competences and the future of curriculum: a global reference for curricula transformation. http://www.ibe.unesco.org/sites/default/files/resources/02_future_competences_and_the_future_of_curriculum_30oct.v2.pdf. Accessed 10 May 2018
Marope M (2017b) Reconceptualizing and repositioning curriculum in the 21st century: a global paradigm shift. http://www.ibe.unesco.org/en/news/document-reconceptualizing-and-repositioning-curriculum-21st-century. Accessed 10 May 2018
Schmidt W, Houang R, Cogan L (2002) A coherent curriculum. American Education, pp 1–17
Schmidt WH, McKnight CC, Raizen S (2007) A splintered vision: an investigation of US science and mathematics education, vol 3. Springer Science & Business Media
Webb L, Webb P (2008) Introducing discussion into multilingual mathematics classrooms: an issue of code switching? Pythagoras 2008(1):26–32
Yarzebinski E, Ogan A, Rodrigo MMT, Matsuda N (2015) Understanding students' use of code-switching in a learning by teaching technology. In: International conference on artificial intelligence in education. Springer, pp 504–513

Part IV
Sketch Recognition in STEM

Chapter 5
Qualitative Assessment of CogSketch Worksheets in Introductory Geoscience Laboratory Courses: An Argument for Expanded Use

Wayne T. Marko

Abstract The use of computer-assisted instruction to tutor students in the geosciences is not common, in part because practical programs capable of assessing sketches relevant to introductory geoscience subjects are relatively new. One such program, CogSketch, is an open-domain sketch understanding system that is capable of tutoring students on sketch-based exercises and grading their work. This chapter reports on the mixed use of paper-based exercises and tablet PCs equipped with Cog Sketch worksheets in introductory geoscience laboratory courses. Potential benefits of using CogSketch worksheets include increased group focus and reduced barriers to starting laboratory exercises. Grading efficiency was not affected. However, increasing the proportion of CogSketch worksheets used during lab sessions will improve grading efficiency and amplify benefits in classroom social dynamics and teaching efficiency that may lead to learning gains.

5.1 Introduction

The use of sketches in teaching science, technology, engineering, and mathematics (STEM) courses is common practice and evidence for improved learning and the development of students' spatial skills from sketching diagrams is promising (Ainsworth et al. 2011; Gagnier et al. 2017). It seems natural that sketching migrates to a digital format as portable touch screen devices are now becoming ubiquitous in the daily lives of students and a number of sketch evaluation programs have been developed for the purposes of tutoring or coaching students in STEM subjects by having students create sketches (see Forbus et al. 2008 and Forbus et al. 2011 for examples).

CogSketch is an open-domain sketch understanding software that contains a tutoring system intended to be used in engineering and science disciplines. These disciplines commonly use sketching to communicate and to learn concepts that depend on

W. T. Marko (✉)
Engineering, Math & Physical Sciences Division, College of Lake County,
19351 W. Washington St., Grayslake, IL 60030, USA
e-mail: wmarko@clcillinois.edu

T. Hammond et al. (eds.), *Inspiring Students with Digital Ink*, Human–Computer Interaction Series, https://doi.org/10.1007/978-3-030-17398-2_5

evaluating spatial layout, visual conceptual relationships, and scaling (Forbus et al. 2017). The program uses analogy mapping (Falkenhainer et al. 1989; Forbus et al. 2008) to compare solution sketches created by the worksheet designer with those of students and is able to make qualitative and quantitative assessments of their ink.

The use of sketch-tutoring software in the geosciences is not widely practiced at any educational level, but the educational benefits of rapid feedback in the classroom and computer grading for instructors are alluring. It is not, however, expected that the application of innovative and intuitively useful technology in the classroom will always be successful (e.g., Murphy 2011). If digital touch-based sketching is to be widely used in future geosciences courses, then some fundamental multifaceted questions should be addressed: (1) What is the full range of effects generated using computer-assisted instruction and sketching exercises? (2) How can benefits to learning outcomes be maintained or increased, while minimizing drawbacks? (3) When should such teaching strategies be implemented? These are not the only questions to be addressed, and the observations and interpretations presented below are not sufficiently rigorous to answer these questions explicitly, but they can be used to generate research questions and to guide the classroom use of computer-assisted tutoring in the geosciences.

This chapter reports on the deployment of CogSketch along with a number of introductory college-level physical geology worksheets that have been recently developed for the program and are now available at the Science Education Resource Center at Carleton College (SERC)[1] website. Exercises that were used in this study covered the following subjects: topographic maps; geologic time; the principle of faunal succession; identification and kinematics of joints, faults, and folds; earthquake slip; flooding and flood recurrence; and glacial movement. The qualitative results focus on overall teaching efficiency and classroom social dynamics as compared to a traditional face-to-face physical geology laboratory course that uses paper-based exercises.

5.2 Previous Work

CogSketch combines concept sketching with the ability of the participant to receive immediate corrective feedback (Forbus et al. 2017). Concept sketches are annotated cartoon diagrams that depict the spatial relationships among geologic features (Johnson and Reynolds 2005). Johnson and Reynolds developed the definition of a concept sketch and described how it could be successfully applied to a learning cycle. Their work, as well as the work of others (e.g., Reusser et al. 2012) has produced useful methods for evaluating a student's understanding of concepts and documenting student learning progress.

Computer-assisted tutoring in the form of instant feedback has been shown to influence learning. Shofield et al. qualitatively noted higher levels of student engagement,

[1]https://serc.carleton.edu/NAGTWorkshops/intro/browse_activities.html.

higher levels of risk-taking in students, and that slower geometry students received more assistance from their instructor when an intelligent tutor was used in the classroom (Schofield et al. 1990). Koedinger and Anderson demonstrated improvement in students' learning of geometry proofs when computer-assisted tutoring was combined with an instructor who knew the tutoring software and was actively engaging students during the learning process (Koedinger and Anderson 1993). Anderson et al. documented increased rates of learning and improved performance on a final assessment for students in computer science (Anderson et al. 1995).

Twenty-six geoscience worksheets were developed by Garnier et al. (2014) to be used with CogSketch. Worksheets are similar to concept sketches, but with some differences. Unlike concept sketches, where the student or the instructor is required to generate most of the content, including the annotations, geoscience worksheets begin with a fairly sophisticated background and a curated selection of labels and annotations. Worksheets introduce a problem to students in the form of an uncompleted sketch and ask them to complete and annotate the drawing.

CogSketch geoscience worksheets have been used and tested in classroom pilot studies and in experiments. In pilot studies of geoscience worksheets, assignments were given to students as homework or extra credit in EARTH 201 courses at Northwestern University (Yin et al. 2010) as well as in in-class activities in an introductory geology course at Carleton College (Garnier et al. 2013). Reports from the implementation of the program and the exercises indicate that students quickly learned how to use CogSketch worksheets and could complete multiple geoscience worksheets within an hour.

Experiments with CogSketch and worksheets have targeted cognitive research and educational topics. Jee et al. compared the sketches of experts (graduate and undergraduate geoscience students) and nonexperts (undergraduate psychology students) and found that CogSketch could be used as a tool to distinguish the degree of spatial understanding among users with different levels of expertise (Jee et al. 2009). In a large-scale study, Garnier et al. demonstrated that CogSketch could be used to conduct frequent sketching with minimal instruction and in some instances produced learning gains (Garnier et al. 2014). Finally, Miller et al. identified learning strategies related to user feedback and connected them to the degree of learner gains (Miller et al. 2014).

This study is different from previous contributions in several ways. First, it considers how geoscience worksheets are integrated into the broader teaching process. Second, it compares the experience of using paper-based and digital worksheets as part of a single lab. Finally, it serves to document an independent and relatively large deployment of geoscience worksheets that was not directly influenced by the worksheet development process or experimental design.

5.3 Methodology

Qualitative observations were made in six different laboratory sections of an EARTH 201 Earth Systems Revealed course taught at Northwestern University between fall 2015 and fall 2016. All sections were taught by the same instructor, but the teaching assistants were different for each course. A majority of the students that participated in these courses were junior or senior undergraduates in the school of engineering.

Data used in this study consist of notes on the teaching experience that were collected by the author during the teaching process and notes that were made by the author after reviewing student worksheets. Observations were initially categorized as being related to teaching efficiency and broken out into subcategories. However, during this process, observations related to social interactions in the classroom also appeared to be prominent and were included as a separate category with a set of subcategories. Thematic content analysis (see Libarkin and Kurdziel (2002) for a summary) was applied to the observations. Observations were interpreted, restated, and coded as potential benefits, neutral outcomes, and potential drawbacks with respect to activities and interactions experienced with paper-based exercises. Potential benefits are observed behaviors that improved teaching or learning efficiency by decreasing the time necessary to complete a task or which amplified collaborative interaction between participants in the classroom. Neutral influences did not have a detectable effect on the classroom experience as perceived by the instructor. Possible drawbacks are those effects which reduced teaching or learning efficiency, made tasks more complex or time-consuming relative to a traditional lab, or dampened the frequency of social interactions. Table 5.1 presents examples of categorized observations, their interpretation, and coded themes. The results of the analysis are presented in Sect. 5.4.

5.3.1 *Using CogSketch*

Students used 10.5-in. Microsoft Surface Pro tablets to complete CogSketch worksheets which were preloaded onto the tablets. All six lab sections used the program

Table 5.1 An example of relationships among categories, observations, and coded themes

Category	Observation	Interpretation and coding
In-class use	Rarely, if ever, did students request assistance with a blank worksheet or fail to use feedback	Possible benefit: Fewer barriers to beginning worksheets
Lab teardown	Instructor never perceived cleanup time to be excessive given lab length	Neutral: Teardown time was not noticeably increased
Lab preparation	At least once between quarters, a time was scheduled to clean desktops	Potential drawback: Tablet desktops must be cleaned up

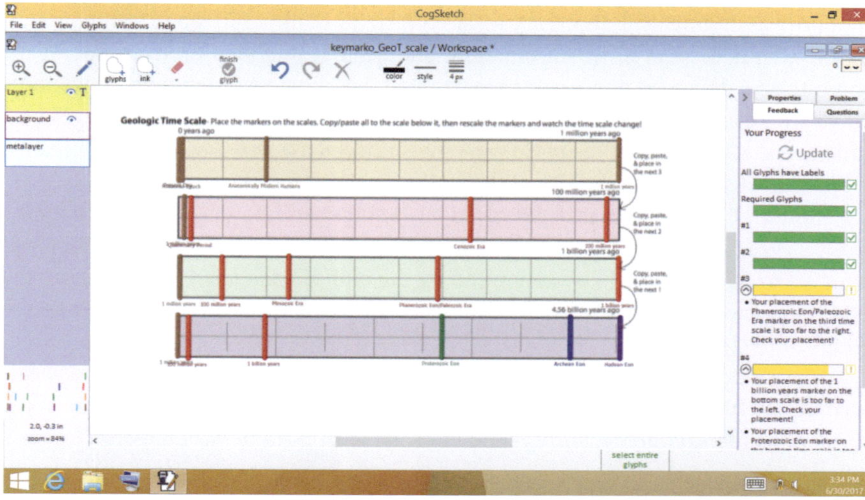

Fig. 5.1 Image of workspace with feedback meters shown on right side. Feedback text is shown below the related bar

and class sizes ranged from 9 to 22 students. Over the course of three-quarters, 492 exercises were assigned to 82 students.

Students used a stylus to create ink that was then designated as a glyph or they manipulated existing glyphs and moved them into the correct position. The glyphs were either conceptual (i.e., contour lines, glacial profiles) or annotations (i.e., arrows indicating relationship and kinematics). Glyph labels and annotation designations were assigned by the student as part of the exercise and were used by CogSketch, in addition to the ink, to evaluate the sketch against the designer's solution sketch and rubric.

Students received text and graphic feedback (Fig. 5.1). Text responses were predetermined and authored by the worksheet designer. The feedback tool measured the proportion of tasks that had been completed. The length of the feedback bar as well as its color indicated the degree of student progress. The color of the bar also indicated the degree of completion. A green bar indicated that the completed tasks were correct. A yellow bar indicated that some tasks were either not complete or were incorrect. The program provided a hierarchy of bars and text feedback. There were bars for "all glyph labels," "required glyphs," and "overall sketch" as well as feedback bars that measured the completeness of specific subtasks within a sketch.

5.3.2 *Course Design*

CogSketch was used in the laboratory because there were enough tablets to outfit one lab section and because the sketch exercise content fits well with typical introductory laboratory assignments. Laboratory sessions lasted 110 min. Fifteen to thirty minutes of time was dedicated to an introductory lecture that provided an overview of the lab exercises, delivered conceptual background, and demonstrated worked example problems. None of this time was specifically dedicated to discussing CogSketch worksheets. Students used the basic worksheet tutorial to learn how to use CogSketch and practiced submitting their work digitally.

Laboratory problems consisted of paper-based exercises designed or compiled by the instructor and one or two CogSketch worksheets. Ideally, lab content was designed to be completed and submitted by the end of each laboratory session, but some students finished their exercises outside of lab. Students typically worked in groups of two or three.

Tablets were used in six of the nine laboratory meetings. Specific worksheets were chosen based on their topical relevance and the ability of the instructor to apply the exercise to the course learning outcomes. At least 20 min was budgeted for each exercise.

5.3.2.1 Grading

Exercises were graded using pass/fail criteria that included two parts. (1) All elements or steps in a problem must be attempted. (2) Most (ideally 70%) of the exercise must be correct. Students used the feedback tool to measure their progress and estimated whether these criteria had been met. They were not provided with the numeric rubric that is part of each exercise. Exercises were submitted in two ways: (1) Images of the final sketch were exported as "JPEG" files which were then electronically uploaded to the Canvas[2] educational support program. (2) CogSketch files with the ".skw" file extension were transferred to memory sticks at the end of each lab session by students. Exercises were manually loaded into the gradebook tool that is part of the CogSketch software.

Grading of exercises was done through Canvas using the SpeedGrader tool. This tool allowed the instructor to survey the entire sketch or zoom in to examine sketch details. It also allowed the instructor to sort through a collection of images quickly, provide comments, and enter a score. Because CogSketch provided feedback to each user, no additional comments were given during the grading process.

5.4 Results

Deploying CogSketch on tablet PCs in the laboratory environment impacted teaching and learning efficiency as well as the social dynamics in the classroom. A summary of potential drawbacks, neutral outcomes, and benefits pertaining to lab preparation, in-class use, teardown, and grading are summarized in Table 5.2.

[2]https://www.canvaslms.com/.

Table 5.2 Summary of effects on teaching efficiency

Areas of teaching	Possible benefit	Neutral	Possible drawback
Lab preparation			Tablet desktops must be cleaned up
In-class use		Transition from paper to tablet use was smooth	It can be more difficult to quickly diagnose worksheet problems on a tablet PC
		There was minimal off-task use of tablets	The program did not always recognize changes made to a worksheet
	Fewer barriers to beginning worksheets		
Lab teardown		Teardown time was not noticeably increased	
Grading and reporting	Worksheets removed the need to decipher handwriting	No perceptible changes in grading time	Incorrect submissions must be opened and graded
	No need to handle and track hardcopies		

Beneficial effects were observed in the areas of in-class use, lab teardown, and grading and reporting. During class, few if any students were unable to start an exercise. This observation was common to all three-quarters of teaching. Using CogSketch worksheets also limited the need to decipher cryptic handwriting because labels and annotations are added as typed text. Finally, the digital submission process produced less paperwork to collect, sort, carry, staple, identify, and return to students.

Areas of teaching where drawbacks were felt included lab preparation, in-class use, and grading and reporting. The combined influence of CogSketch worksheets and tablets made it more time-consuming to track problems with student work. One issue is that tablet screens are relatively small compared to traditional paper-based exercises. Another issue is that the feedback presented by CogSketch is detailed (Fig. 5.1). Taken together, it was more time-consuming to evaluate the feedback and to link feedback to a problem in a student's sketch. This experience was common with the exercise that concerned the scaling of geologic time and was noted every quarter. Another drawback is that in some cases, CogSketch failed to recognize corrected glyphs and/or labels that were added and updated by the student. Typically, between zero and two students, per lab session, had a problem completing a sketch. However, most students had figured out the correct answer. Typically, saving, closing, reopening, and requesting feedback from CogSketch updated the worksheet. Restarting the worksheet from the beginning also solved the problem and redrawing a sketch only took a few minutes. Lastly, between 1 and 12% of the students submitted their work

Table 5.3 Summary of effects on social dynamics

Participants	Possible benefit	Neutral	Possible drawback
Group [students]	Increased focus when using tablets		
Instructor–student interaction			Frequency of student questions decreased
			Instructor role shifted toward technology support as students used tablets
Student–student interaction			Decrease in student interaction

in the incorrect file format. This slowed the online grading process because the files had to be downloaded and opened in CogSketch before they were graded. The largest number of worksheets submitted in the wrong file format occurred during the first quarter of teaching.

Using CogSketch on tablets produced no effect in some areas of teaching. In class, the transition from paper to digital exercises was smooth because there were enough tablets for each student in the class and students appeared to remain focused on finishing the lab assignment. Packing up tablets and styluses was not different from packing up other types of teaching supplies such as maps. Most notably, the author's approach to grading did not allow for any perceptible gains inefficiency.

The use of CogSketch exercises on tablet PCs also influenced group, instructor–student, and student–student classroom social dynamics. A summary of these observations is presented in Table 5.3. A potential benefit was an observed increase in group focus. Possible drawbacks were experienced by all participants. Most notable was the nature and frequency of student questions. The overall perception is that the frequency of questions from students decreased. This observed behavior is consistent with the findings of Garnier et al. who noted that students did not need much help with worksheets (Garnier et al. 2014), but the interpretation that this behavior is a drawback is at odds with their findings for learning gains. This inconsistency is discussed below. Other observations indicate that the nature of the questions shifted toward solving both perceived and real technology-related problems with tablets and with CogSketch. However, questions varied with exercises. With topographic maps, there were almost no questions from students during any of the quarters. Questions regarding the scaling of geologic time were focused on precisely positioning glyphs on the worksheet and those regarding structural outcrops were both technology-related and related to the exercise content. Such questions occurred during every quarter of teaching. Finally, students interacted with each other less frequently when using the tablets.

5.5 Discussion

Integrating tablet-based exercises into the lab was fairly straightforward because the program is easy to learn how to use and the available exercises have learning outcomes that could be combined with traditional paper-based laboratory assignments. Exercises are also relatively short and can be inserted into a traditional laboratory design which allows exercises to be added or deleted as time allows. The section below considers how alternative techniques and methods of deployment could improve on the application of CogSketch in laboratory courses.

Examining student work in class may be best managed by using additional technology. For example, it may be possible to use software, such as SMART Sync,[3] to allow the instructor to view student work on their own tablet or laptop and remove the need to look over the shoulders of students in the classroom. Other drawbacks such as managing tablet desktops, maintaining clean worksheet files, and fielding questions about technology will need to be absorbed into the teaching process and can potentially be offset by efficiency gains made in areas such as grading.

The instructor used the pass/fail rubric and grading method described above to manually grade CogSketch exercises. This style of grading allowed students to finish and submit their work before the end of the lab period with fewer technical issues. As it turned out, the instructor could grade worksheets as fast as CogSketch. This was because additional comments were not made, scores were not tallied, and some of the common minor mistakes, such as mislabeled glyphs, were ignored. As such, using the automated grading tool in a mixed-format course with a quantitative rubric should yield a modest increase in grading efficiency.

One approach to significantly improving efficiency would be to remove traditional paper-based exercises altogether. All exercises could then be graded automatically by CogSketch and students would not need to submit JPEG files. There are other potentially important benefits that may be amplified by this approach. For example, using more worksheets will require students to seek automated feedback more frequently and may move students through lab assignments more quickly, it may also influence which students receive assistance from the instructor. For example, the instructor may be able to focus their attention on students who are struggling with fundamental concepts and thus are making limited progress on their lab assignment as a whole. Finally, more frequent use of CogSketch and tablets could motivate some students to become more self-sufficient when solving basic technical problems.

Teaching geoscience labs using only CogSketch worksheets will require the development and testing of new exercises to target the multiple learning objectives that are commonly covered by a typical laboratory assignment. This is a significant drawback to only using CogSketch worksheets. One approach to this daunting problem is to take on laboratory topics individually and create batches of exercises for a specific topic. These exercises could be deployed as a single "digital format" lab among paper-based labs, but the entire set of exercises could be graded by CogSketch. This

[3] https://support.smarttech.com/software/other-software/smart-sync.

will change the workflow for grading lab assignments and result in perceivable time savings for the instructor.

The reduced frequency of content-related questions and the reduction in student–student interaction may be amplified by increasing the number of worksheets used per lab. However, it is also possible that such behaviors will not dampen potential learning gains (Garnier et al. 2014) generated by using more worksheets. Other positive effects like increased focus and the benefits of instant feedback (see Miller et al. (2014)) may simply compensate for working in a less collaborative environment.

5.6 Future Work

The qualitative summary of observations presented above highlights several interesting elements of social dynamics and teaching efficiency that may influence learning. Lines of future investigation should focus on accurate and quantitative characterization of increased student focus and the ability of students to begin exercises. The causes of these behaviors may not be simple. For example, the improved focus could be related to receiving immediate feedback, using the tablet, worksheet content, or some combination of these elements. Similarly, there are also several explanations for the apparent lowering of barriers to getting started on exercises. These include receiving automated feedback, the content of the exercises, the ability of students to tackle spatial problems, or some combination of these reasons. Until CogSketch's influences on classroom social dynamics and teaching efficiency are better understood, it will be difficult to predict if and how increasing the number of worksheets per lab will influence learning among the different student populations taking introductory geoscience courses.

5.7 Conclusions

CogSketch worksheets and tablet PCs were deployed in traditional face-to-face physical geology lab sections and used along with paper-based worksheets with minimal adjustment to the instructional dynamics of the course. Worksheets were easily integrated into a traditional geoscience laboratory design and content, and produced a mixture of potential benefits and drawbacks with regard to teaching efficiency and classroom social dynamics. Potential benefits include increased group focus and reduced barriers to starting laboratory exercises. The mixed-use course design and rubric used here did not allow for noticeable gains in grading efficiency. However, significant improvements in grading efficiency may be achieved by modifying the course design to increase the proportion of CogSketch worksheets used in class. This approach also has the potential to improve learning by making it possible for students to move through exercises more quickly and by allowing instructors to focus their attention on students who need it most.

Acknowledgements This research was made possible by the Department of Earth and Planetary Sciences and the Qualitative Reasoning Group at Northwestern University. Thanks to Patricia Beddows for introducing me to members of the research group and thanks to Maria Chang and Madeline Usher for their technical support with CogSketch and tablet PCs. Ken Forbus provided the impetus for this chapter, as well as needed insight into research on CogSketch. This chapter was improved and benefited greatly from the comments of two anonymous reviewers.

References

Ainsworth S, Prain V, Tytler R (2011) Drawing to learn in science. Science 333:1096–1097

Anderson JR, Corbett AT, Koedinger KR, Pelletier R (1995) Cognitive tutors: lessons learned. J Learn Sci 4(2):167–207

Falkenhainer B, Forbus KD, Gentner D (1989) The structure-mapping engine: algorithm and examples. Artif Intell 41(1):1–63

Forbus KD, Usher JM, Lovett AM, Lockwood K, Wetzel J (2008) CogSketch: open-domain sketch understanding for cognitive science research and for education. SBM 8:159–166

Forbus K, Usher J, Lovett A, Lockwood K, Wetzel J (2011) CogSketch: sketch understanding for cognitive science research and for education. Top Cogn Sci 3(4):648–666

Forbus KD, Chang M, McLure M, Usher M (2017) The cognitive science of sketch worksheets. Top Cogn Sci 9(4):921–942

Gagnier KM, Atit K, Ormand CJ, Shipley TF (2017) Comprehending 3d diagrams: sketching to support spatial reasoning. Top Cogn Sci 9(4):883–901

Garnier B, Ormand CJ, Chang M, Matlen B, Tikoff B, Shipley TF, Forbus K (2014) Testing CogSketch geoscience worksheets as an effective spatial learning tool in introductory geoscience courses. Geol Soc America Abs Programs 46(6):671

Garnier B, Ormand CJ, Chang MD, Tikoff B, Shipley TF, Forbus KD (2013) Using sketching software with a virtual tutor to increase sketching and spatial skill development in a classroom environment. Geol Soc America Abs Programs 45(7):656

Jee BD, Gentner D, Forbus K, Sageman B, Uttal DH (2009) Drawing on experience: use of sketching to evaluate knowledge of spatial scientific concepts. In: Proceedings of the 31st Annual Conference of the Cognitive Science Society, Amsterdam, The Netherlands

Johnson JK, Reynolds SJ (2005) Concept sketches—using student-and instructor-generated, annotated sketches for learning, teaching, and assessment in geology courses. J Geosci Educ 53(1):85–95

Koedinger KR, Anderson JR (1993) Effective use of intelligent software in high school math classrooms. In: Proceedings of the World Conference on Artificial Intelligence in Education, Edinburgh, Scotland, pp 241–248

Libarkin JC, Kurdziel JP (2002) Research methodologies in science education: qualitative data. J Geosci Educ 50(2):195–200

Miller BW, Cromley JG, Newcombe N, Chang MD, Forbus KD (2014) Using CogSketch to support student science learning through sketching with automatic feedback. Accessed from 30 April 2018, from the AERA Online Paper Repository

Murphy GD (2011) Post-PC devises: a summary of early ipad technology. E-J Bus Educ Scholarsh Teach 5(1):18–32

Reusser LJ, Corbett LB, Bierman PR (2012) Incorporating concept sketching into teaching undergraduate geomorphology. J Geosci Edu 60(1):3–9

Schofield JW, Evans-Rhodes D, Huber BR (1990) Artificial intelligence in the classroom: the impact of a computer-based tutor on teachers and students. Soc Sci Comput Rev 8(1):24–41

Yin P, Forbus KD, Usher JM, Sageman B, Jee BD (2010) Sketch worksheets: a sketch-based educational software system. In: Proceedings of the 22nd IAAI Conference, Atlanta, GA, pp 1871–1876

Chapter 6
Flow2Code: Transforming Hand-Drawn Flowcharts into Executable Code to Enhance Learning

Samantha Ray, Jorge Iván Herrera-Cámara, Matthew Runyon and Tracy Hammond

Abstract Flowcharts serve as a great tool for new students learning programming logic in a language-independent fashion. However, current software tools for creating flowcharts on the computer have various shortcomings. UI-based solutions make creating flowcharts difficult through inefficient drag-and-drop menus. Sketching-based solutions take a more intuitive approach but don't help the students beyond having pseudocode to start with. Flow2Code, on the other hand, enables students to draw flowcharts and translate them into code in a helpful way of bridging the gap between the two languages. Flow2Code can identify and interpret flowcharts drawn on paper using an algorithm for recognizing various shapes used in flowcharts. It fills a gap in the current solutions by converting the flowcharts into executable code and by having an intuitive and interactive interface where the users can edit both their flowchart and its resulting code.

6.1 Problem Statement and Context

6.1.1 Problem Statement

6.1.1.1 Barrier to Entry for New Students

There exists a new and alarming trend in computer science education of undergraduate students failing introductory programming classes at a rate of around

S. Ray (✉) · J. I. Herrera-Cámara · M. Runyon · T. Hammond
Sketch Recognition Lab, Department of Computer Science and Engineering, Texas A&M University, College Station, TX, USA
e-mail: sjr45@tamu.edu

J. I. Herrera-Cámara
e-mail: jorgeivan000@gmail.com

M. Runyon
e-mail: mattrunyon@tamu.edu

T. Hammond
e-mail: hammond@tamu.edu

T. Hammond et al. (eds.), *Inspiring Students with Digital Ink*, Human–Computer Interaction Series, https://doi.org/10.1007/978-3-030-17398-2_6

33% (Bennedsen and Caspersen 2007). High failure rates in an introductory course suggest a problem in the course's design as the students should not need any background in the subject to perform well.

Introduction to programming classes can be one of the two types. The first involves starting directly in a coding language, learning to write code in that language, and focusing on learning the semantics and details of using that language, e.g., pointers in C++. The second starts with learning how to create flowcharts and focuses on gaining problem-solving skills and practicing writing the step-by-step processes of a program (Powers et al. 2006).

Due to the focus on learning syntax and details about specific programming languages, students in the first type of class may not learn fundamental programming skills. The program itself remains an abstract concept to the struggling students. They do not understand the purpose of algorithms or data structures and cannot identify them in existing programs. As a result, they learn snippets of code akin to a foreign-language learner only learning select phrases and try to mash them together into programs. Eventually, the class will progress to the point where this brute-force strategy will fail.

Flowcharts, on the other hand, help students learn the design and logic of programming in a language-neutral way. They serve as a visual representation of an algorithm, so students have an easier time understanding what a given program does. The different shapes help distinguish different data structures and key words and flowcharts do not have any special/unique syntax. Additionally, flowcharts can be used as an outline for a program.

6.1.1.2 Proposed Solution

Flow2Code combines the two methods to take advantage of the flowchart's intuitive design and to help students learn beginner programming by using a system that converts their hand-drawn flowchart into code. The user draws their flowchart on paper and takes a photo to upload their flowchart into the application. Flow2Code processes the flowchart and generates executable code that the user can edit. The physical act of writing or drawing reinforces the concepts in a person's memory, helping students learn programming logic. This system bridges the gap between flowcharts and code in a form that directly connects the two domains. Additionally, the user can edit the code to correct the program or experiment. As a result, this system fully realizes the goal of using flowcharts as a tool for learning how to write code.

6.1.2 Context

The work in our system acknowledges and expands upon the current software systems for learning programming using flowcharts. Existing tools for flowchart creation fall short as a method for learning programming due to their design shortcomings and/or lack of connection to code.

6.1.2.1 Traditional Systems

Courses that use flowcharts as a learning tool for programming take one of two approaches: using flowcharts as an outline or using flowcharts as training wheels. The difference in methods comes from how the course treats flowcharts after coding has been introduced. Both of these methods begin by teaching the students only about flowcharts and algorithmic logic. Generally, students will be restricted to only using flowcharts even if the student has some understanding of programming. For the sake of simplicity, the course often has the students draw flowcharts on paper instead of software solutions (Farrugia et al. 2005). Additionally, drawing flowcharts on paper has the benefit of reinforcing the concepts into the student's memory due to the connection between the physical act of writing and retention (Buxton 2007).

The outline approach uses flowcharts as the starting point for writing any program. These courses focus on program design and understanding programming logic over learning how to code in a specific language. Writing a program in these courses follows a 3-step process. First, the student draws the flowchart. Next, the student translates the flowchart into pseudocode. Finally, the student converts the pseudocode into the specific language the course uses.

The training wheels approach uses flowcharts as an introduction to programming and transitions to a code-only method by the end of the course. The flowchart and programming language systems remain independent within the course and the student must bridge the gap on their own. Naturally, these courses tend to be more language focused.

Both of these methods begin by teaching the students only about flowcharts and algorithmic logic. Generally, students will be restricted to only using flowcharts even if the student has some understanding of programming. First, the student draws the flowchart. Next, the student translates the flowchart into pseudocode. Finally, the student converts the pseudocode into whatever language the course uses.

These traditional systems generally use minimal technology to aid or enhance the usefulness of flowcharts. The flowchart serves only as a starting point for writing a program; it does not matter if the student creates the flowchart on paper or in a software application. The student will write the code or pseudocode on their own.

6.1.2.2 Menu-Driven Systems

Many software systems for creating flowcharts use drag-and-drop or point-and-click menu systems. These approaches have the advantage of editing the flowchart with relative ease as individual parts of the flowchart can be moved, added, or deleted. Another benefit to generating flowcharts using software lies in the beautification of the result. All of the elements will be uniform and unambiguous. The cost of these benefits comes from learning the user interface which can consist of complicated, nested menus. This design will lead to frustration if the user cannot find the flowchart element they need or if the interface proves cumbersome to use.

Some of these systems have the capability to generate code from the user's flowcharts. The available languages depend on the age and purpose of the system: BACCII (Calloni et al. 1994) can translate into C++ and the older languages Pascal, and FORTRAN. Raptor (Giordano and Carlisle 2006) can translate into Ada, C++, C#, and Java.

These systems help students learn programming skills with respect to problem-solving and writing algorithms rather than learning the syntax of a language. On one hand, this helps students develop a foundation in programming logic without having to struggle through syntax bugs. On the other hand, these systems do not help the student learn to write the program themselves.

None of these systems have the ability to execute the code generated from the flowcharts. At best, these systems generate uneditable code. To verify if their program works as intended, the user must run the code in another source. At worst, these systems do not allow the user to access the generated code, making them less useful for learning how to program.

6.1.2.3 Sketching Systems

Some software solutions seek to bridge the gap between traditional sketching and menu-driven software. These methods use sketch recognition to generate flowcharts from the user's drawings. Drawing has the advantage of being intuitive to the user. These systems enable users to draw their flowcharts by hand using either online or offline frameworks.

Online systems specialize in recognizing hand-drawn, online flowcharts, i.e., sketch recognition. Because of the nature of online drawings having effectively no noise, the major recognition hurdle for online systems comes from time constraints. Improvements to this style of software focus on improving the user's ability to edit and correct their drawings in addition to improving the recognition algorithms. Currently, these methods require significant processing power for their recognition algorithms and as such do not work as real-time systems on all computing devices. An example of such a system comes from Wu et al.'s SmartVisio system (Wu et al. 2015) which has a 94.9% accuracy in recognizing strokes and an 83.2% accuracy in recognizing symbols when tested on an online database of de-noised images.

Offline systems specialize on recognizing flowcharts drawn on paper. The main challenge these systems face lies in stroke extraction from noisy drawings in order to do shape recognition. A variety of methods have been used to achieve this goal including fuzzy logic set membership (Novak et al. 1999) and the A* search algorithm (Delling et al. 2009). An example of this type of system comes from Carton (Carton and Lemaitre 2013) which has a 92.4% accuracy in recognizing strokes and a 75% accuracy in recognizing shapes when tested on an online database of de-noised images.

6.2 Method Employed

Drawing flowcharts on paper remains the most natural and intuitive way to create flowcharts. Flow2Code improves on traditional methods by enhancing the flowcharts with technological conveniences such as code generation and drawing beautification and organization. To address and surpass limitations in current software solutions for flowchart creation, the proposed system focuses on real-time, offline recognition that works on photos from a smartphone camera. The system has high accuracy, usability, and novelty as shown in the initial user studies and during a classroom evaluation.

Flow2Code uses the following steps:

(1) Sketch flowchart on paper using a pencil.
(2) Take photo of flowchart using smartphone.
(3) Flow2Code processes flowchart and produces color-coded, classified result.
(4) User reviews shape classification and makes corrections if needed.
(5) User confirms correctness of text classification and makes corrections if needed.
(6) Flow2Code generates executable code.
(7) User executes code and can modify code to experiment with results.
(8) User can save and manage the flowchart and code.

6.2.1 Preprocessing

First, the student draws out their flowchart on paper. The constraints on these drawings include (1) not tracing over previously drawn lines, (2) drawing arrows in two strokes to differentiate the shaft from the head, and (3) have positive conditional logic arrows point downward and negative conditional arrows point left or right. The users do not need to completely close the shapes for them to be recognized as a closed shape. Stroke collision can create confusion between shapes and arrow shafts and create false positives in the closed shape recognizer. Additionally, people do not always close their shapes when drawing, so this requirement does not go against instinctive drawing habits.

When the user finishes drawing their flowchart, the user will take a photo using their smartphone. This photo will go through preprocessing steps to generate a digital flowchart based off the user's that will move on to the recognition phase of the application. The system works best when the drawing contrasts against the paper, so flowcharts drawn on white paper work best. However, the photo does not need to be of perfect quality for the system to accurately process the flowchart. Figure 6.1 depicts an example photo where the lighting causes a blue effect and the pencil lines vary in darkness.

First, the user crops their photo to adjust their flowchart to maximize the flowchart's visibility and remove noise around the border of the photo. After cropping, the resulting image goes through a resizing step to standardize the flowchart into a 600×400 pixel rectangle. Figure 6.2 shows how this step affects the initial

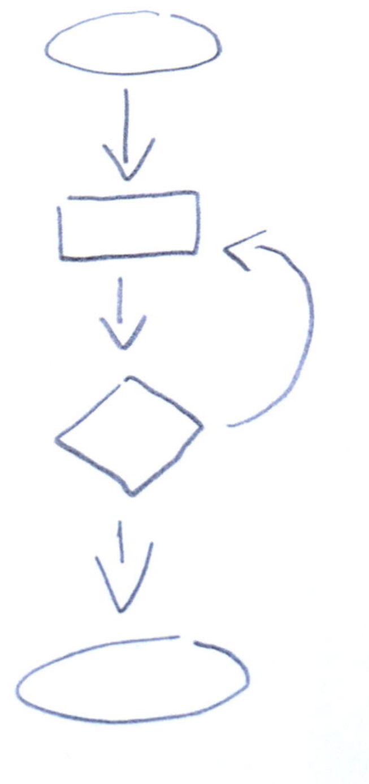

Fig. 6.1 An example hand-drawn flowchart drawn on white paper in natural light

flowchart's appearance. Any shape distortion will not alter the logic depicted by the flowchart.

Next, the photo gets converted to grayscale to remove all color and then converted to black and white using binary thresholding to standardize the image. This removes any uneven brightness and environmental effects on the lighting as shown in Fig. 6.3. This step makes it possible for the user to take a photo without any special requirements for the lighting or drawing utensil as long as the flowchart contrasts against the background.

Then, the image gets cleaned up by removing the salt and pepper noise, i.e., removing any black or white dots to make all the lines solid black and the background solid white. This type of noise occurs in all photos (Bovik 2005); the selected method of adaptive Gaussian threshold works best for this application's subject matter of photos of varying conditions and properties. Figure 6.4 shows how this step improves the contrast of the flowchart against the paper.

Lastly, the image goes through a skeletonization step to normalize the line thickness in the drawings. All of the lines become one pixel wide. This minimizes the noise in the image and makes edge detection easier. Flow2Code focuses on high accuracy and speed, so we selected the Zhang–Suen thinning algorithm (Zhang and Suen 1984) for this step. The flowchart in Fig. 6.5 shows the final result of the preprocessing.

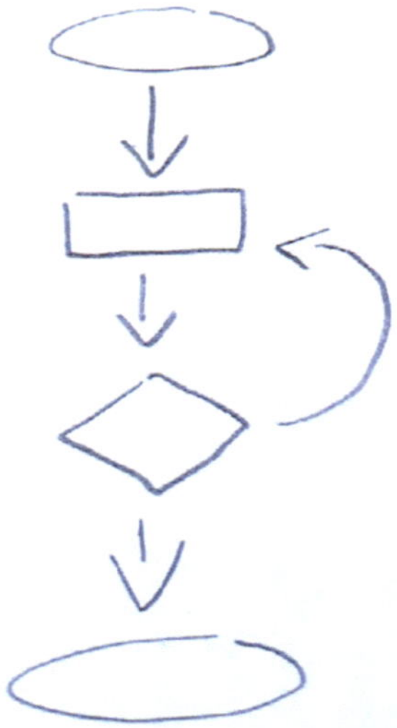

Fig. 6.2 The flowchart from Fig. 6.1 after size normalization

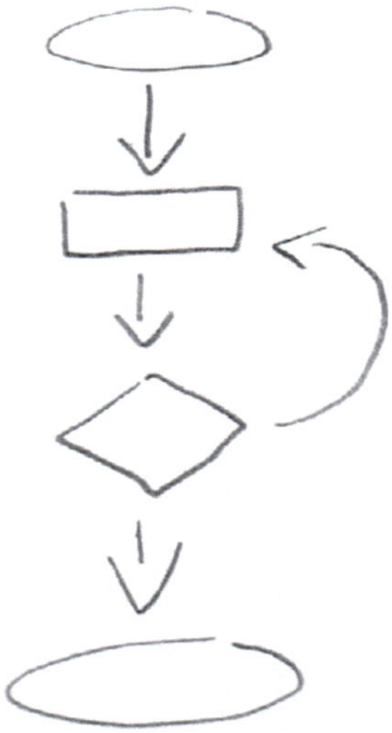

Fig. 6.3 The flowchart from Fig. 6.2 after grayscale conversion

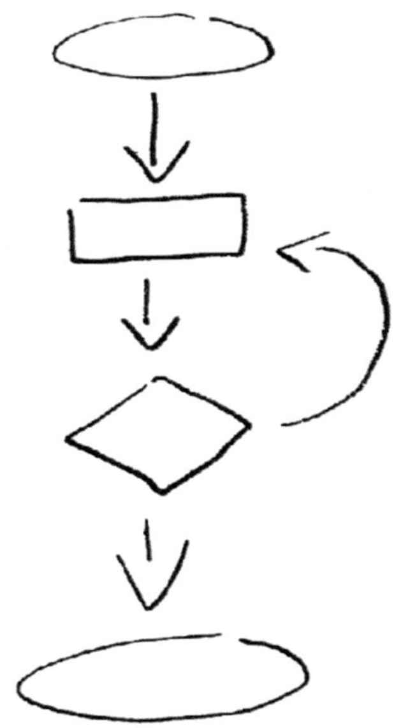

Fig. 6.4 The flowchart from Fig. 6.3 after thresholding

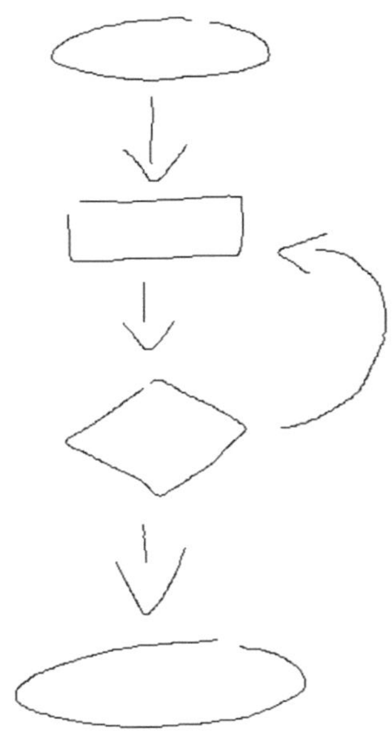

Fig. 6.5 The flowchart from Fig. 6.4 after skeletonization

6.2.2 Recognition

6.2.2.1 Stroke Extraction

The system now has a cleaned-up flowchart for the recognition phase. Now the individual parts of the image must be recognized and classified in order to identify the logic represented by the flowchart. First, the system must extract the strokes and line segments from the image using an algorithm similar to Paulson et al. (2008), Rajan et al. (2010). This generates a bitmap in the form of a matrix for the image where a 0 signifies a white (off) pixel and a 1 signifies a black (on) pixel. The stroke extraction algorithm takes this matrix as input and iterates through it using a nested loop starting from the top left and ending at the bottom right. When the system detects an index containing a 1, it applies a recursive algorithm, adds this point to a list of points, and changes the value from 1 to 0 to prevent revisiting the pixel. The recursive method examines the 8-pixel window surrounding the point. During each recursion, it checks for the following three cases: one on neighbor, multiple on neighbors, or zero on neighbors.

In the one on neighbor case, only one pixel adjacent to the center pixel contains a 1. The algorithm calls its recursive method on this neighbor, continuing its discovery of the stroke, and adds the pixel to the stroke's list of points. This case serves as the ideal discovery scenario: the algorithm has found the start point of a stroke or sub-stroke that has no branching paths. Ideally, the algorithm will exclusively encounter this case and will travel along the stroke to its end point without discovering any points of ambiguity. However, because the algorithm iterates through the bitmap from left to right, top to bottom, there exists a significant probability that the search will discover a point in the middle of a stroke as shown in Fig. 6.6. Similarly, strokes may collide, creating branching paths during stroke discovery.

In the multiple on neighbors case, the 8-pixel window has multiple pixels containing the value 1. As a result, the algorithm faces an ambiguity problem for determining which neighbor continues the stroke. This case has two sub-cases depending on whether the ambiguity occurs at the beginning or during a stroke discovery.

If the current list of points contains only one point, i.e., the recursive method just started, then this constitutes the "First Point of Stroke" sub-case. In this sub-case, the system adds this point to a new list called the ignored point list, preserves the current pixel's original value in the matrix, and skips the current pixel. By ignoring the pixel

Fig. 6.6 An example of the "Middle of Stroke" sub-case

during this iteration, the algorithm will visit it again once the search discovers the start or end point of the stroke and thereby enters the one on neighbor case.

On the other hand, if the current list contains multiple points, then this constitutes the "Middle of Stroke" sub-case. In this sub-case, the algorithm found a juncture within a stroke, so the search has multiple paths it can take. To decide which route to take next, the system calculates the angle between the current pixel and each of its on neighbors and picks the neighbor with the angle with the least amount of change from the current stroke path.

In the zero on neighbors case, the algorithm found no pixel with value 1 within the 8-pixel window. This case functions as the base case of the recursive method. The method terminates and returns the list of points, declaring it a stroke.

Finally, after iterating through the entire bitmap, the system iterates through the ignored point list and tries to detect any strokes it accidentally ignored. Completely closed strokes have no distinct start or end points, so the recursive method will ignore the entire stroke by repeatedly entering the "First Point of Stroke" sub-case in the multiple on neighbors case. Therefore, the system performs a similar algorithm for stroke detection on the ignored point list without concern for points of ambiguity. This allows the algorithm to efficiently and robustly detect both mostly closed and completely closed shapes.

6.2.2.2 Shape Recognition

Now that the system has identified all of the strokes in the image, the system now must determine what shapes these strokes create. A person can intuitively recognize a shape by its appearance. For example, different shapes have varying numbers of corners, e.g., a triangle has three, a quadrilateral four, and a hexagon six. To replicate this process in a machine, it must correctly approximate the number of corners within a stroke. A method for achieving this comes from the ShortStraw (Wolin et al. 2008) paper. ShortStraw begins by calculating the distance between each sampling point based on the total length of the stroke and the total desired amount of sample points for that stroke. Next, it resamples the entire stroke based on these parameters so that the newly sampled points all have equal distance from one another. Then it creates a list of "straws" by calculating the distance for each point in the range of $i \pm w$ where i signifies the ith point in a set of n points and w represents the offset value set at 3. Next, it calculates the mean length of a straw and passes the straws through a filter to determine which straws fall below the mean. These short straws detect corners as the distance between two points with a corner in the middle being shorter than the distance between two points along a straight line. The selected short straws go through a false-positive filter to remove straight straws that coincidentally had a length shorter than the mean length and made it through the first filter. Lastly, the short straws go through a corner filter to remove straws that detect the same corner so that the list only has one short straw per corner. The algorithm returns the number of corners based on the remaining number of short straws in the list (Figs. 6.7 and 6.8).

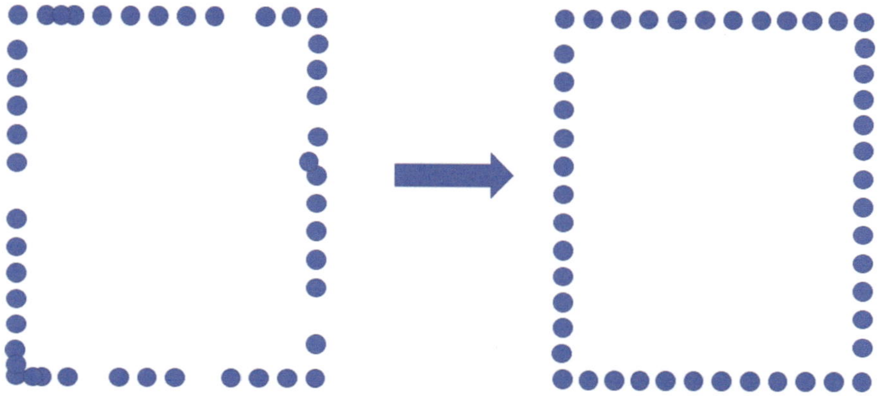

Fig. 6.7 Before and after resampling the points in the stroke

Fig. 6.8 Example of corner detection. Orange straws detect corners, and purple straws detect straight sub-strokes

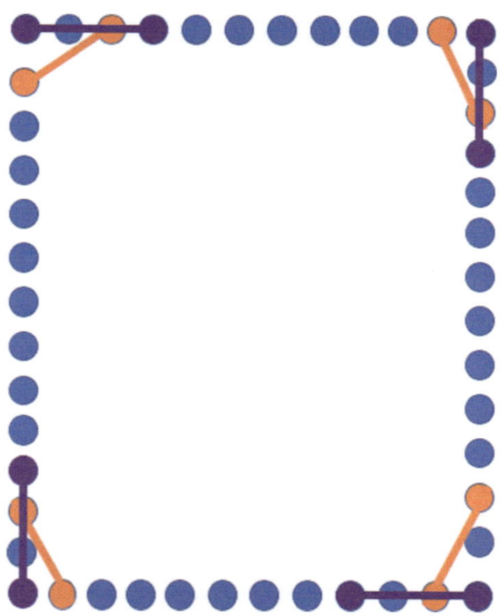

Different shapes have unique characteristics that can be used as features for classification. Rubine (1991a, b) defined a set of 13 features computable in constant time per input point. The shape recognizer uses the five features most relevant to flowchart shapes: start point, end point, stroke length, total rotation squared, and the distance between start and end point.

Several of these features have intuitive definitions. Start and end point refer to the points at the beginning and end of the stroke, respectively. Uniquely to the stroke extraction algorithm, the start point signifies the first point in the point list for a stroke and naturally, the end point signifies the last point in that list. Stroke length refers to its literal meaning, but it equivalently refers to the size of the point list as Shortstraw normalizes the distance between each point. For context, Rotational Change measures the curve of a stroke by calculating the angle of the line formed between the start and end points of a stroke. This value can distinguish a horizontal line from a vertical line, but it cannot tell the difference between a curvy line and a straight line with the same start and end points. As such, most closed shapes will have similar Rotational Change as the end point returns to the start point. However, not all closed shapes contain the same types of angles, so using Rotational Change Squared will distinguish smooth shapes from angled shapes. The Rotational Change Squared accentuates differences in smoothness by giving more weight to corners whereas Rotational Change alone would be identical among closed shapes. In conclusion, Rotational Change Squared measures the curvature of a stroke: the higher the score, the rounder the shape.

These features quickly and easily differentiate most closed shapes relevant to flowcharts with the exception of diamonds and other quadrilaterals as they have the same number of corners. High-level constraint-based geometrical methods can be used to resolve the problem at the cost of being computationally expensive (Johnston and Hammond 2010). Therefore, this system has implemented a new feature, the Axis Aligned Score (AAS), to quickly differentiate diamonds from other quadrilaterals.

AAS takes the four corners detected by ShortStraw and sorts them in adjacency order, clockwise or counterclockwise. Next, it finds the center point of the entire shape by averaging the x and y values of the corner points and the maximum and minimum x and y values. Using these values, AAS generates four new points to represent the xy-axis: (x_{avg}, y_{max}), (x_{avg}, y_{min}), (x_{max}, y_{avg}), and (x_{min}, y_{avg}). AAS calculates the distances from the axis points to the shape points so that it can uniquely map each axis point to one of the corner points. To find the most accurate alignment of the shape with the xy-axis, AAS selects the mapping which has the smallest sum of those distances and uses the sum as its value.

Using this information about the orientation of the shape relative to the xy-axis, the classifier can determine if the corners belong to a diamond or another quadrilateral. The points of a diamond lie on or close to the xy-axis, so the AAS value should be close to zero. If the smallest sum of the distances totals to less than 80 pixels, the algorithm classifies the shape as a diamond (Fig. 6.9). This number comes from the fact that other quadrilaterals produce a sum of distances well above 100 pixels. AAS proved itself a useful feature for solving this case of shape ambiguity in a computationally cheap manner.

After classifying diamonds, the remaining quadrilaterals consist of rectangles and parallelograms. The ratio of the diagonals connecting nonadjacent corners differentiates rectangles from parallelograms as the ratio should be close to one for rectangles (Fig. 6.10).

Once the system computes all the aforementioned features, it applies prescribed geometric rules to categorize the strokes into a complete shape or as an unrecognized stroke if it cannot satisfy the features of any of the shapes. The classification process follows a sequential order to optimize the decision tree: Circle/Ellipse, Diamond, Rectangle, Parallelogram, and Arrow. Closed shapes like Circle/Ellipse have appar-

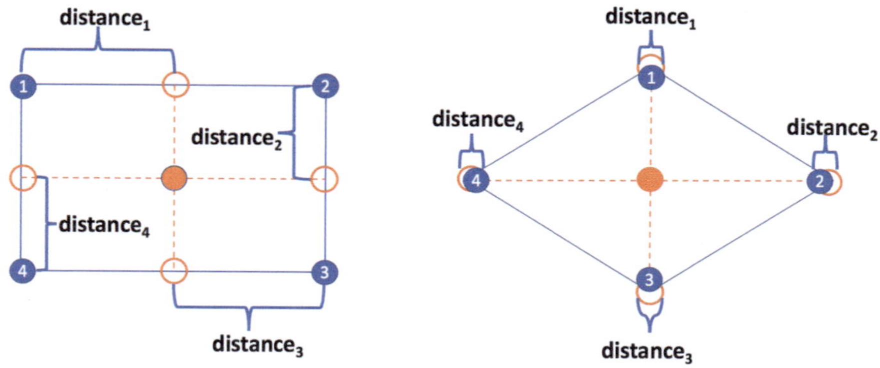

Fig. 6.9 Axis Aligned Score (AAS) calculation for a rectangle and a diamond

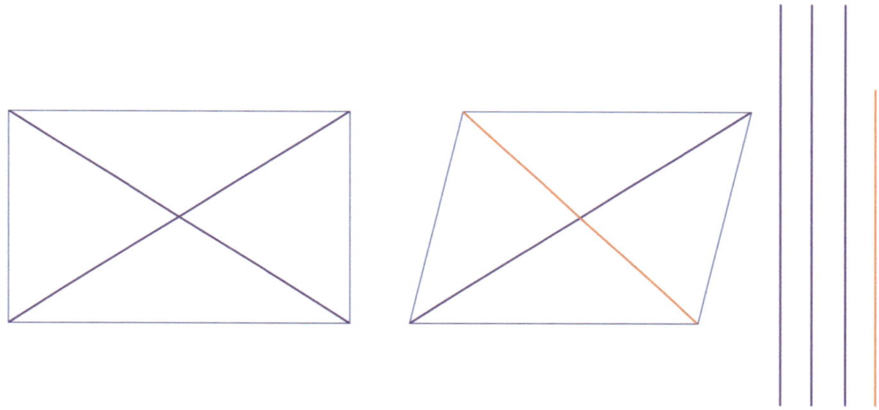

Fig. 6.10 Example of how the diagonals of rectangles and parallelograms compare

ent characteristics which require no extra computation to classify while others like the quadrilateral family require some attention to differentiate the shapes.

The system defines closed shapes to be a single stroke with a distance between start and end points of less than 20 pixels. As mentioned, users often do not fully close shapes when drawing, so the margin of error allows for robust detection of closed shapes.

If the shape satisfies the following conditions, then the closed shape recognizer classifies it as an ellipse:

- Zero to three corners
- Rotational Change Squared > 40

Theoretically, an ellipse has zero corners, but ShortStraw can give false positives due to extreme angular change being mistaken as a corner like the strong curves at the short sides of an ellipse. Ellipses have the highest Rotational Change Squared and the fewest corners among the flowchart shapes, so the closed shape recognizer picks out all the ellipses first to make classifying the next shapes easier.

The closed shape recognizer looks for quadrilaterals next. Quadrilaterals must satisfy the following conditions:

- Three or four corners
- Rotational Change Squared > 20

In the case of three corners, the classifier attempts to find the fourth corner by calculating the midpoint between the start and end points and treating it as a corner. As a nearly closed shape, this approximation does not alter the overall shape of the stroke: it simply completes the stroke in the same way the human eye would fill in the negative space. If successful, the classifier declares the stroke a quadrilateral and moves onto the subclassifiation to differentiate diamonds, rectangles, and parallelograms.

To check for diamond classification, the system takes the coordinates of all four corners of the quadrilateral shape as input. Then, it checks the AAS of the potential diamond. If the AAS < 80 pixels, the classifier declares the quadrilateral a diamond.

If the quadrilateral does not satisfy the features of a diamond, the classifier then tries to classify the quadrilateral as a rectangle or parallelogram. It does this by first checking the Diagonal Difference Ratio. If the Diagonal Difference Ratio approximately equals 1, then the classifier declares the quadrilateral a rectangle. Otherwise, if the ratio holds a value within an experimentally determined threshold, then the classifier declares the quadrilateral a parallelogram.

For text recognition, the system assumes all strokes found within an ellipse or a parallelogram to be text and groups them accordingly. It then uses Tesseract (Smith 2007), an open-source library (Rosen 2005), for Object Character Recognition to identify the text in each group of strokes. Released under the Apache License Version 2.0 (Apache Software Foundation 2004), the library has been under development and sponsored by Google since 2006 and many consider it to be one of the most accurate open source OCR engines.

The system performs arrow recognition after exhausting all other classification options, ensuring that the unrecognized strokes must be either the shaft or the head of an arrow. Currently, the classifier cannot recognize arrows drawn in a single stroke due to the collisions and ambiguity caused by over-tracing lines. The head and the shaft of the arrow cannot connect; however, the classifier can detect wavy and traveling arrow shafts. Arrow recognition first performs a recursive algorithm on unrecognized strokes to identify the shafts and arrows and adds them together using Euclidean distance threshold. As a result, this joins the arrow head and with the shaft. Also, it determines the orientation of the head of the arrow and the orientation for the head and end of the shaft.

Finally, at this point, the system has two major sets: the recognized shapes and the unrecognized strokes. To handle any unrecognized strokes, it implements a top-down approach by applying recursion on the set of unrecognized strokes to try and join any neighboring strokes together. This recursion has a limited depth of four to avoid a stack overflow. The recursive process goes as follows: join any strokes within a certain distance of each other and apply the recognition rules. If it cannot satisfy any of the shape conditions, the process tries again with the strokes closest to the previously combined stroke. As the recursion progresses, the system keeps track of all the joined strokes to avoid repetition. If any compound stroke meets the shape recognition rules, then the recursion terminates and the algorithm adds the newly recognized shape to the shapes set and removes the compound strokes from the unrecognized stroke set.

6.2.3 Post-processing

Once the shape recognition phases complete, the system presents the user a 2D colored rendering of the skeletonized image. The color scheme denotes the shape or symbol classification that the strokes create as determined by the shape recognizer during processing. If the recognizer did not successfully classify the flowchart, the user has two options. The first option consists of canceling this classification, restarting the process, and drawing a new flowchart on paper. This option works best for users who did not follow the sketching constraints, e.g., not tracing over lines. By extension, this option works best in the case that the system filtered out a stroke during preprocessing.

The second option consists of reclassifying the mislabeled shapes. This option works best in the case where the classification has minimal errors or all of the errors consist of mislabeling shapes. This saves the user the time of redrawing the entire flowchart. Additionally, the user can correct any misunderstood text. Text recognition has an ambiguity problem with some characters, so the system elects to have the user correct the text in the application versus attempt to rewrite the text and restart the classification process. Furthermore, this system focuses on the accurate classification of flowchart elements, not textual elements.

When the user finishes the review phase, the system generates pseudocode by recursively iterating through the flowchart, treating it like a tree. The algorithm first finds the START block to find the beginning of the program. To find the next block to translate into pseudocode, the algorithm searches for the nearest end point of the arrow(s) coming from the current block. This system keeps track of which blocks have already been visited in order to detect loops. If a block has multiple arrows, then the algorithm interprets the connected blocks as conditional logic with positive logic following downward arrows and negative logic following sideways arrows. The algorithm terminates when all blocks and arrows have been visited.

If the user selects to execute the code, the Mozilla Rhino Library will execute the pseudocode, interpreting it as Javascript. The user can edit the generated code and execute it as well so that they can practice, experiment, and learn.

6.3 Results and Evaluation

The evaluation of the system consists of both an initial user study to gauge accuracy and usability and a classroom evaluation to gauge the applicability and usefulness of the system in its intended environment. The initial user study used both qualitative and quantitative data to determine the performance of the system. The quantitative data comes from the accuracy of the system in correctly classifying flowcharts in the first try. The qualitative data comes from a combination of usability surveys using a combination of the standard System Usability Scale (SUS), user interviews, and grounded theory. During the classroom evaluation, the focus shifted to the accuracy of the system when used by inexperienced programmers without special instructions on how to use the system.

6.3.1 Experiment

The participants for the study consisted of undergraduate and graduate students who had all been previously exposed to using flowcharts as a model for programming. A total of 20 people participated in total: 18 males, 2 females; 4 undergraduate, 16 graduate. Their ages ranged from 19 to 30, evenly distributed.

Familiarity with flowcharts and programming skill varied significantly among the participants. Sixteen of the participants had previously taken courses that covered flowchart design; only 12 had used a graphical software tool for the purpose of software design. Table 6.1 displays the self-reported skills of the participants.

The participants received the supplies they would need at the experiment center: a single desk and chair, pencil, pencil sharpener, eraser, five sheets of white paper, a set of drawing guidelines, and the Flow2Code application installed on an Android smartphone. The drawing guidelines contained the list of flowchart shapes and their meanings, an example flowchart and corresponding pseudocode for those out of practice with flowcharts, a brief description of how to use the application, and tips for drawing recognizable flowcharts. To aid in recognition, the guidelines requested that participants not over-trace or overlap their shapes, draw arrows in two strokes to differentiate the head from the shaft, and use down arrows for positive logic and right arrows for negative logic. For the privacy of the participants and convenience of the researcher, the participants all used the supplied smartphone. During the activity, the researcher played the role of observer, only speaking to the participant if they did not

Table 6.1 Participant demographics

Skill	Very poor (%)	Poor (%)	Mediocre (%)	Good (%)	Very good (%)
Flowchart	5	15	50	15	15
Programming	10	0	30	35	25

understand an instruction or wanted more paper to accurately record the participant's unprompted interaction with the exercise.

The experiment contained three exercises for the participants to draw flowcharts to solve.

(1) Print Hello: Print "Hello" X number of times if $X < 10$
(2) Fibonacci: For a given input N, output the first N Fibonacci numbers
(3) Factorize: For a given input K, output the factors of K

6.3.2 Data Collected

To judge the accuracy of the system on the 60 flowcharts collected from the 20 participants, the experiment used two evaluation metrics to judge the accuracy of the system: shape-wise and all-or-nothing accuracy. Shape-wise accuracy primarily evaluates the accuracy of the shape recognizer; this evaluation metric serves as the standard for classifier algorithms. All-or-Nothing accuracy evaluates the system accuracy for recognizing every element in the flowchart correctly in a single run and consequently serves as a more representative but difficult evaluation metric. Users can edit the system's classifications, but the goal remains that the system will correctly identify each flowchart element on the first attempt.

As per the standard for classification algorithms, the evaluation uses the F1-score as the accuracy calculation in addition to basic accuracy. The shape recognizer must both correctly label each shape (precision) and not miss any strokes/shapes during classification (recall). A good predictor must maximize true positives (TP) and true negatives (TN) while minimizing false positives (FP), e.g., assign to the wrong group, and false negatives (FN), e.g., failure to detect or incorrectly assign to "None."

$$Accuracy = \frac{TP + TN}{TP + TN + FP + FN} \tag{6.1}$$

$$Precision = \frac{TP}{TP + FP} \tag{6.2}$$

$$Recall = \frac{TP}{TP + FN} \tag{6.3}$$

$$F1\text{-}Score = \frac{2TP}{2TP + FP + FN} \tag{6.4}$$

Tables 6.2, 6.3, and 6.4 show the confusion matrices for the shape classifier for each of the exercises and Table 6.5 shows the summary of said data. Overall, the system displayed great accuracy during the shape-wise evaluation. All of the classifications had greater than 0.95 basic accuracy. Excluding the none category, all of the elements had F1-scores greater than 0.93. As shown in Tables 6.6, 6.7, 6.8, and 6.9, the low

Table 6.2 Confusion matrix for (1) Print Hello

		P	R	E	D	I	C	T	Total
		Elli	Para	Rect	Diam	Arro	Text	None	
A	Elli	**37**	0	0	0	0	0	3	40
C	Para	1	**51**	5	0	0	0	1	58
T	Rect	0	0	**22**	0	0	0	0	22
U	Diam	1	1	0	**38**	0	0	0	40
A	Arro	0	0	0	0	**168**	0	12	180
L	Text	0	0	0	0	0	**156**	4	160
	None	0	0	0	0	0	0	**19**	19
	Total	39	52	27	38	168	156	39	

Table 6.3 Confusion matrix for (2) Fibonacci

		P	R	E	D	I	C	T	Total
		Elli	Para	Rect	Diam	Arro	Text	None	
A	Elli	**35**	0	2	1	0	0	2	40
C	Para	1	**35**	2	1	0	0	1	40
T	Rect	0	1	**77**	0	0	0	2	80
U	Diam	0	1	1	**17**	0	0	1	20
A	Arro	0	0	0	0	**167**	0	14	181
L	Text	0	0	0	0	0	**174**	6	180
	None	0	0	0	0	1	0	**10**	11
	Total	36	37	82	19	168	174	36	

Table 6.4 Confusion matrix for (3) Factorial

		P	R	E	D	I	C	T	Total
		Elli	Para	Rect	Diam	Arro	Text	None	
A	Elli	**38**	0	0	0	0	0	2	40
C	Para	0	**39**	1	0	0	0	0	40
T	Rect	0	0	**78**	0	0	0	2	80
U	Diam	0	1	0	**19**	0	0	0	20
A	Arro	0	0	0	0	**172**	0	8	180
L	Text	0	0	0	0	0	**176**	4	180
	None	0	0	0	0	1	0	**13**	14
	Total	38	40	79	19	173	176	29	

Table 6.5 Confusion matrix for all exercises

		P	R	E	D	I	C	T	Total
		Elli	Para	Rect	Diam	Arro	Text	None	
A	Elli	**110**	0	2	1		0	7	120
C	Para	2	**125**	8	1	0	0	2	138
T	Rect	0	1	**177**	0	0	0	4	182
U	Diam	1	3	1	**74**	0	0	1	80
A	Arro	0	0	0	0	**507**	0	34	541
L	Text	0	0	0	0	0	**506**	14	520
	None	0	0	0	0	2	0	**42**	44
	Total	113	129	188	76	509	506	104	

Table 6.6 Evaluation of (1) Print Hello

	TP	TN	FP	FN	Accuracy	Precision	Recall	F1-Score
Elli	37	477	2	3	0.9904	0.9487	0.9250	0.9367
Para	51	460	1	7	0.9846	0.9808	0.8793	0.9273
Rect	22	492	5	0	0.9804	0.8148	1.0000	0.8980
Diam	38	479	0	2	0.9961	1.0000	0.9500	0.9744
Arro	168	339	0	12	0.9769	1.0000	0.9333	0.9655
Text	156	359	0	4	0.9923	1.0000	0.9750	0.9873
None	19	480	20	0	0.9615	0.4872	1.0000	0.6552
Total	491	3086	28	28	0.9846	0.9461	0.9461	0.9461

Table 6.7 Evaluation of (2) Fibonacci

	TP	TN	FP	FN	Accuracy	Precision	Recall	F1-Score
Elli	35	511	1	5	0.9891	0.9722	0.8750	0.9211
Para	35	510	2	5	0.9873	0.9459	0.8750	0.9091
Rect	77	467	5	3	0.9855	0.9390	0.9625	0.9506
Diam	17	530	2	3	0.9909	0.8947	0.8500	0.8718
Arro	167	370	1	14	0.9728	0.9940	0.9226	0.9570
Text	174	372	0	6	0.9891	1.0000	0.9667	0.9831
None	10	525	16	1	0.9692	0.3846	0.9091	0.5405
Total	515	3285	27	37	0.9834	0.9502	0.9330	0.9415

Table 6.8 Evaluation of (3) Factorial

	TP	TN	FP	FN	Accuracy	Precision	Recall	F1-Score
Elli	38	514	0	2	0.9964	1.0000	0.9500	0.9744
Para	39	513	1	1	0.9964	0.9750	0.9750	0.9750
Rect	78	473	1	2	0.9946	0.9873	0.9750	0.9811
Diam	19	534	0	1	0.9982	1.0000	0.9500	0.9744
Arro	172	373	1	8	0.9838	0.9942	0.9556	0.9745
Text	176	374	0	4	0.9928	1.0000	0.9778	0.6047
None	13	524	16	1	0.9693	0.4483	0.9286	0.9657
Total	535	3305	19	19	0.9902	0.9657	0.9657	0.9657

Table 6.9 Evaluation of all exercises

	TP	TN	FP	FN	Accuracy	Precision	Recall	F1-Score
Elli	110	1502	3	10	0.9920	0.9735	0.9167	0.9442
Para	125	1483	4	13	0.9895	0.9690	0.9058	0.9363
Rect	177	1432	11	5	0.9902	0.9415	0.9725	0.9568
Diam	74	1543	2	6	0.9951	0.9737	0.9250	0.9487
Arro	507	1082	2	34	0.9778	0.9961	0.9372	0.9657
Text	506	1105	0	14	0.9914	1.0000	0.9731	0.9864
None	42	1529	52	2	0.9668	0.4468	0.9545	0.6087
Total	1541	9676	74	84	0.9861	0.9542	0.9483	0.9512

Table 6.10 All-or-Nothing accuracy

		Accuracy
(1)	Hello	0.20
(2)	Fibonacci	0.25
(3)	Factorial	0.50
	Average	0.3166

F1-score for the none category results primarily from the system not recognizing arrow strokes as evidenced by the large number of arrows classified into the "None" category. In general, the system correctly identifies the shapes it detects, resulting in high true positives and few false positives, but it can fail to detect a shape or stroke, resulting in false negatives. In other words, the system has excellent precision for the shape categories but has room for improvement in recall as the low precision in the "None" category results comes from false negatives in the other categories.

The results of the all-or-nothing evaluation given in Table 6.10 show that the system normally does not recognize every element in the flowchart in the first attempt. However, the significant increase in accuracy across the three exercises shows that the system accuracy improved with user experience with the system. If a user did not completely follow the initial guidelines, e.g., draw arrows in two strokes, the system would have a higher probability of failed shape recognition. By the third exercise, the users would know which shapes the system did not recognize in earlier exercises and would subsequently sketch them more carefully. We predict that the accuracy would continue to increase with more exercises.

6.3.3 *Qualitative Results*

After the three exercises, participants completed a post-experiment survey using the System Usability Scale (SUS) to give feedback on their experience (Brooke 1996). SUS serves as the standard usability metric for both hardware and software and gives accurate results even with a small sample of participants, e.g., less than 15. As such, the 20 participants constitute a large enough group to use SUS reliably.

The SUS questionnaire consists of 10 questions using the Likert (1932) scale with a 5-point range: Strongly Disagree, Slightly Disagree, Neutral, Slightly Agree, and Strongly Agree. To ensure that the participants read the questions carefully, the questions switch from positive to negative sentiment so that users cannot blindly give the same answer repeatedly. For example, one question may ask if the interface was confusing (the negative "Strongly Disagree" gives positive feedback) and the next could ask if the user found the application easy to use (the positive "Strongly Agree" gives positive feedback). SUS scores the system on a 0–100 scale. Despite looking like a percentage score, the SUS score does not give a measure of usability. The score indicates the maximum points that the users gave the system. In Fig. 6.11, the SUS score determines if the design received an acceptable score and further gives a relative description of the score from "excellent" to "terrible." The SUS has an average score of 68; the minimum strongly acceptable score starts at 70 points. Great scores range from 80 to 90 points (Bangor 2009). The scores given by the participants, shown in Table 6.11, averaged at 84.25 which reaches the range of excellent scores.

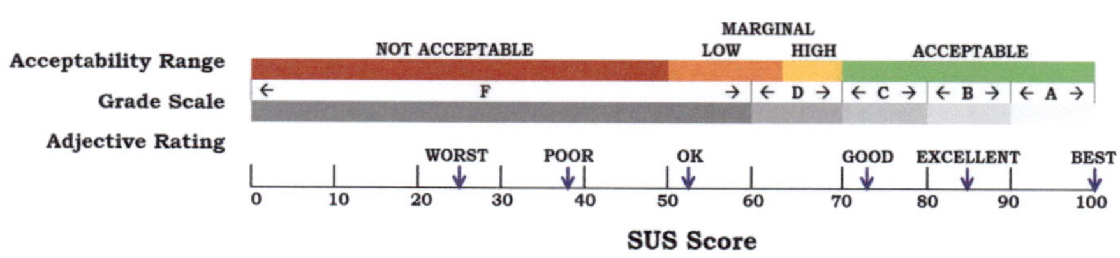

Fig. 6.11 SUS score

Table 6.11 SUS questionnaire scores

			Q	U	E	S	T	I	O	N		Total	Weighted
		Q1	Q2	Q3	Q4	Q5	Q6	Q7	Q8	Q9	Q10		
	P01	2	4	3	3	3	2	4	3	2	4	30	75
	P02	2	3	3	2	3	3	3	1	3	2	25	62.5
	P03	3	4	3	3	4	4	4	3	3	4	35	87.5
	P04	4	3	3	4	4	4	3	4	4	4	37	92.5
P	P05	2	3	3	3	4	2	4	2	3	4	30	75
A	P06	3	3	4	4	3	4	4	4	3	4	36	90
R	P07	3	4	2	4	4	4	4	3	4	4	36	90
T	P08	4	4	4	3	4	4	4	3	4	4	38	95
I	P09	4	3	3	4	3	4	4	4	4	3	36	90
C	P10	3	4	3	4	4	4	4	4	4	3	37	92.5
I	P11	3	4	4	3	4	4	3	4	3	3	35	87.5
P	P12	1	3	3	4	3	4	3	3	3	4	31	77.5
A	P13	3	4	3	4	4	4	4	4	4	3	37	92.5
N	P14	4	4	4	4	4	4	4	4	4	3	39	97.5
T	P15	3	3	4	3	4	4	4	4	3	4	36	90
S	P16	3	3	3	3	3	3	3	3	2	3	29	72.5
	P17	3	4	3	4	3	4	3	4	3	3	34	85
	P18	3	3	2	4	2	3	3	3	2	3	28	70
	P19	3	3	3	4	0	3	3	3	3	0	25	62.5
	P20	4	4	4	4	4	4	4	4	4	4	40	100
												Average:	84.25

6.3.4 Grounded Theory

In addition to the SUS questionnaire, the participants also took part in a semi-structured interview in order to get feedback on the participant's detailed opinions on the system. After using Grounded Theory (Strauss and Corbin 2008) with the open coding strategy (Flick 2009) to draw conclusions on the unquantifiable data, the answers summarize into nine categories: Usability, User Experience, Difficulties, Educational, Tool, Usefulness, Suggestions, Drawing, and Tedious. As supported by the SUS results, the participants found the system to be a user-friendly drawing tool. One participant specifically voiced that he thought the tool would help students. Two of the novice programmers enjoyed the flowchart processing and code execution. However, the answers also included negative feedback regarding the flowchart drawing process as they found it tedious. The participants who did not learn programming with flowcharts did not see the value in flowcharts and consequently did not care for the application. Other feedback included the desire for more flowchart beautification and fewer drawing restrictions.

6.3.5 Classroom Evaluation

To evaluate its potential as a learning tool, an introductory programming course at Texas A&M University, CSCE 206, used Flow2Code during one of its class sessions. This programming course satisfies the programming requirement for non-computer science majors in the college of engineering. The participating course section of 71 students primarily contained industrial engineering majors, and all had little to no flowchart experience. Before completing the same exercises from the initial evaluation, the 45 participating students received a 5-min lesson on flowcharts. The students did not receive any special instructions or drawing guidelines for Flow2Code.

This evaluation focused on first-pass recognition for the shapes. Table 6.12 shows the accuracy for each shape across the 135 flowcharts. As students did not receive drawing guidelines, many drew arrows in one stroke instead of two, resulting in low accuracy for arrow recognition. Excluding arrows, the results show great accuracy of greater than or equal to 0.95.

The teaching assistant for the course reported that the students enjoyed using Flow2Code because drawing flowcharts did not feel like classwork. Some of the students went on to switch into the computer science major after completing this course.

Table 6.12 Shape-wise accuracy

	Ellipse	Parallelogram	Rectangle	Diamond	Arrow
Accuracy	0.950	0.970	0.968	0.972	0.778

6.4 Contributions

In this chapter, we describe a flowchart drawing tool to help novice programmers learn fundamental programming skills by guiding them through the process of drawing flowcharts to writing code. The main contributions of the work include code generation and execution, ability to edit hand-drawn flowcharts in the application for the ease of the user, and improved real-time flowchart element recognition when compared to existing solutions.

Acknowledgements The authors thank the Mexican Chamber of Electronics, Telecommunications, and Information Technologies (Spanish: Cámara Nacional de la Industria Electrónica de Telecomunicación) (CANIETI), and Microsoft (Surface Hub Grant) for their support. The conclusions, findings, opinions, and recommendations described in this chapter do not necessarily reflect those of CANIETI nor Microsoft. Additionally, the authors thank the Sketch Recognition Lab for their feedback and support of this project. Special thanks go to Duc Hoang for his part in writing this chapter.

References

Apache Software Foundation (2004) Apache license version 2.0. https://www.apache.org/licenses/LICENSE-2.0

Bangor A, Kortum P, Miller J (2009) Determining what individual SUS scores mean: adding an adjective rating scale. J Usability Stud 4(3):114–123. http://dl.acm.org/citation.cfm?id=2835587.2835589

Bennedsen J, Caspersen ME (2007) Failure rates in introductory programming. SIGCSE Bull 39(2):32–36. https://doi.org/10.1145/1272848.1272879

Bovik AC (2005) Handbook of image and video processing (Communications, networking and multimedia). Academic Press Inc, Orlando, FL, USA

Brooke J (1996) SUS: a quick and dirty usability scale

Buxton B (2007) Sketching user experiences: getting the design right and the right design. Morgan Kaufmann Publishers Inc., San Francisco, CA, USA

Calloni BA, Bagert DJ (1994) Iconic programming in BACCII vs. textual programming: which is a better learning environment? SIGCSE Bull 26(1):188–192. https://doi.org/10.1145/191033.191103. http://doi.acm.org/10.1145/191033.191103

Carton C, Lemaitre A, Coüasnon B (2013) Fusion of statistical and structural information for flowchart recognition. In: 12th International conference on document analysis and recognition (ICDAR) (2013). IEEE, Washington, DC, USA, pp 1210–1214

Delling D, Sanders P, Schultes D, Wagner D (2009) Engineering route planning algorithms. In: Lerner J, Wagner D, Zweig KA (eds) Algorithmics of large and complex networks. Springer, Berlin, Heidelberg, pp. 117–139. https://doi.org/10.1007/978-3-642-02094-0_7. http://dx.doi.org/10.1007/978-3-642-02094-0_7

Farrugia PJ, Borg JC, Camilleri KP, Christopher S et al (2005) Experiments with a cameraphone-aided design (CPAD) system. In: ICED 05: 15th international conference on engineering design: engineering design and the global economy. Engineers Australia, Melbourne, Australia, p 737

Flick U (2009) An introduction to qualitative research. SAGE Publications, London, UK. https://books.google.com/books?id=sFv1oWX2DoEC

Giordano JC, Carlisle M (2006) Toward a more effective visualization tool to teach novice programmers. In: Proceedings of the 7th conference on information technology education, SIGITE

'06. ACM, New York, NY, USA, pp 115–122. https://doi.org/10.1145/1168812.1168841. http://doi.acm.org/10.1145/1168812.1168841
Johnston J, Hammond T (2010) Computing confidence values for geometric constraints for use in sketch recognition. In: Proceedings of the seventh sketch-based interfaces and modeling symposium, SBIM '10. Eurographics Association, Aire-la-Ville, Switzerland, pp 71–78. http://dl.acm.org/citation.cfm?id=1923363.1923376
Likert R (1932) A technique for the measurement of attitudes. Arch Psychol 22(140):1–55
Novak V, Mockor J, Perfilieva I (1999) Mathematical principles of fuzzy logic. Kluwer international series in engineering and computing science. Kluwer, Boston, MA. https://cds.cern.ch/record/425778
Paulson B, Rajan P, Davalos P, Gutierrez-Osuna R, Hammond T (2008) What!?! no Rubine features?: using geometric-based features to produce normalized confidence values for sketch recognition. In: HCC Workshop: sketch tools for diagramming (VL/HCC), p. 57-63. VL/HCC, Herrsching am Ammersee, Germany
Powers K, Gross P, Cooper S, McNally M, Goldman KJ, Proulx V, Carlisle M (2006) Tools for teaching introductory programming: what works? In: Proceedings of the 37th SIGCSE technical symposium on computer science education, SIGCSE '06. ACM, New York, NY, USA, pp 560–561. https://doi.org/10.1145/1121341.1121514. http://doi.acm.org/10.1145/1121341.1121514
Rajan P, Taele P, Hammond T (2010) Evaluation of paper-pen based sketching interface. In: Proceedings of the 16th international conference on distributed multimedia systems (DMS). Knowledge Systems Institute, Oak Brook, IL, pp 321–326
Rosen LE (2005) Open source licensing: software freedom and intellectual property law. Prentice Hall PTR. https://books.google.com/books?id=HGokAQAAIAAJ
Rubine D (1991) Specifying gestures by example. In: Proceeding of the 18th annual conference on computer graphics and interactive techniques, SIGGRAPH 91, pp 329–337
Rubine D (1991) Specifying gestures by example. In: Proceedings of the 18th annual conference on computer graphics and interactive techniques, SIGGRAPH '91. ACM, New York, NY, USA, pp 329–337. https://doi.org/10.1145/122718.122753. http://doi.acm.org/10.1145/122718.122753
Smith R (2007) An overview of the Tesseract OCR engine. In: Proceedings of the ninth international conference on document analysis and recognition (ICDAR), vol 2. IEEE, pp 629–633
Strauss AL, Corbin J (2008) Basics of qualitative research: techniques and procedures for developing grounded theory. SAGE Publications, Los Angeles, London, New Delhi. http://opac.inria.fr/record=b1133423
Wolin A, Eoff B, Hammond T (2008) Shortstraw: a simple and effective corner finder for polylines. In: Proceedings of the fifth eurographics conference on sketch-based interfaces and modeling, SBM'08. Eurographics Association, Aire-la-Ville, Switzerland, pp 33–40. https://doi.org/10.2312/SBM/SBM08/033-040. http://dx.doi.org/10.2312/SBM/SBM08/033-040
Wu J, Wang C, Zhang L, Rui Y (2015) Offline sketch parsing via shapeness estimation. In: Proceedings for the 35th international joint conference on artificial intelligence (IJCAI). IJCAI, Buenos Aires, Argentina, pp 1200–1207
Zhang TY, Suen CY (1984) A fast parallel algorithm for thinning digital patterns. Commun ACM 27(3):236–239. http://dblp.uni-trier.de/db/journals/cacm/cacm27.html#ZhangS84

Chapter 7
FreeStyle: A Sketch-Based Wireframing Tool

Savinay Narendra, Sheelabhadra Dey, Josiah Coad, Seth Polsley and Tracy Hammond

Abstract User interfaces have classically involved WIMP (windows, icons, mouse, and pointing) paradigm. Current wireframing tools in the early stages of web interface design focus on using drag-and-drop features, that is, selecting elements from a menu and inserting them in the interface. Most designers prefer to sketch early interface ideas on paper. A system that allows them to draw sketches would make the process more intuitive, thus going beyond traditional methods of website interface designing. We have developed an interactive tool called FreeStyle that allows designers the ability to quickly sketch a web-based interface electronically. The designer can draw web-based HTML elements on the canvas and in response, FreeStyle transforms the sketch into an interface. Additionally, we also provide the functionality of downloading the code developed from the sketch.

7.1 Introduction

As computers grow more powerful, less expensive, and more widely available, people are expecting them not only to perform obvious computational tasks but also to assist in people-oriented tasks, such as writing, drawing, and designing. This shift

S. Narendra · S. Dey · J. Coad
Department of Computer Science & Engineering, Texas A&M University,
College Station, TX, USA
e-mail: savinay@tamu.edu

S. Dey
e-mail: sheelabhadra@tamu.edu

J. Coad
e-mail: josiahcoad@tamu.edu

S. Polsley (✉) · T. Hammond
Sketch Recognition Lab, Department of Computer Science and Engineering,
Texas A&M University, College Station, TX, USA
e-mail: spolsley@tamu.edu

T. Hammond
e-mail: hammond@tamu.edu

T. Hammond et al. (eds.), *Inspiring Students with Digital Ink*, Human–Computer Interaction Series, https://doi.org/10.1007/978-3-030-17398-2_7

is causing some user-interface (UI) researchers to rethink the traditional reliance on methods that are more machine-oriented and to look at ways to support properties like ambiguity, creativity, and informal communication. The idea is to bend computers to people's way of interacting, not the other way around.

When professional designers first start thinking about a visual interface, they often sketch rough pictures of the screen layouts. Their initial goal is to work on the overall layout and structure of the components, rather than to refine the detailed look and feel. Designers use these sketches and other "low-fidelity technique" to quickly consider design ideas, later shifting to interface construction tools or handing off the design to a programmer. Unfortunately, this transition forces the designer to specify too many details. Much of the design literature recommends drawing rough sketches of design ideas, yet most interface construction tools, and even prototyping tools, require the designer to specify much more of the design than a rough sketch allows. These tools force designers to bridge the gap between how they think about a design and the detailed specification they must create.

Another key lesson from the design literature is the value of iterative design. It is important to iterate quickly in the early stages of design because that is when radically different ideas can and should be examined. The need to turn out new designs quickly is hampered by tools that require detailed designs. This over-specification can be tedious and may also lead to a loss of spontaneity. Thus, the designer may be forced to abandon computerized tools until later in the design process or forced to change design techniques in a way that is not conducive to early creative design.

Additionally, research indicates that the use of the current interactive tools in the early stages of development places too much focus on design details like color and alignment rather than on the major interface design issues, such as structure and behavior. Wong (1992) discovered that colleagues give more useful feedback when evaluating interfaces with a sketchy look. The designers reported that the current user interface construction tools are a hindrance during the early stages of interface design. What designers need are computerized tools that allow them to quickly sketch rough design ideas.

We have developed an interactive web-based wireframing tool that allows website designers to quickly sketch a website having certain HTML elements and in response, our tool has developed a website containing all the sketches that the user drew that were converted into the corresponding HTML elements having custom values. Designers can test the interface at any point, not just when they finish the design. When they are satisfied with their early prototypes, they can have FreeStyle transform the sketch into an operational interface using real widgets, according to a particular look and feel.

7.2 Prior Work

Our work draws inspiration from SILK (Sketching Interfaces Like Krazy) Landay (1996), an informal sketching tool that combines many of the benefits of paper-based sketching with the merits of current electronic tools. With SILK, designers can quickly sketch an interface using an electronic pad and stylus, and SILK recognizes widgets and other interface elements as the designer draws them. Unlike paper-based sketching, however, designers can exercise these elements in their sketchy state. SILK also supports the creation of storyboards, that is, the arrangement of sketches to show how design elements behave such as how a dialog box appears when the user activates a button. Storyboards are important because they give designers a way to show colleagues, customers, or end users early on how an interface will behave. After the designer tests the interface and iterates the design as needed, SILK transforms the rough design to a more finished looking implementation. But, our system resembles a more real-world scenario which automatically generates the website in real time while sketching the HTML elements on the canvas. This provides real-time feedback to the website designers, thereby improving their efficiency and quality of work.

Our work is based on an approach developed by Fonseca et al. (2002) which presents a fast, simple, and compact approach to recognize scribbles (multi-stroke geometric shapes) drawn with a stylus on a digitizing tablet. Regardless of the size, rotation, and the number of strokes, the method identifies the most common shapes used in drawings, allowing for dashed, continuous or overlapping strokes. The method combines temporal adjacency, fuzzy logic, and geometric features to classify scribbles with measured recognition rates over 97%. In 1963, Sutherland (1964) presented Sketchpad, the first interactive system that used one light pen to draw diagrams directly over the screen surface. Nevertheless, due in part to ergonomic problems with the light pen and the invention of the mouse in 1964, current graphical interfaces relegated pen-based interactions to specific CAD applications. Things changed with the appearance of the first pen computers in 1991, even though pens were used mainly to input text through handwriting recognition.

The Newton system (Menuez and Kounalakis 1993), one of the first hand-held pen-based computers, incorporates handwriting, shape, and gesture recognizers. While the shape recognizer only handles uni-stroke, axis-aligned shapes, the gesture recognizer is more suitable for text editing than for drawing schematics. An approach to recognize schematic drawings was developed at the University of Washington (Apte et al. 1993), which recognized a small number of non-rotated shapes and did not distinguish open/closed, dashed or bold shapes. Zhao (1993) described an interactive editor based on the StateCharts formalism (Harel 1987). Although the editor used a mouse and direct manipulation, many of the ideas described in Zhao (1993) express an approach based on diagram recognition guided by syntax. Gross (1996) described a system fundamentally based on sketches that are partially interpreted for use in architecture drawings, using a recognizer substantially simpler and less robust than ours. Although this recognizer is trainable, the number of identified shapes is apparently smaller than ours. Landay (1996) used a recognizer developed by Rubine (1991) to sketch graphical arrangements of bidimensional documents. Rubine's recognizer is a trainable single-stroke gesture recognizer that uses a classic linear discriminator training algorithm. Other authors have proposed more complex methods, involving neural networks (Ulgen et al. 1995), to identify a small number of geometric shapes (rectangles, squares, circles, ellipses, and triangles). These shapes are recognized independent of size and rotation, but they cannot be drawn using dashed or bold lines. Even though the authors claim good performance for their method, the paper does not present clear measurements of the results. The PaleoSketch system supports as many primitive shapes, combining recognition with beautification, although it integrates a large number of different shape recognizers to achieve this (Paulson and Hammond 2008).

7.3 System Overview

The domain for which we developed the sketch recognition system required us to identify simple shapes such as rectangles, triangles, circles, and line segments. A geometric recognizer that recognizes multi-stroke shapes perfectly suits our application. We decided to use the technique described by Fonseca et al. (2002) in their paper to identify shapes.

7.3.1 Finding the Convex Hull

The first step of our algorithm involves finding the convex hull of a set of points using the Jarvis March algorithm (Jarvis 1973). It helps in removing ambiguity of shapes that are not drawn perfectly since most of the times, when drawing with free hand, it is difficult to generate perfect figures. Taking the convex hull of the set of data points, obtained in a stroke, approximates it to the actual shape that the user intended to draw. In the next step, our algorithm calculates the bounding box of the figure by finding the extreme points of the figure. So, in the drawn sketch if the maximum x coordinate is given by x_max, the maximum y coordinate is given by y_max, the minimum x coordinate is given by x_min, and the minimum y coordinate is given by y_min, the coordinates of the corner points of the bounding box will be (x_min, y_min), (x_max, y_min), (x_max, y_max), and (x_min, y_max) (Figs. 7.1 and 7.2).

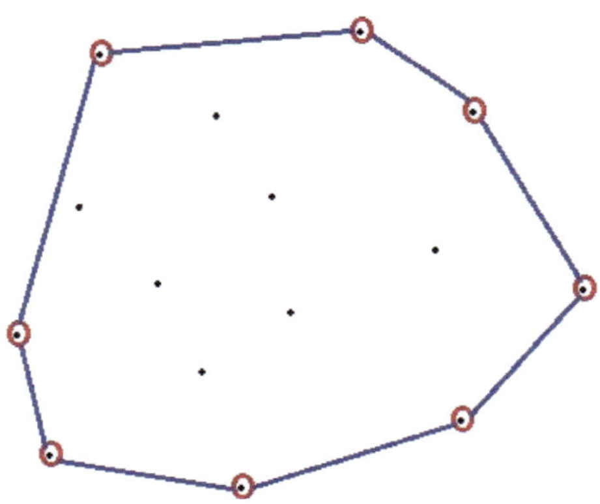

Fig. 7.1 Convex Hull—indicated by the blue lines

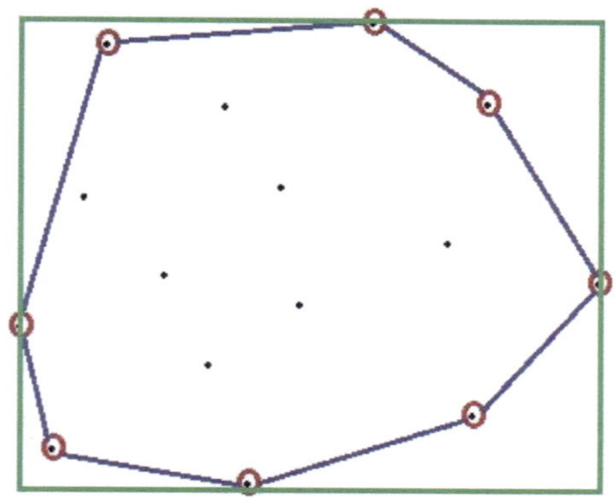

Fig. 7.2 Bounding Box—indicated by the green lines

7.3.2 *Recognition of Elementary Shapes*

For classification, we compute a feature that is unique for each shape that we are concerned with. Once we are done finding the convex hull and the bounding box of the sketch, we compute their areas. The ratio (ρ) of the area of the convex hull to the area of the bounding box is one of the features that can be helpful for classification.

$$\rho = \frac{Area\ of\ the\ Convex\ Hull}{Area\ of\ the\ Bounding\ Box}$$

In the ideal case, ρ would be 1, $\pi/4$, 0.5, and 0 for a rectangle, a circle, a triangle, and a line segment, respectively. This method of classification is pretty intuitive and foolproof for identifying the elementary shapes that we are concerned with since it is based on the geometrical properties.

Humans usually do not draw shapes perfectly and hand-drawn sketches often contain a lot of noise. Due to this reason, most of the times the ideal values for ρ are not obtained. To resolve the issue, we consider a range in which ρ would lie. Experimentally, we found that the bounds for ρ lie between 0.8 and 1 for a rectangle, between 0.7 and 0.8 for a circle, between 0.4 and 0.6 for a triangle, and between 0 and 0.1 for a line segment.

Based on the value of these ratios, we built a set of decision rules that were used to classify the drawn figures as a rectangle, a circle, a triangle, and a line segment. These decision rules provided the correct classification when the shapes were drawn using a single continuous stroke (Figs. 7.3 and 7.4).

7.3.3 *Recognition of Complex Shapes*

Wireframing tools consist of complex shapes other than the elementary shapes that we have listed above. A shape drawn inside another shape can be considered a complex

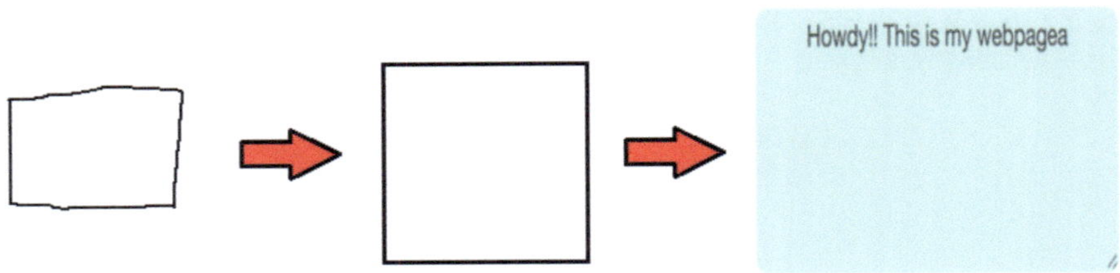

Fig. 7.3 A rectangle drawn is beautified to generate a text area element

Fig. 7.4 A circle drawn is beautified to generate a radio button element

shape. Once we are done drawing a shape in a single stroke, our recognition algorithm recognizes the shape and waits for the user to draw another figure for a time threshold of 2 s. If the user draws a figure after the 2 s, then the algorithm identifies the figure drawn previously and the current figure as separate wireframing elements. Otherwise, the previously drawn shape and the current shape are considered to be a part of a single wireframing element. The shape that is drawn after drawing another figure in the case of complex shapes is usually drawn inside the first figure. So, the size of the shape drawn second is in general smaller than the first figure. This helps us decide if the shape drawn second is actually a part of a complex figure by comparing the size of its bounding box with the previously drawn figure. If the two shapes are found to combine together to form a single wireframing element, then we run the recognition algorithms on the two shapes separately. This identifies the two shapes. Thereafter, we extract some other features such as the location of the second shape with respect to the 1st shape, the slope, and the length of the stroke. This helps us form the decision rules to identify the wireframing elements. For example, if the recognizer identifies that the first shape drawn is a rectangle and the second shape drawn is a triangle, there are two possible wireframe elements that they could refer to a video element or a drop-down menu. But, if we observe Fig. 7.5, the video element has the triangle at the center of the figure drawn first while the drop-down element shown in Fig. 7.11 has the triangle drawn toward the right end side of the figure drawn first. This allowed us to introduce an attribute, the relative location of the second shape with respect to the first shape, and differentiate a video element from a drop-down menu element (Figs. 7.6, 7.7, 7.8, 7.9 and 7.10).

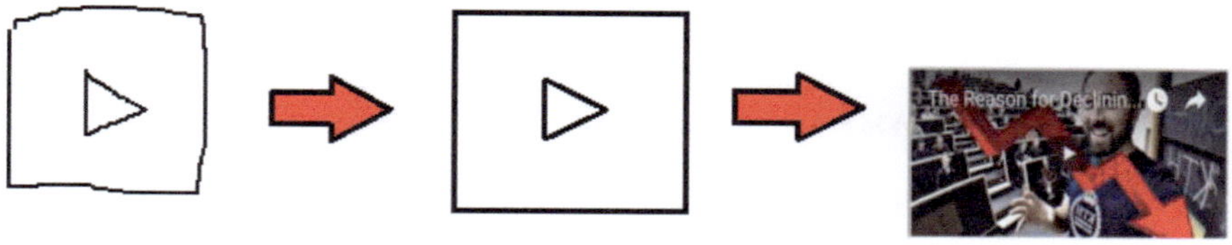

Fig. 7.5 A shape with a triangle drawn inside a rectangle is beautified to generate a video element

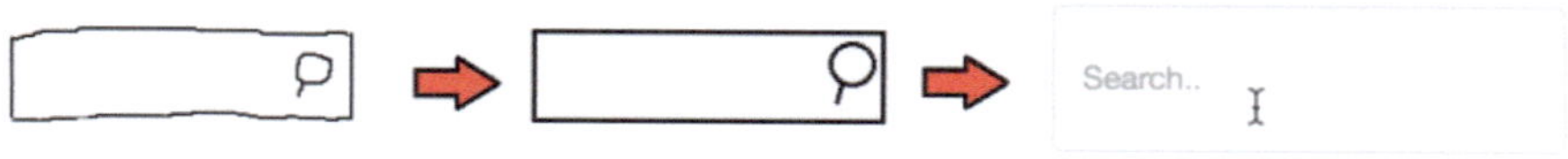

Fig. 7.6 A shape with a lens shape drawn inside a rectangle is beautified to generate a search box element

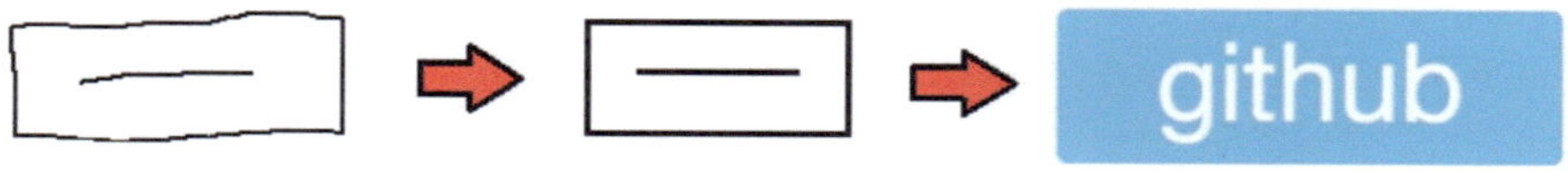

Fig. 7.7 A shape with a horizontal line drawn inside a rectangle is beautified to generate a button element

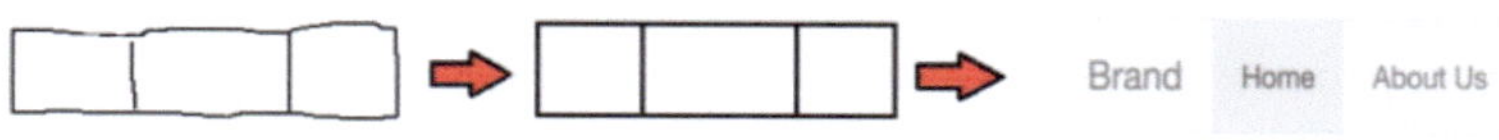

Fig. 7.8 A shape with vertical lines drawn inside a rectangle is beautified to generate a navigation bar element

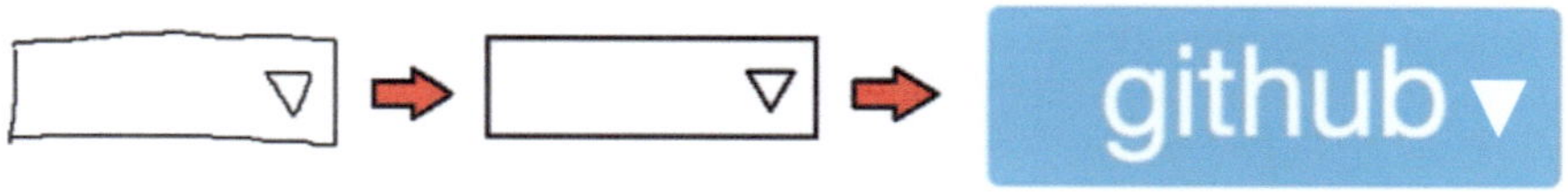

Fig. 7.9 A shape with a triangle drawn inside a rectangle toward the right end is beautified to generate a drop-down menu element

Fig. 7.10 A shape with a tick mark drawn inside a rectangle is beautified to generate a checkbox element

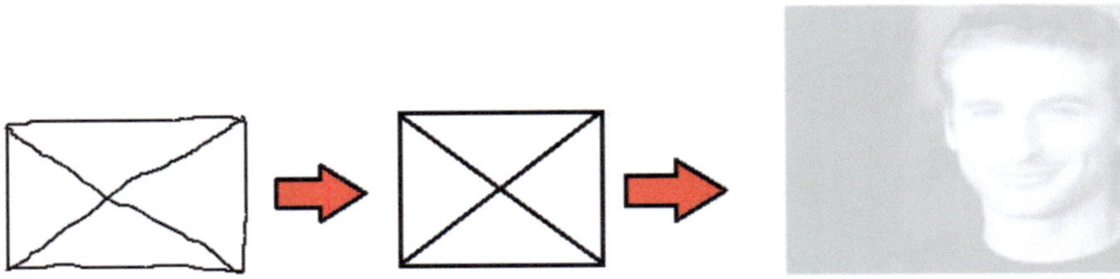

Fig. 7.11 A shape with a cross mark drawn inside a rectangle is beautified to generate an image element

7.3.4 *Beautification of Elements*

Once the shapes are correctly recognized and are classified as the correct wireframing elements, we beautify the elements, in order to provide a more responsive interface. Although there are certain advantages to leaving the canvas unaltered, beautifying lends clarity to the wireframing elements and also provides us the freedom to add customizable features. The beautified element is introduced in place of the hand-sketched element. The size of the beautified element is equal to the size of the bounding box of the shape that the user drew. Thereafter, we allow the user to customize elements according to her preference. For example, on identifying that a particular shape refers to a video, the user can insert the link to the video that she intends to insert. The video will be embedded in the area created for the video element. Similarly, once a cross drawn inside a rectangle is identified as an image element, the user has the freedom to insert the link to an image and the image is displayed in the area created for the image element. This makes the layout of the website to be visually appealing. Since our project also targets amateurs who are new to web designing or people who just wish to design their own website, this feature provides an interesting visual feedback to the user. It helps them anticipate what their website might actually look like (Fig. 7.12).

Professional designers will look for features where they can alter or tinker with the HTML code of the elements that they sketched. We have introduced a feature where once the element drawn by the user is identified, the HTML code for the element is displayed on the right hand of the canvas. Users can use the HTML code to alter the features of the wireframing elements. FreeStyle works by giving the user a blank white canvas which they can sketch freely on. The recognition algorithm can recognize up to nine distinct elements at this time. These elements are standardly identified as a developer would draw them. For example, a rectangle drawn with crossed diagonal lines inside is an image element. Once identified, the recognizer removes the drawn sketch and replaces it with the code element that the sketch represents (which in the case of an image drawn would be the $< img >$ tag). Inside the HTML tag is information about the size and the position to match the element which was drawn. The code associated is shown temporarily on the side of

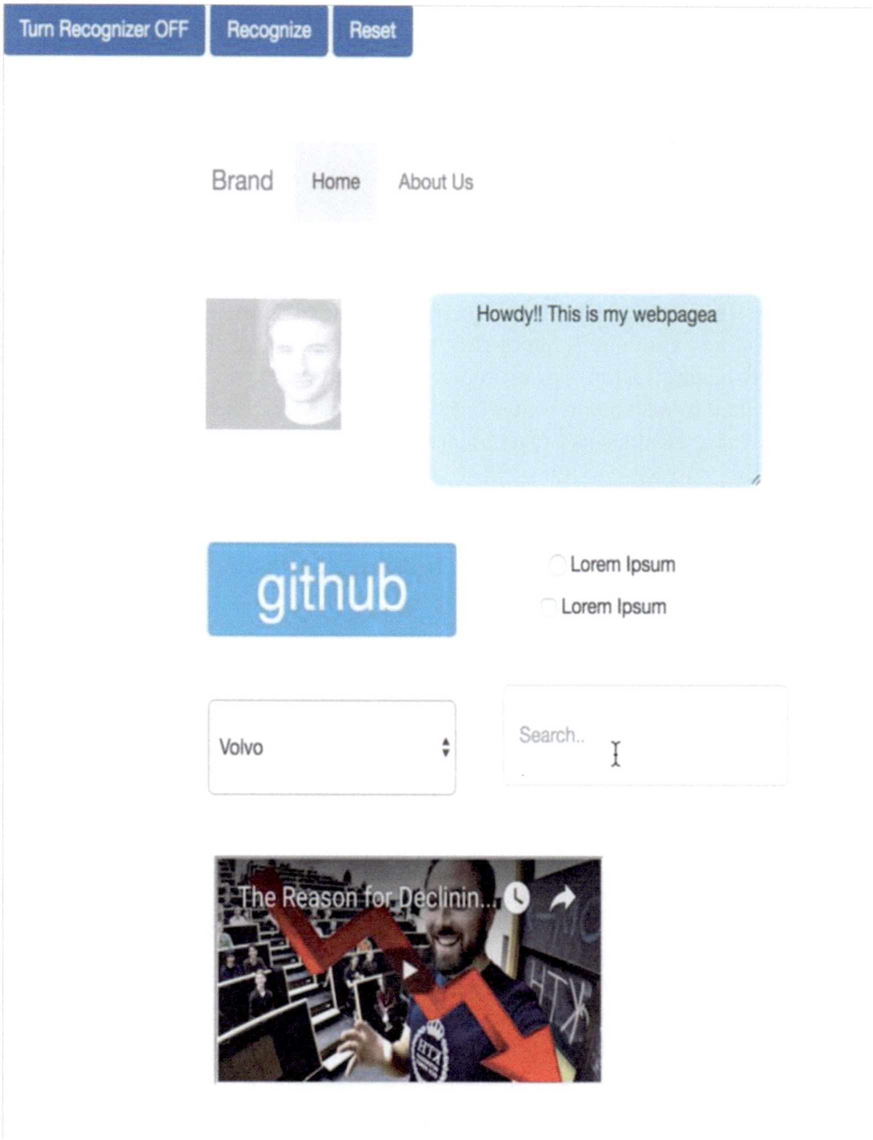

Fig. 7.12 A basic website created in our interface using wireframing elements

the screen at the time of insertion. The code generated as a result of the design is easily downloadable at any time through the click of a button.

7.3.5 Dynamic Functionality

While FreeStyle is designed to be as quick and easy as possible to create a website design, we have also added additional functionality to the beautified elements that allows the website to go beyond a concept assistant to a functional website builder. Each element has a unique functionality which is accessible through selecting the element after beautification. For example, when a user first draws the symbol for a button (a rectangle with a horizontal line drawn inside), the sketch goes away and a button icon image is added as a placeholder for the actual button. Based on the user's intentions, this may be enough or they could choose to select the beautified icon which it then prompts for a button link and text to display. At this point, the button becomes a live link, that is a clickable button. Each element has similar functionality that would allow someone with minimal technical knowledge the ability to make a basic yet functional website.

7.4 Evaluation

Although a good user interface is essential for our software to provide a delightful experience to the users, it is not possible to quantify satisfaction. Hence, the criterion that we used for testing our application is to measure the accuracy of the recognition of the shapes. For a small user study evaluation, we recruited five graduate Computer Science students by convenience sampling to draw shapes that were defined by us on the canvas. We took a small sample since we wanted to only test a working prototype of our application. All the participants were briefed regarding the working of our system. The experiments were performed in a controlled manner in which the participants were asked to draw shapes that were close to ideal shapes with low variance. Each of them drew each shape in the canvas four times. On running the recognizer for the nine shapes corresponding to navbar, video, image, text area, dropdown, search bar, checkbox, radio button, and button for twenty times each, we obtained the confusion matrix as depicted in Fig. 7.13. We find that our recognizer has a pretty high accuracy for recognizing shapes. The recognizer was able to identify not only the simple shapes but some complex shapes as well including radio button, dropdown, and search bar with an accuracy of 100%. Sometimes, it misclassified a radio button as a checkbox, a dropdown as a search bar, and a search bar as an image. However, the error percentage was low and we were able to get accurate results most of the time. The conditions in which the experiments were done can be considered as ideal and real-life user study of our recognizer may show lower accuracy recognition.

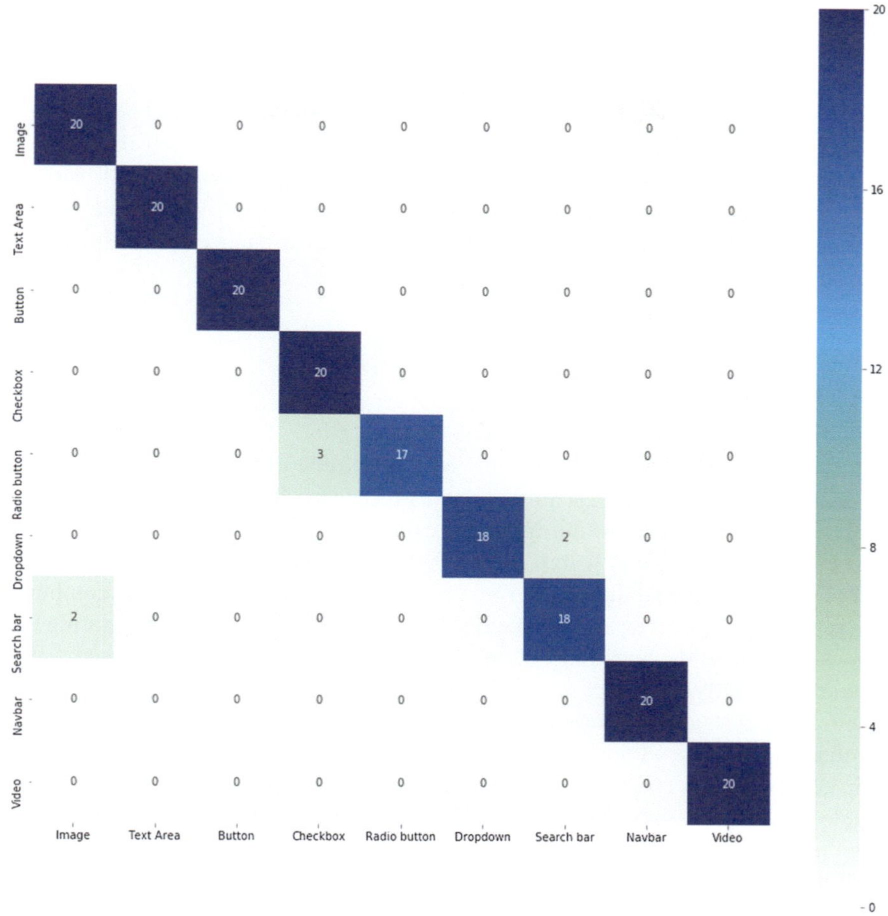

Fig. 7.13 Confusion matrix

7.5 Future Work

We wish to make FreeStyle accessible to all as an effective tool. In this vein, we plan to make additions which would aid in ease of use and extend functionality. We would like to add the move, edit, and delete functionality through drawing circles around elements and scribbling elements out. We also wish to apply a similar system to what is shown in SILK of multiple page navigation through drawing arrow from page to page. Additionally, we plan to build into our algorithm, a normalized confidence feedback. We have experimented with this by using the shapes features to create a type of shape profile which can then be statistically compared against the attributes of each ideal shape profile. By producing such feedback, we would be able to tell if the user is trying to draw an element or leave an annotation, in which case we would leave whatever they sketched on the canvas without beautification. To improve FreeStyle's accuracy, we plan to make a data-driven recognizer that employs a deep neural network. FreeStyle currently lives up to its name by really allowing its users to sketch anywhere on the canvas but our research indicated that users and professional developers would like the option to switch on a grid system which their drawn elements would snap to. We plan to implement a customizable grid with various containers, much like the open-source CSS project "Bootstrap". Finally, we plan to continue to further our research in FreeStyle through case studies with both website building newcomers and professional developers.

7.6 Conclusion

The current drag-and-drop wireframing tools accessible to website developers lack the feel of pen and paper which often proves restrictive in the early brainstorming stage of website interface design. We believe that the FreeStyle system is an effective use of sketch recognition research. Our recognition techniques are effective in shape identification which can then further recognize more complex shapes as a combination of simple shapes. Our current methods identify simple shapes by comparing the ratio of the area of the bounding box to the area of the convex hull. Additionally, our method of identifying complex shapes through their relative position to each other, their relative size, and their orientation has been shown to be effective for identifying wireframing sketches. FreeStyle has applications much larger than the tool for the website designer. It can be scaled to be the tool for anyone who wants to make a simple personal website with little or no technical experience; it could also be used as an educational tool bridging the gap between visually designing a website and illustrating the code that runs behind it.

References

Apte A, Vo V, Kimura TD (1993) Recognizing multistroke geometric shapes: an experimental evaluation. In: Proceedings of the 6th annual ACM symposium on user interface software and technology. ACM, pp 121–128

Fonseca MJ, Pimentel C, Jorge JA (2002) CALI: an online scribble recognizer for calligraphic interfaces. In: AAAI spring symposium on sketch understanding, pp 51–58

Gross MD (1996) The electronic Cocktail Napkin—a computational environment for working with design diagrams

Harel D (1987) Statecharts: a visual formalism for complex systems. Sci Comput Progr 8(3):231–274

Jarvis RA (1973) On the identification of the convex hull of a finite set of points in the plane. Inf Process Lett 2(1):18–21

Landay JA (1996) SILK: sketching interfaces like krazy. In: Conference companion on human factors in computing systems. ACM, pp 398–399

Menuez D, Kounalakis M (1993) Defying gravity: the making of Newton. Beyond Words Pub

Paulson B, Hammond T (2008) Paleosketch: accurate primitive sketch recognition and beautification. In: Proceedings of the 13th international conference on Intelligent user interfaces. ACM, pp 1–10

Rubine D (1991) The automatic recognition of gestures. PhD thesis, Carnegie Mellon University

Sutherland IE (1964) Sketchpad a man-machine graphical communication system. Trans Soc Comput Simul 2(5):R–3

Ulgen F, Flavell AC, Akamatsu N (1995) Geometric shape recognition with fuzzy filtered input to a backpropagation neural network. IEICE Trans Inf Syst 78(2):174–183

Wong YY (1992) Rough and ready prototypes: lessons from graphic design. In: Posters and short talks of the 1992 SIGCHI conference on human factors in computing systems. ACM, pp 83–84

Zhao R (1993) Incremental recognition in gesture-based and syntax-directed diagram editors. In: Proceedings of the INTERACT'93 and CHI'93 conference on human factors in computing systems. ACM, pp 95–100

Part V
Teaching Sketching Skills

Chapter 8
Improvement in Freehand Sketching Application for Spatial Visualization Training

Elizabeth Cowan, Nathan Delson, Bob Mihelich and Lelli Van Den Einde

Abstract Spatial visualization is the cognitive ability of mentally representing and manipulating two-dimensional and three-dimensional figures. This is a learnable cognitive skill that has been correlated with increased GPA's and retention in science, technology, engineering, and math (STEM) disciplines. Traditional spatial visualization training includes freehand sketching assignments, which require human grading. A spatial visualization training application (app) was developed in which students freehand sketch on a touchscreen and an automatic grading algorithm provides immediate feedback. In spring 2014, the app was used with iPads in a one-unit spatial visualization course where students took pre- and post-spatial visualization assessment tests. In 2014, 46% of the students who scored low on the pre-assessment had a significant improvement of 10% or more on the post-assessment. This chapter describes how the app was modified to increase student gains: the user interface and assignments were modified, taking advantage of color and cues that are not present in the traditional paper-based sketching assignments; and gamification was added to motivate increased persistence. The course was taught with the newly modified app in 2017, during which 82% of incoming students with low spatial skills showed significant improvement. The increase from 46 to 82% is attributed to the capability of pen and touch technology to be adapted effectively for educational purposes.

E. Cowan (✉)
eGrove Education, 5037 Seagrove Cove, San Diego, CA 92130, USA
e-mail: lizzy@egrove.education

N. Delson · L. Van Den Einde
UCSD, 9500 Gilman Dr, La Jolla, CA 92093, USA
e-mail: ndelson@ucsd.edu

L. Van Den Einde
e-mail: lellivde@ucsd.edu

B. Mihelich
McHenry County College, 8900 US Route 14, Crystal Lake, IL 60012, USA
e-mail: bmihelich@mchenry.edu

T. Hammond et al. (eds.), *Inspiring Students with Digital Ink*, Human–Computer Interaction Series, https://doi.org/10.1007/978-3-030-17398-2_8

8.1 Introduction

Spatial visualization is the ability to mentally represent and manipulate two-dimensional (2D) and three-dimensional (3D) figures. These skills are required in many professions (Smith 1964). They have been correlated with increased grade point averages in STEM-related fields including math, engineering, computer programming, and science (Sorby 2009) and a study following over 7000 students showed that spatial visualization training is correlated with increased graduation rates (Sorby 2012). Spatial visualization skills are learnable (Sorby 2009); however, most students do not receive formal instruction as spatial visualization concepts are not a focus of contemporary K-12 curriculum. Research has shown that a single unit spatial visualization course has increased retention in STEM majors, especially for women and other underrepresented minorities (Hill et al. 2010).

Typical spatial visualization training is a combination of multiple-choice and freehand sketching assignments (Sorby 2011). Multiple-choice-based instruction is a more manageable system for instructors to incorporate into the classroom because of its ease of grading, ability to provide students with relatively quick feedback, and its ability to be administered both traditionally with paper and pencil, and incorporated into an online learning management systems (LMS). However, multiple-choice assignments are subject to the process of elimination and are not an accurate representation of how these skills would be applied in a real-world application. Spatial visualization training using freehand sketching exercises has shown greater benefits over solely multiple-choice assignments for developing students' spatial visualization reasoning (Sorby 2009), as well as improving students' technical communication ability and creativity (Do and Gross 1996; Song and Agogino 2004). However, incorporating sketching assignments on paper requires instructor time for manually grading, and students do not receive immediate feedback on their performance.

To bridge the gap between the more practical multiple-choice instruction and the more valuable freehand sketching training, an iPad application, called Spatial Vis, was developed in 2012 to address these concerns (Delson 2015). Spatial Vis automatically grades freehand sketching assignments, removing the need for human grading, providing instantaneous feedback to students, creating a more manageable solution for teachers and a more beneficial solution for students.

The initial pilot in 2014 yielded interesting results. In addition to freehand sketching, the element of persistence also plays a significant role in the development of spatial skills (Delson 2015). The use of a touchscreen with stylus or finger sketching has led to the development of an alternative to multiple-choice learning technology. This chapter will discuss application modifications focused on increasing student engagement and persistence made after the 2014 pilot that has led to significantly improved results in a 2017 pilot. The enhancements include; user interface modifications, assignment additions and design modifications, and the introduction of gamification.

8.2 Spatial Vis 2014 Training Application

8.2.1 App Overview

The Spatial Vis application has several key components, including; the assignment window, sketching window, toolbar, and save button (Fig. 8.1). The assignment window describes the task students are to complete. The sketching window is where students draw their solution to the assignment. The sketching window and the assignment window each have a reference dot to prompt the student to know where in the sketching window they need to draw their solution in order for the grading algorithm to correctly score their solution. The toolbar features an eraser, pencil, and help button. When the user selects the save button in the top right corner, the grading algorithm is initiated. The grading algorithm produces a pop-up window that gives the student immediate feedback if their solution is correct or not. If the solution is correct, the student moves on to the next assignment. If the solution is incorrect, the

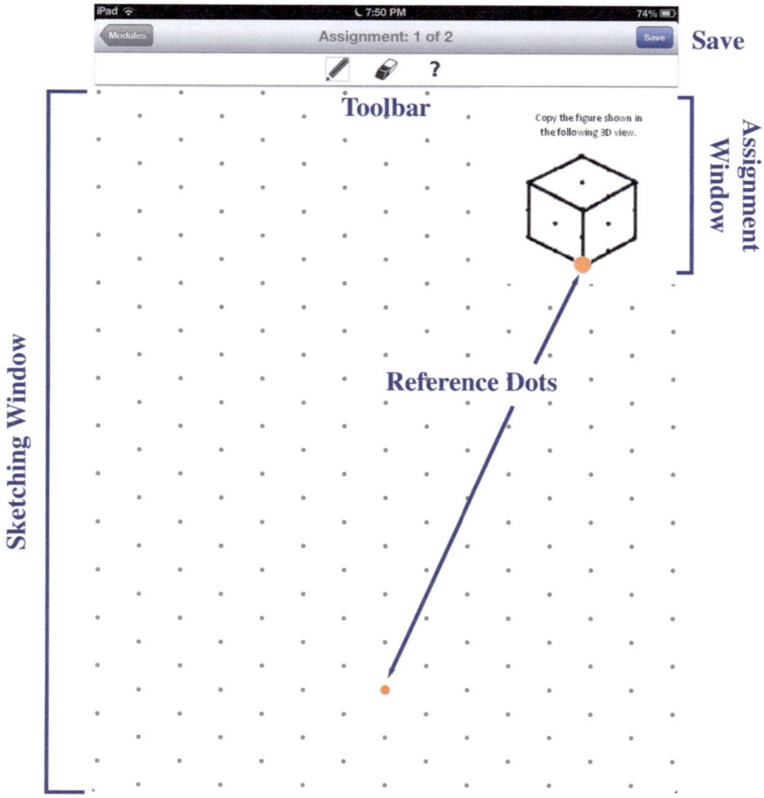

Fig. 8.1 2014 assignment and sketching window

student can either retry the assignment or peek at the solution. If the student chooses to peek at the solution, the sketching window will show which lines are correct or incorrect, and which lines are missing from their sketch for it to be graded as correct.

8.2.2 2014 Pilot

The 2014 pilot course was a one-unit, pass/no pass course at the University of California, San Diego consisting of 52 students who met once a week for ten weeks. Prior to being introduced to the Spatial Vis application, students were given the Purdue Spatial Visualization Test: Rotations (PSVT:R) as a pre-assessment of their incoming spatial visualization skills. The PSVT:R (Maeda et al. 2013) is a timed, 20 minute assessment consisting of thirty multiple-choice questions of three-dimensional rotation tasks (Fig. 8.2). The students then went through the one-unit course and completed the Spatial Vis application. Upon the conclusion of the course, the PSVT:R was administered as a post-assessment allowing us to compare their scores. The primary focus was on students who scored 70% and below on the pretest because they were considered most at risk for dropping out of a STEM major. Out of the 52 students that took the one-unit course, 13 of them scored 70% and below on the pretest. Those 13 students were the focus of the analysis.

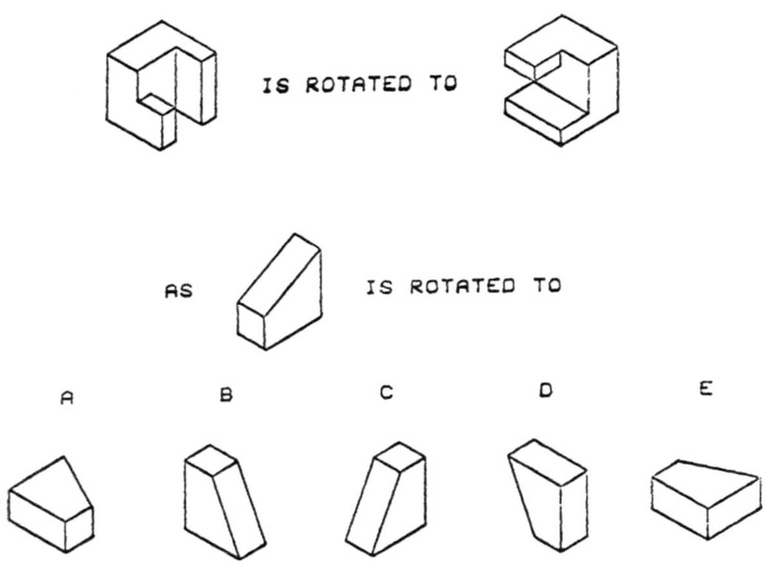

Fig. 8.2 The Purdue Spatial Visualization Test: Rotations (PSVT:R) sample test assignment (Guay 1977)

8.2.3 2014 Results

The results showed that the low pretest group of students had an average test improvement of 18%. However, Table 8.1 shows a noticeable split between the individual

Table 8.1 2014 test performance of students in the low pretest group

2014 (n = 13)

Individual students with low pretest categorized into two groups	Pretest score (max = 100)	Posttest score (max = 100)	Test improvement (%)
Low pretest: no/low improvement	57	60	6
Low pretest: no/low improvement	57	60	6
Low pretest: no/low improvement	67	67	0
Low pretest: no/low improvement	67	67	0
Low pretest: no/low improvement	43	43	0
Low pretest: no/low improvement	70	60	−14
Low pretest: no/low improvement	57	47	−18
Average	**60**	**58**	**−3**
Low pretest: significant improvement	60	93	56
Low pretest: significant improvement	40	60	50
Low pretest: significant improvement	40	57	42
Low pretest: significant improvement	50	70	40
Low pretest: significant improvement	57	77	35
Low pretest: significant improvement	57	77	35
Average	**51**	**72**	**43**

students. 54% of the students had no or low improvement, while the other 46% of students had significant improvement (10% or more).

Possible reasons why some students improved while others did not improve were further investigated. Multiple performance metrics were compared and the largest difference between the two groups was the number of times they tried again without using the peek feature. When a student got an assignment incorrect, they were given two options: they could retry the assignment or peek at the solution. The students with significant improvement would retry assignments without peeking 74% more often than those who had low or no improvement (Delson 2015). Accordingly, the percentage of time a student would retry assignments without peeking was used to quantify persistence.

8.3 Spatial Vis Training Application Modifications

The 2014 version of the application used assignments from a traditional paper and pencil spatial visualization training curriculum (Delson 2015). Since the 2014 pilot, digital and touchscreen affordances have been leveraged by making several design changes with the goal of increasing student engagement, persistence, and spatial visualization skills. These alterations include enhancements to the user interface, assignment design modifications, and the introduction of gamification.

8.3.1 User Interface Changes

Several user interface changes were made between Spatial Vis 2014 and Spatial Vis 2017 (Fig. 8.3). One major change was the addition of color. The color makes the application seem more game-like and less like an assignment. The changes in color create a more fun and engaging atmosphere for students.

The assignment window was also separated from the sketching window so that a larger assignment could be created that would stay in view if students wanted to zoom-in on the sketching window. By giving the assignment window more area on the interface, additional instruction about an assignment could be added.

Another improvement was the change in grid structure. Initially, both the orthographic and isometric grids that were used to guide the students in making accurate, proportioned sketches were individual black dots. This grid type is common in traditional hand sketching exercises because it does not overpower the student's pencil lines, allowing graders and students to easily see their sketches. The digital interface is not restricted by color so the lack of contrast between black print and gray pencil lines was no longer a concern, allowing for the use of a full halftoned gray grid paired with a contrasting blue digital pen color. This subtle change not only helps students improve their freehand sketching ability by giving them lines to follow, but also

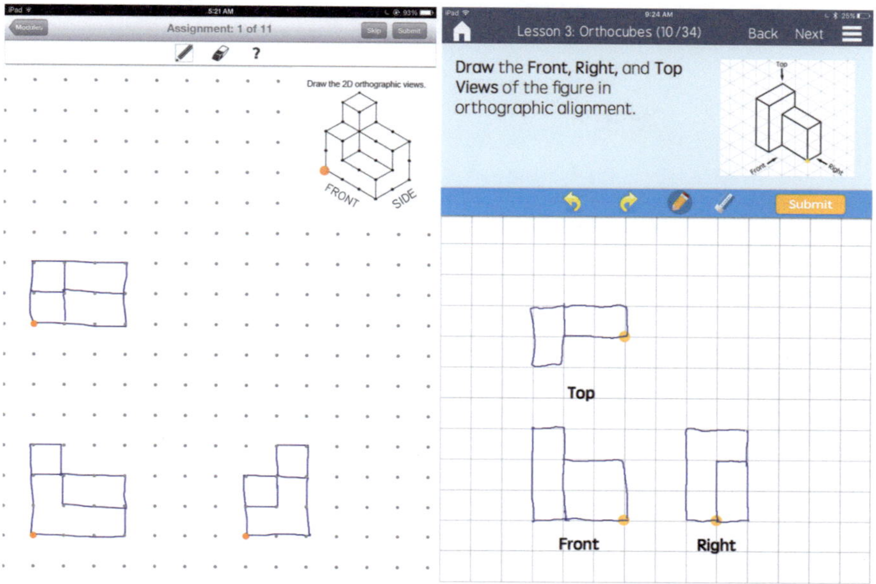

Fig. 8.3 Comparison of 2014 (left) and 2017 (right) interfaces

makes the potential solution more visible in the high contrast color and lineweight between the light-gray background grid and their heavier blue sketched lines.

8.3.2 Assignment Redesign

In terms of assignment redesign, moving to pen and touch technology has many affordances over traditional, analog pen and paper. According to the 2014 student survey, students found sketching on the iPad about the same to sketching on paper (Delson 2015). Because of the survey results and studies showed the value of sketching assignments over multiple-choice assignments, the number of sketching assignments in the application was increased. Table 8.2 shows the breakdown of assignment types within the two versions of the application.

Table 8.2 2014 and 2017 assignment types

	Total assignments	Percent multiple-choice (%)	Percent freehand sketching (%)
2014	341	76	24
2017	306	8	92

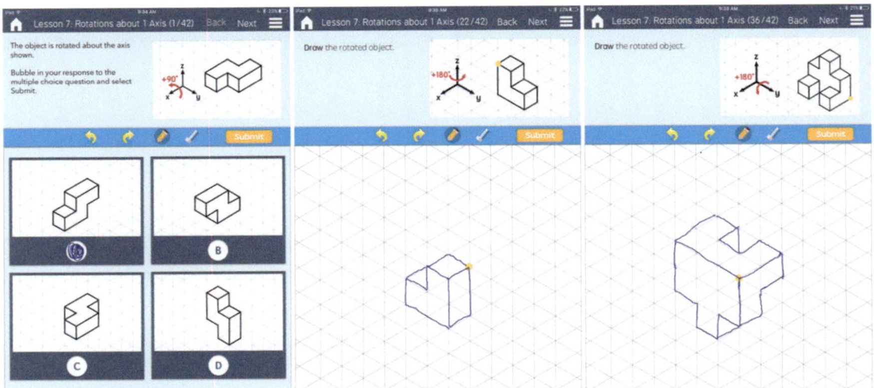

Fig. 8.4 Progression of difficulty within a lesson

In addition to having primarily hand sketching assignments, another focus of the Spatial Vis 2017 application was that it was intuitive enough to be able to stand-alone and not need additional instruction. Because of the variability of the students' incoming spatial visualization skill, a stand-alone application is ideal because it allows students to work at their own pace. Additionally, it creates a more flexible spatial visualization solution for instructors because it can be used in the classroom or as a homework assignment.

In order to achieve this, the assignments started very simple and gradually progressed in difficulty (Fig. 8.4). Assignments could not progress too gradually or students would lose interest. There were several criteria for making an easy assignment. Easy assignments consist of simple shapes, multiple reference dots, labels, or a multiple-choice format. To make an assignment more difficult, the shape would increase in complexity and aids such as extra reference dots and labels were removed.

Similar to the user interface overhaul, the color was strategically added to aid students in their understanding of the foundational concepts each individual lesson teaches. For example, traditional approaches to teaching multiview (orthographic) projection include surface and vertices numbering and/or lettering. The app simplified this concept by using multiple colored dots to help prompt students to recognize the relationship between the 2D orthographic projection drawing they are to create from the 3D isometric pictorial drawing given in the assignment window (Fig. 8.5).

An intermediate level of help was also added (Fig. 8.6). For 2014, when students got an answer incorrect they were given the option to retry the assignment or peek at the solution. In the 2017 app, a hint feature was added. The hint tells the user which parts of their drawing are correct by highlighting them in green and removing the incorrect lines. If a student used a hint and most of their submission remained in the workspace then the student is close to the solution. Alternatively, if the student uses a hint and most of their submission disappears then they know they need to rethink the problem, ask for help, or possibly use a peek.

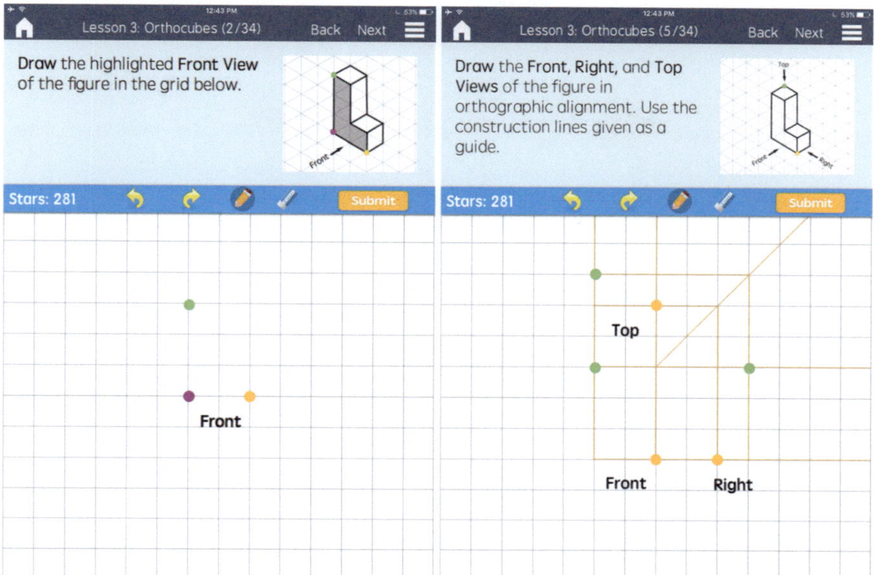

Fig. 8.5 Enhancing student scaffolding with color

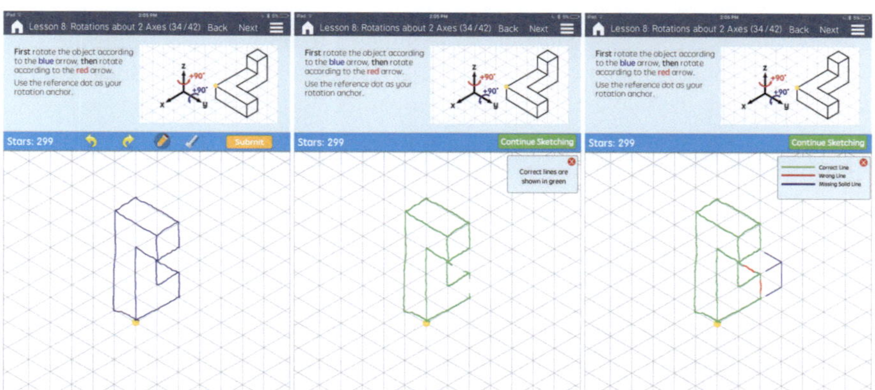

Fig. 8.6 Original Submission (right), hint feedback (middle), and peek feedback (right)

The final three assignments of each lesson were considered "Test Assignments". These assignments were of moderate difficulty and the hint and peek features were disabled. This served as an incentive for students to learn what the lesson was teaching, rather than rely on the hint and peek features. They were aware that they would have to eventually complete three assignments without help features before they could move on to the next lesson.

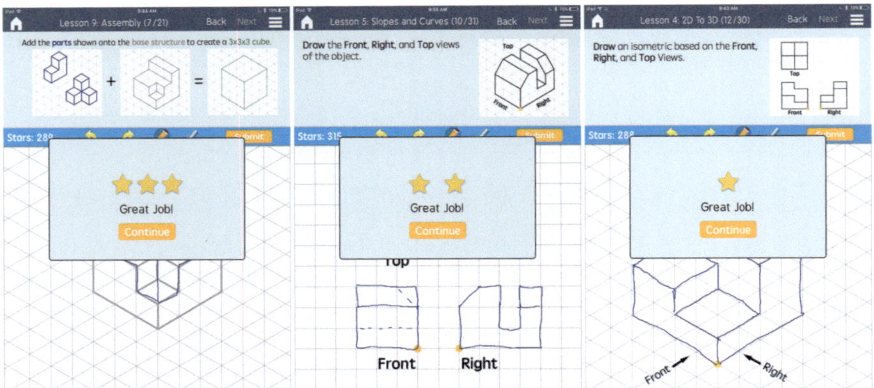

Fig. 8.7 Stars and help features

8.3.3 Gamification

Lastly, a gamification aspect to the application was added to encourage persistence. A goal was to have students retry often and limit their use of the hint and peek features, so stars were added as incentive. The maximum stars a student could receive on an assignment was three stars. Students were allowed to retry as many times as they would like without a penalty (Fig. 8.7 left). If a student used the hint feature on an assignment, then the maximum stars they could receive was two stars (see Fig. 8.7 middle). If a student used a peek, then the maximum stars they could receive was one star (Fig. 8.7 right).

8.4 2017 Pilot

After the changes were made to the application, another one-unit pilot course study was conducted at the University of California, San Diego. Like the 2014 pilot, students met once a week for ten weeks. Before the students were introduced to the application, the students completed the same Purdue Spatial Visualization Test. They then completed the course featuring the Spatial Vis application and took the Purdue Spatial Visualization Test again so that their pre- and posttest scores could be compared. Because the focus of the 2014 pilot was on the students who scored 70% and below on the pretest, students who met the same criteria were evaluated in 2017 for consistency. In the class, 11 of the 32 students during this pilot tested into the low pretest group.

8.4.1 2017 Results

The results showed that the low pretest group of students had an average test improvement of 39%. When you look at the students individually (see Table 8.3), there is no

Table 8.3 2017 test performance of students in the low pretest group

2017 (n = 11)

Individual students with low pretest categorized into two groups	Pretest score (max = 100)	Posttest score (max = 100)	Test improvement (%)
Low pretest: no/low improvement	70	70	0
Low Pretest: no/low improvement	67	57	−15
Average	**68**	**63**	**−7**
Low Pretest: significant improvement	30	73	144
Low Pretest: significant improvement	47	93	100
Low Pretest: significant improvement	63	90	42
Low Pretest: significant improvement	57	80	41
Low Pretest: significant improvement	70	90	29
Low Pretest: significant improvement	70	87	24
Low Pretest: significant improvement	70	87	24
Low Pretest: significant improvement	67	80	20
Low pretest: significant improvement	63	73	16
Average	**60**	**84**	**49**

Table 8.4 Comparison of 2014 and 2017 low pretest group averages

Low pretest students: 70% and below				
Year	Average pretest score (%)	Average posttest score (%)	Average test improvement (%)	Students with significant improvement (10%+) (%)
2014 (n = 13)	55	64	18	46
2017 (n = 11)	61	80	39	82

longer a noticeable split between students with no or low improvement and students with significant improvement.

When comparing the results of the 2014 to the 2017 study, there is a 78% increase of incoming low spatial skilled students that show significant improvement (see Table 8.4).

In addition to using the pretest and posttest method to evaluate student performance 26 of the 32 students that enrolled in the course took a survey after completing the course. Overall, 92% of students reported noticing an improvement in their spatial visualization skills as a result of taking the course and 96% of students would recommend the course to their peers.

8.5 Discussion

The design changes made to the user interface following the 2014 pilot led to an improvement in test scores of students with low incoming spatial visualization skills in 2017. The addition of color and gamification helped create a "low stress, interesting, and fun" (2017 Pilot Student) experience. Additionally, the focus on the assignments building in difficulty with the use of scaffolding and a clear assignment progression allowed for the students to work independently; creating a more flexible and manageable spatial visualization training method for the classroom.

While the combination of the design changes has led to better test scores, it is not clear if one specific design change had a greater impact on the results than the others. In addition, these were relatively small studies with n = 13 in 2014 and n = 11 in 2017. Additional studies with larger numbers of students will be needed to validate the results. It is interesting to note that although the focus was on students with low pretest scores, students from all pretest groups felt they improved over the duration of the course. When surveying the entire class, 92% of students (n = 26) that took the course reported a noticeable improvement in their spatial visualization skills with some saying they "feel more confident in their visualizing skills" (2017 Pilot Student).

8.6 Future Work

In addition to the previously discussed design changes impacting the posttest scores of students, we plan on further looking at the 2017 student submission data to determine if there is a difference in the student persistence metrics between 2014 and 2017. We will also look closely at the student data metrics surrounding specific assignments, which will influence future assignment designs.

We plan to continue our research around Spatial Vis at the University of California, San Diego as well as making the application available to other universities, high schools, camps, and afterschool programs. The Spatial Vis App is currently being ported to Apple and Android phones and tablets, Chromebooks, and Windows Computers.

8.7 Conclusions

Touchscreen devices provide a unique environment which allow for an electronic stand-alone method of teaching a skill that has previously been reliant on analog methods and human grading. Not only can spatial visualization exercises be digitized, but the unique affordances of the digital platform allow for color, animations, personalized feedback, and gamification to play a role in student learning and motivation. The flexibility of these devices allows the application to be used in a classroom, independently, or a hybrid setting.

A prior study had indicated that sketching assignments can be used to quantify student persistence, which in turn was tied to the effectiveness in learning. This study shows how changes in the user interface designed to increase persistence have led to increases from 46% to 82% in the number of students with significant posttest gains.

8.8 Disclosure

Nathan Delson and Lelli Van Den Einde have equity interest in eGrove Education, Inc., a company that may potentially benefit from the research results. The terms of this arrangement have been reviewed and approved by the University of California, San Diego in accordance with its conflict of interest policies. In addition, a Small Business Innovation Research (SBIR) grant was awarded to eGrove Education, Inc, by the NSF (Award # 1648534), that also supported the research effort of this publication.

Acknowledgements We would like to thank Stephanie Hernandez and Michael Hohl for contributing to the application's graphics, and Justyn Bell and Sean Patno for their programming efforts. We would also like to thank Jackie First, Stephanie Hernandez, Edward Lan, Samuel Lechtman, and Patricia Tan for administering and coordinating the MAE7 course. These studies were supported by the University of California, San Diego, Department of Mechanical and Aerospace Engineering, Department of Structural Engineering, and a grant from the NSF (SBIR Award # 1407123).

References

Delson N (2015) Tracking student engagement with a touchscreen app for spatial visualization training and freehand sketching. ASEE 26:1

Do EYL, Gross MD (1996) Drawing as a means to design reasoning. In: AI and design

Guay R (1977) Purdue spatial visualization test-visualization of views. Purdue Research Foundation, West Lafayette, IN

Hill C, Corbett C, St Rose A (2010) Why so few? Women in science, technology, engineering, and mathematics. ERIC

Maeda Y, Yoon SY, Kim-Kang G, Imbrie P (2013) Psychometric properties of the revised PSVT:R for measuring first year engineering students' spatial ability. Int J Eng Edu 29(3):763–776

Smith IM (1964) Spatial ability: its educational and social significance. RR Knapp

Song S, Agogino AM (2004) Insights on designers' sketching activities in new product design teams. In: ASME 2004 international design engineering technical conferences and computers and information in engineering conference. American Society of Mechanical Engineers, pp 351–360

Sorby S (2011) Developing spatial thinking workbook and accompanying developing spatial thinking software by Anne Frances Wysocki. Cengage Learn ISBN-13 1470606071

Sorby SA (2009) Educational research in developing 3-d spatial skills for engineering students. Int J Sci Edu 31(3):459–480

Sorby SA (2012) Spatial skills training to improve student success in engineering. Chemistry 1(2.47):0–024

Chapter 9
Teaching Engineering Students Freehand Sketching with an Intelligent Tutoring System

Ethan Hilton, Blake Williford, Wayne Li, Tracy Hammond and Julie Linsey

Abstract Sketching is an essential skill in engineering design. However, the instruction of sketching in engineering curriculum has greatly diminished in recent decades. Previous studies have shown that teaching an Industrial Design-inspired version of free hand sketching is effective in engineering courses, but engineering professors are often untrained to teach this method effectively. This chapter studies the effect of supplementing instructor-taught sketching with an online sketching tutor that utilizes artificial intelligence to provide human-like feedback to user sketches. To measure the impact of the introduction of this program, the authors compared students who used the online tutor against students who only completed paper-based sketching homework using pre- and post-course spatial visualization evaluations and sketching quizzes. The results show that the students using the online tutor significantly improve their spatial visualization skills at a level equivalent to students who had more practice with pen-and-paper sketching.

E. Hilton (✉)
College of Engineering and Science, Louisiana Tech University, Ruston, LA, USA
e-mail: ehilton@latech.edu

B. Williford · T. Hammond
Sketch Recognition Lab, Department of Computer Science & Engineering,
Texas A&M University, College Station, TX, USA
e-mail: bwilliford@gmail.com

T. Hammond
e-mail: hammond@tamu.edu

W. Li
School of Industrial Design, Georgia Institute of Technology, Atlanta, GA, USA
e-mail: wayne.li@design.gatech.edu

J. Linsey
George W. Woodruff School of Mechanical Engineering, Georgia Institute of Technology,
Atlanta, GA, USA
e-mail: julie.linsey@me.gatech.edu

T. Hammond et al. (eds.), *Inspiring Students with Digital Ink*, Human–Computer Interaction Series, https://doi.org/10.1007/978-3-030-17398-2_9

9.1 Introduction

Engineers use hand-drawn sketches in a variety of contexts. They are a key component of the language of engineering design (Dym et al. 2005) and an integral part of the engineering design process (Ullman et al. 1990). Sketching has been found to improve communication in collaborative design (Goldschmidt 2007; Shah et al. 2001). Using sketches is also an effective means of working through a design problem as sketching has been found to improve conceptual understanding of a subject (Gobert and Clement 1999), aid in understanding ill-defined problems (Cross and Roy 1989), and assist in the idea-generation phase of product development (Yang 2009). Sketching is even a proven method for improving spatial visualization skills, a key skill in engineering (Olkun 2003; Sorby 2009). Despite all of these findings, instruction in sketching has been given less emphasis as Computer-Aided Design (CAD) programs have become more prevalent (Dym et al. 2005). Teaching students sketching techniques help to remove their inhibition to use sketching (Booth et al. 2016). For this reason, an Introduction to Engineering Graphics (IEG) course at Georgia Tech has been redesigned in recent years to incorporate pedagogy for teaching sketching based on methods typically found in Industrial Design curricula (Hilton et al. 2016a).

Introduction to Engineering Graphics consists of 5 weeks of instruction in sketching while the remaining 12 weeks of the semester focuses on teaching students solid modeling. Before the redesign of the sketching portion of the course, students learned a more traditional version of engineering drawing. This version of the course is referred to as the Traditional version for the remainder of the paper. The Traditional version takes an approach to teach engineering drawing more commonly found in engineering curricula. Students learn basic drafting techniques using straight edges and grid paper to guide their drawings. The primary objective of the sketching portion of the Traditional version is to prepare students to use CAD programs to generate renderings of a product idea and to improve their spatial visualization skills. After the redesign, three of the four instructors of the IEG course taught the sketching portion using the pedagogy inspired by Industrial Design. This method is referred to as the Perspective version for the remainder of the paper. The Perspective method of the course teaches students to generate realistic renderings of a product via sketch before using a CAD program. Students learned more advanced sketching techniques such as sketching in perspective views, shading, and raytracing to generate realistic depth and shadows. Figure 9.1 is an example of a student's final sketching assignment.

Teaching this method is difficult in engineering curricula as there is a lack of expertise in this pedagogy among engineering faculty. The amount of time needed to grade these types of sketches and provide feedback to students is also higher than more traditional methods. This led to the development of SketchTivity, a web-based Intelligent Tutoring System (ITS) that utilizes pen-and-tablet technology to teach students sketching through a series of sketching exercises with feedback. The goal of this program is to enhance the sketching ability of students with less instructor interaction.

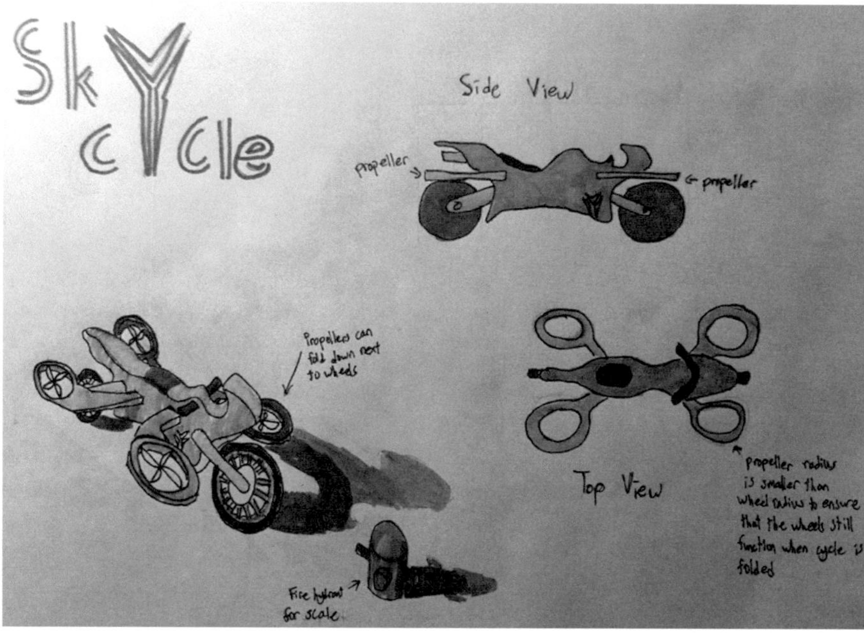

Fig. 9.1 Student work from perspective version of IEG course

9.2 Previous Work

Since the introduction of the Perspective method, there have been several studies on the effectiveness of the new method and ways to continue improving the sketching portion of the IEG course. These studies include looking at the impact of the Perspective method on engineering students and the development of a tool to teach students perspective sketching with less interaction from an instructor.

9.2.1 Evaluating the Impact of the Perspective Method

In a previous study, researchers studied the Traditional and Perspective methods to determine the impact of teaching engineering students with the Industrial Design-based pedagogy, by comparing students who were taught each version of the course in various key skills including spatial visualization (Hilton et al. 2016a) and sketching ability (Hilton et al. 2017a). The first study used the Purdue Spatial Visualization Test of Rotations (PSVT:R) to evaluate the students' spatial visualization skills both before and after taking the course (Bodner and Guay 1997). The study found the Traditional and Perspective methods impacted students' spatial visualization equally. Both methods significantly improved students' spatial skills, especially for those stu-

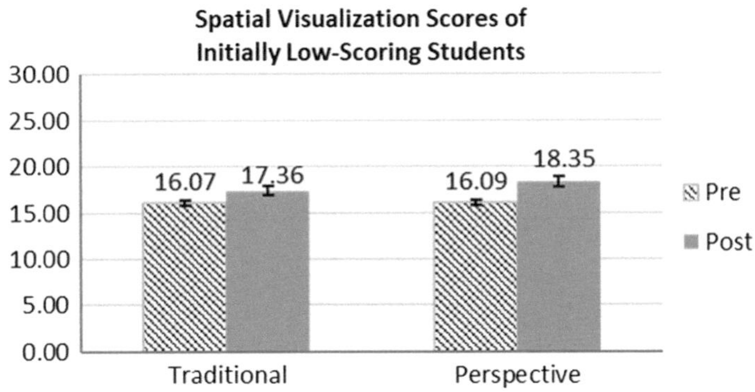

Fig. 9.2 Pre-to-post comparison of PSVT scores of initially low-scoring students shown with standard error bars

dents initially categorized as having low spatial visualization skills. Figure 9.2 shows the pre- to post-course improvements of students with initially low spatial visualization skills. The second study found that the Perspective method was significantly more likely to improve students' sketching ability than the Traditional Method. Ultimately, these previous studies by Hilton et al. (2016a, b), show that the Perspective method allows students to learn additional skills in the same timeframe while maintaining the development of key skills gained from the Traditional method (Hilton et al. 2017b).

9.2.2 *SketchTivity*

SketchTivity is a web-based intelligent tutoring system that utilizes pen-and-tablet technology to teach students perspective-based sketching through a mastery-based pedagogy (Williford et al. 2016). The system is broken into several modules that allow users to master simple skills such as drawing consistent straight lines and more advanced exercises such as sketching primitives in perspective space (Keshavabhotla et al. 2017). Figure 9.3 shows the SketchTivity lesson overview for primitive shapes.

SketchTivity provides immediate feedback to users on the accuracy of their lines through colored lines indicating where the line was intended to be drawn versus where the user drew the line. After completing eight exercises, the system provides additional feedback to the user indicating their average accuracy, line quality (smoothness) and speed when completing the exercises.

At the time of this study, SketchTivity included modules on Basic, Perspective, and Primitive Lessons. The Basic lessons included straight and curved lines, squares, and circles. The Perspective lessons included planes and ellipses. The Primitive lessons included Cubes and Cuboids. As the user advances through the lessons, the system

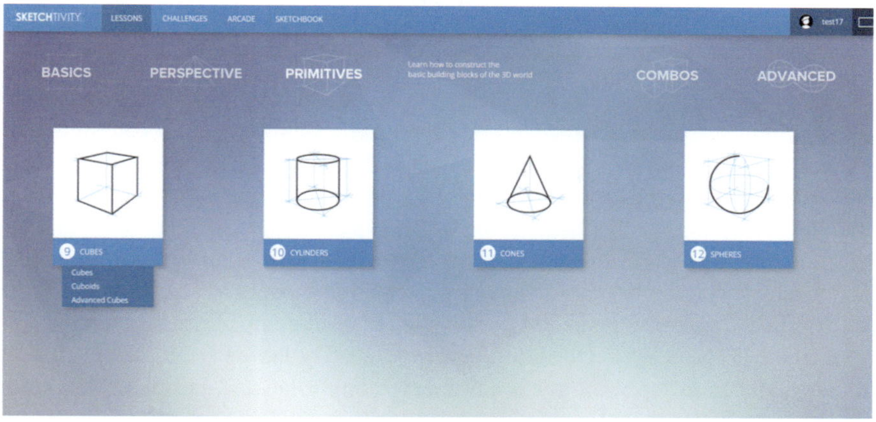

Fig. 9.3 SketchTivity lesson overview for primitive shapes

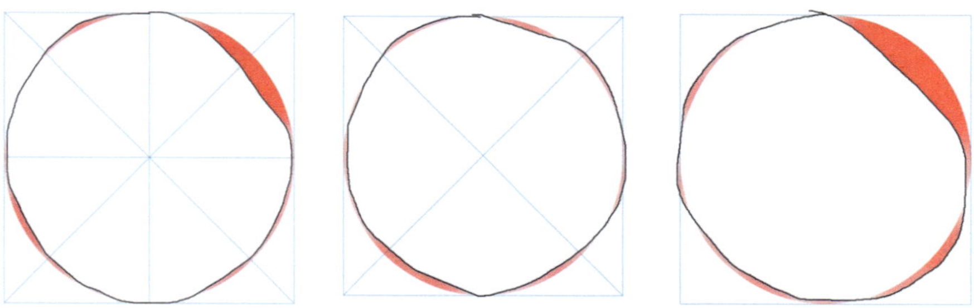

Fig. 9.4 Example of circle exercise with progressively less scaffolding

provides progressively less scaffolding. Figure 9.4 shows an example from three different levels of the circle exercise with full, some, and no scaffolding.

9.3 Research Question

Researchers observed the Perspective method to be an effective way to teach engineering students sketching. With the development and implementation of SketchTivity into the Perspective version of the course, there is interest in determining the impact of using the system on the user's sketching ability. This chapter explores the impact of SketchTivity with the following research question:

Does using an online sketching tutor influence spatial visualization and sketching skills gained by students?

9.4 Methodology of Evaluation

One instructor implemented SketchTivity into one section of the Introduction to Engineering Graphics course taught using the Perspective method over two semesters. The IEG course consists of two 50-min lecture periods and one 3-h lab period each week. The entire class had the opportunity to participate in a study using a new method of teaching sketching. A random selection of the students who agreed to participate in the study determined 20 students used the SketchTivity program, and the remaining participants only completed assignments using pen-and-paper and made up the Paper group. All students who agreed to participate received compensation in the form of extra credit in the course. During three of the weekly lab periods, the students in the SketchTivity group went to a touchscreen monitor lab and completed the modules of SketchTivity that aligned with that week's lecture and sketching assignment. The students in the Paper group remained in the regular lab space with the graduate teaching assistants for the course where they worked on the sketching assignments. The SketchTivity group was also compared to students in the Traditional group who were taught the more traditional version of engineering drawing.

Three of the five sketching assignments for the Perspective version of the course consisted of two parts: exploration and final composition. The exploration involved sketching at least 25 views of the primitives (cubes, spheres, etc.) in two-point perspective (Fig. 9.5). The final composition was a single sketch using all of the skills taught in class. The students in the SketchTivity group did not complete the exploration portion of the assignment but instead performed the equivalent exercise in the SketchTivity program (see Fig. 9.6) at least 25 times. The students received no human feedback on the portion of the assignment completed in SketchTivity.

9.4.1 *Spatial Visualization*

In order to determine the impact of the system on the students' spatial visualization skills, the students completed a pre- and post-course evaluation. The evaluation used was the Mental Rotation Test (MRT) developed by Vandenberg and Kuse (1978) and revised by Peters et al. (2006). The evaluation consisted of 24 questions with a 12-min time limit. Over the two semesters, the authors collected and analyzed spatial visualization data from 32 students in the SketchTivity group and 42 students in the Control group. The authors analyzed the results of the pre-course evaluation between the two groups to ensure they were initially equivalent and again at the end of the semester to determine if there was a significant change between the two groups.

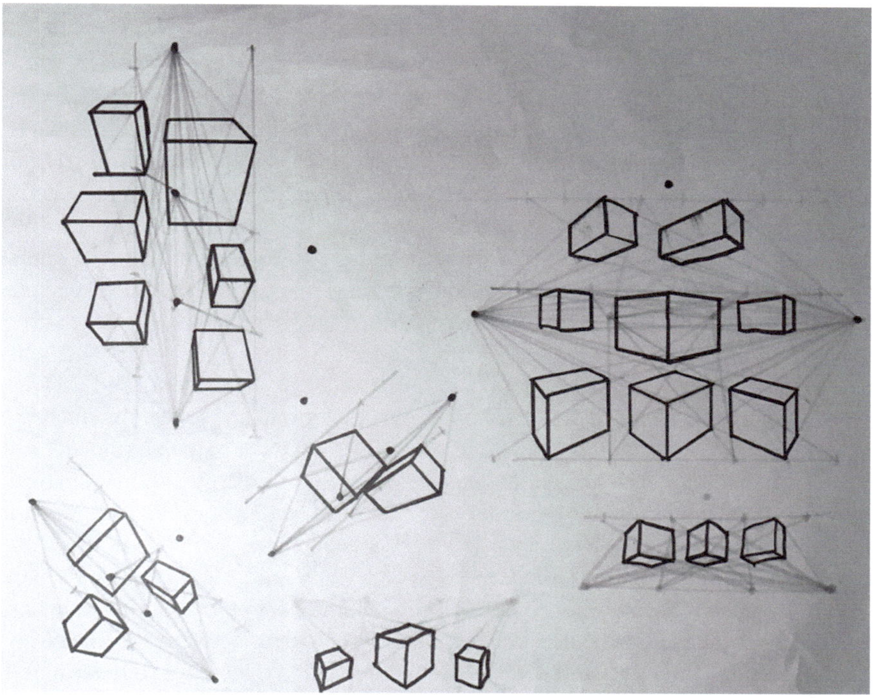

Fig. 9.5 Example of student cube exploration submission

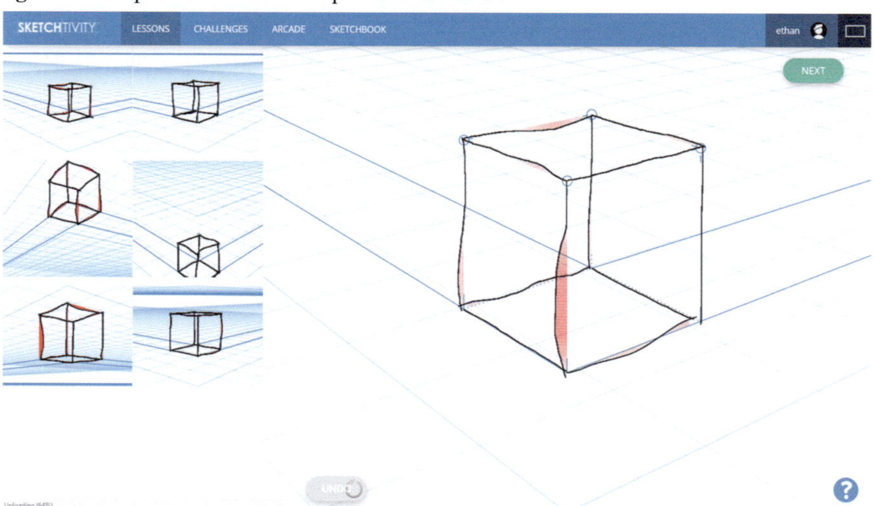

Fig. 9.6 Example of SketchTivity alternate assignment

9.4.2 Sketching Ability

To evaluate the students' sketching ability and the impact of using SketchTivity had on their development, the students completed pre- and post-course sketching quizzes developed. This sketching evaluation quiz was developed in a previous study (Hilton et al. 2016b). The final task in this quiz is to draw a camera in two-point perspective given three face views of the camera (see Fig. 9.7). To evaluate whether or not a student improved in sketching ability, researchers scanned the pre- and post-course camera exercises of each student and uploaded the scans to an online survey presented to two raters. The raters evaluated each student's pre- and post-course sketch by observing two sketches similar to Fig. 9.7 and which sketch they considered better and if it was slightly better or much better. The order of the students and sketches were randomized to avoid a bias toward the students' group and to which sketch was the pre- or post-course sketch. These raters were instructors or graduate students with experience teaching sketching in engineering. For this study, the authors analyzed sketching data from only one semester (the first of the two semesters mentioned in Sect. 9.4.1). The analyzed data consisted of 31 students who were taught the Traditional form of sketching, 16 students in the SketchTivity group, and 26 students in the Control group. To ensure inter-rater reliability, the authors compared the ratings of the two raters. The authors compared the improvement rates between the SketchTivity and Control groups (both taught using the Perspective method) to determine if using SketchTivity was as effective at improving sketching ability as only completing pen-and-paper sketching assignments. The authors also compared the SketchTivity group to the students who were taught the Traditional method to determine if using SketchTivity to teach the Perspective method still improved sketching ability at a higher rate than the Traditional method.

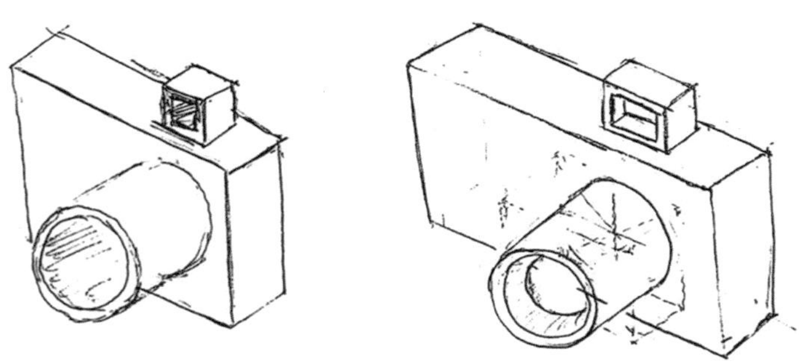

Fig. 9.7 Example of student pre- and post-course sketching quiz

9.5 Results

The authors conducted between-subject analyses to compare the differences in impact to spatial visualization skills between the SketchTivity group and the Control group. The authors also conducted within-subject analyses to determine whether or not each group improved significantly. The authors conducted between-subject analyses of sketching ability between students from the Traditional Group and the SketchTivity group and between students in the SketchTivity Group and the Control group to understand how SketchTivity compared to both styles of teaching sketching.

9.5.1 Spatial Visualization Results

The results of the MRT for the pre- and post-course evaluations for each group can be seen in Fig. 9.8. To determine if the groups were initially equivalent, a t-test was run between the two groups resulting in a p-value of 0.56 ($t = -0.59, df = 78$). This indicates that the two groups were not significantly different initially ($\alpha = 0.05$). The groups were also compared using a t-test on the post-course evaluations which resulted in a p-value of 0.36 ($t = -3.96, df = 47$). This indicates that the two groups are still not significantly different.

A within-subject analysis was also conducted to determine if the groups significantly increased their spatial visualization skills. The paired t-test for the SketchTivity test returned a p-value of less than 0.001 ($t = -4.81, df = 32$) and the Control group's paired t-test also returned a p-value of less than 0.001 ($t = -3.96, df = 47$), indicating that the spatial visualization skills of both groups were significantly increased.

9.5.2 Sketching Ability Results

Comparing the correlation between the two raters resulted in a Pearson correlation of 0.68 when treating the ratings like a continuous rating scale and a Cohen's Kappa of 0.62 when treating the data in a binary pass/fail. According to Cohen (1988),

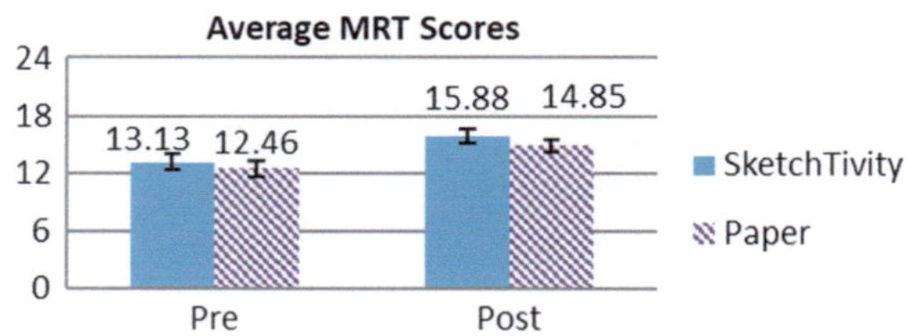

Fig. 9.8 Pre- and post-course average mental rotation test score for each group shown with standard error bars

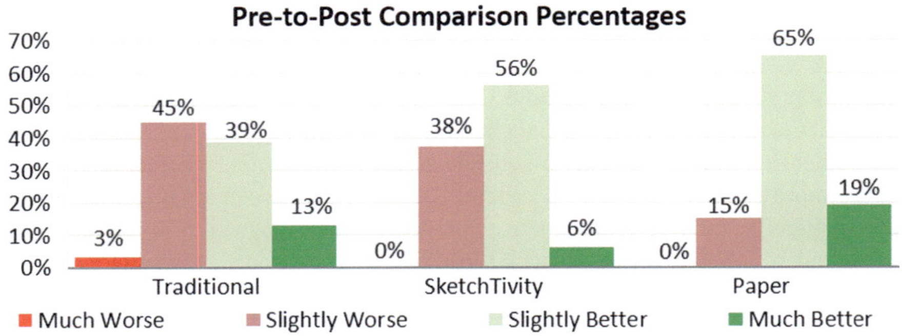

Fig. 9.9 Percentage of pre-to-post sketching comparison ratings for each group

any Pearson correlation above 0.5 is considered a strong correlation in qualitative research, and any Cohen's Kappa between 0.61 and 0.8 is considered substantial. Therefore, the ratings given are reliable as both continuous data and binary data. The remainder of the data shown comes from a single rater.

Figure 9.9 shows the comparison between the percentage of the pre- and post-course sketches among the three groups studied. Pearson's $\tilde{\chi}^2$ test (Pearson 1900) is used to compare the success rates through between-subject analysis of the SketchTivity and Control groups as well as the SketchTivity and Traditional groups. The $\tilde{\chi}^2$ test between the SketchTivity and Paper groups returns a p-value of 0.10 ($Z = 1.63, df = 41$), indicating that the groups are not significantly different, but likely will be different with a larger sample size. The $\tilde{\chi}^2$ test between the SketchTivity and Traditional groups returns a p-value of 0.477 ($Z = 0.711, df = 41$), indicating that the groups are not significantly different.

9.6 Discussion

An analysis of the MRT results indicates that using SketchTivity improves students' spatial visualization skills the same as pen-and-paper sketching. As previous studies find sketching to be an effective way to develop visualization skills, finding sketching digitally to be as effective as analog sketching in this regard is a positive outcome as it shows that the SketchTivity program maintains the development of critical skills gained from analog sketching.

When observing the students' development of sketching abilities, the analyses show two important results. First, the trend of the percentage of students whose sketching ability improves indicates that SketchTivity is more effective at improving sketching ability than the Traditional method, but less effective than the Perspective method with only analog sketching exercises. Second, neither the differences between the SketchTivity group and Traditional group nor the differences between the SketchTivity and Control group were found to be significantly different. These results indicate that while the early version of SketchTivity used by the students in this study was not as effective as analog sketching with more instructor feedback, results do indicate that teaching perspective sketching with SketchTivity may be more effective than teaching traditional engineering sketching.

Ultimately, our results indicate that using SketchTivity maintains improvements in key skills such as spatial visualization while improving students' sketching ability with less instructor feedback to students.

9.7 Future Work

The results indicate that SketchTivity helps to improve students' sketching ability, but a gap exists between the ability gained from students who use SketchTivity and those who only receive feedback from human instructors. This may be due to the increased scaffolding in the SketchTivity lessons (as seen in Fig. 9.6), giving them less practice drawing on a blank surface. Future iterations of the system have included less scaffolding, which should aid in the development of the users' sketching ability. An example of a forthcoming improvement is the advanced cube exercise seen in Fig. 9.10 which requires the user to draw construction lines before sketching a final cube. The system rejects construction lines that are not drawn in the proper location to aid users in developing their mental model of the cube. The user then draws a final cube based on the construction lines they drew. The developers also intend to provide more sophisticated forms of feedback like humanized dialogue. In this way, the system could become closer to a human instructor in effectiveness as well as be an excellent supplementary practice tool for learning design sketching.

There are also several features planned to be included in future versions of SketchTivity. More modules are in development including exercises in combining several primitives. This will allow students to improve their perspective abilities as they place multiple objects in the same perspective plane. Modules allowing users

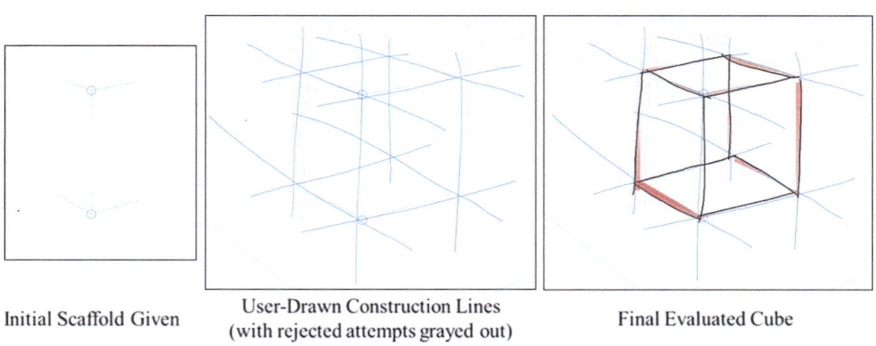

Fig. 9.10 Advanced cube exercise with reduced scaffolding

to sketch with less provided structure are also in development. These will give users more freedom to sketch in perspective but still receive feedback on how well they are maintaining the perspective planes. The inclusion of a user profile will allow users to track their progress over time using SketchTivity. This will help students to identify their own weaknesses to focus on as they perform more exercises. Lastly, a game-based approach is being explored through games like ZenSketch (Williford et al. 2017), a game designed to improve students' line drawing skills, in an effort to better motivate students to practice their sketching fundamentals and be more engaged with the system. Greater engagement generally results in more time spent and greater learning gains.

The authors are also interested in other aspects affected by learning to sketch in perspective from both instructors and SketchTivity. One skill of particular interest is how obtaining sketching skills affects students' creativity, willingness to draw free-body diagrams, and to use sketches to communicate design ideas. Future studies will attempt to understand this impact by measuring students' creative self-efficacy and idea-generation ability.

9.8 Conclusion

Hand-drawn sketches are an important tool in engineering design. Sketches are used to communicate design intent and improve collaboration (Dym et al. 2005; Goldschmidt 2007), and the practice of sketching improves abilities such as spatial visualization (Olkun 2003; Cowan et al. 2019). While previous work has shown that learning perspective-based sketching maintains these benefits while improving sketching ability in engineering students (Hilton et al. 2017a), there are two major drawbacks to include it in engineering curricula. There is a lack of professors who can teach perspective sketching in engineering curricula, and the amount of time required to evaluate and provide feedback on student sketching assignments can be substantial. This chapter shows that the implementation of an online intelligent tutoring system, SketchTivity, achieves the benefits of teaching perspective-based sketching with less instructor interaction.

The results of this study indicate that utilizing SketchTivity maintains the improvement of key skills such as spatial visualization while maintaining or improving the sketching ability of students when compared to students taught using a more traditional method of engineering drawing. However, the authors also observed that SketchTivity might not be as effective at improving sketching ability as teaching the perspective method with only human feedback. Therefore, SketchTivity will continue to be improved, and further analyses will be conducted to measure its future impact.

Acknowledgements The authors would like to express gratitude to all collaborators at the Sketch Recognition Lab at Texas A&M University who contributed to the development and implementation of SketchTivity, with special thanks to Matthew Runyon, Maggie Tanski, and Myela Paige for assisting with the processing of sketch data. Additional thanks are due to Drs. Denis Dorozhkin, Katherine Fu, and Raghuram Pucha, the instructors of Introduction to Engineering Graphics at Georgia Tech, for providing feedback on how to teach perspective sketching and allowing data to be collected from their students. Finally, the authors would like to thank the National Science Foundation. This project was funded through NSF Cyberlearning grant numbers 1441291 and 1441331. The views and opinions expressed in this chapter are solely those of the authors and may not necessarily reflect the National Science Foundation.

References

Bodner GM, Guay RB (1997) The purdue visualization of rotations test. Chem Educ 2(4):1–17

Booth JW, Taborda EA, Ramani K, Reid T (2016) Interventions for teaching sketching skills and reducing inhibition for novice engineering designers. Des Stud 43:1–23

Cohen J (1988) Statistical power analysis for the behavioral sciences, 2nd edn

Cowan E, Delson N, Mihelich B, Van Den Einde L (2019) Improvement in freehand sketching application for spatial visualization training. Inspiring students with digital ink: impact of pen and touch technology on education. In: Hammond T, Prasad M, Stepanova A (eds) Human-computer interaction series. Switzerland, Springer

Cross N, Roy R (1989) Engineering design methods, vol 4. Wiley, New York

Dym CL, Agogino AM, Eris O, Frey DD, Leifer LJ (2005) Engineering design thinking, teaching, and learning. J Eng Edu 94(1):103–120

Gobert JD, Clement JJ (1999) Effects of student-generated diagrams versus student-generated summaries on conceptual understanding of causal and dynamic knowledge in plate tectonics. J Res Sci Teach Off J Natl Assoc Res Sci Teach 36(1):39–53

Goldschmidt G (2007) To see eye to eye: the role of visual representations in building shared mental models in design teams. CoDesign 3(1):43–50

Hilton E, Li W, Newton SH, Alemdar M, Pucha R, Linsey J (2016a) The development and effects of teaching perspective free-hand sketching in engineering design. In: ASME 2016 international design engineering technical conferences and computers and information in engineering conference. American Society of Mechanical Engineers, pp V003T04A013–V003T04A013

Hilton E, Williford B, Li W, McTigue E, Hammond T, Linsey J (2016b) Consistently evaluating sketching ability in engineering curriculum. In: DS86: proceedings of the fourth international conference on design creativity, Georgia Institute of Technology, Atlanta, GA, USA

Hilton EC, Paige M, Williford B, Li W, Hammond T, Linsey J (2017a) Improving the sketching ability of engineering design students. In: DS 87-9 proceedings of the 21st international conference on engineering design (ICED 17), vol 9: design education, Vancouver, Canada, 21–25 Aug 2017

Hilton EC, Paige MA, Williford B, Li W, Linsey JS (2017b) Board# 52: engineering drawing for the next generation: students gaining additional skills in the same timeframe. In: 2017 ASEE annual conference & exposition

Keshavabhotla S, Williford B, Kumar S, Hilton E, Taele P, Li W, Linsey J, Hammond T (2017) Conquering the cube: learning to sketch primitives in perspective with an intelligent tutoring system. In: Proceedings of the symposium on sketch-based interfaces and modeling. ACM, p 2

Olkun S (2003) Making connections: improving spatial abilities with engineering drawing activities. Int J Math Teach Learn 3(1):1–10

Pearson K (1900) X. On the criterion that a given system of deviations from the probable in the case of a correlated system of variables is such that it can be reasonably supposed to have arisen from random sampling. Lond Edinb Dublin Philos Mag J Sci 50(302):157–175

Peters M, Lehmann W, Takahira S, Takeuchi Y, Jordan K (2006) Mental rotation test performance in four cross-cultural samples (n = 3367): overall sex differences and the role of academic program in performance. Cortex 42(7):1005–1014

Shah JJ, Vargas-Hernandez N, Summers JD, Kulkarni S (2001) Collaborative sketching (c-sketch)–an idea generation technique for engineering design. J Creat Behav 35(3):168–198

Sorby SA (2009) Educational research in developing 3-d spatial skills for engineering students. Int J Sci Edu 31(3):459–480

Ullman DG, Wood S, Craig D (1990) The importance of drawing in the mechanical design process. Comput Graph 14(2):263–274

Vandenberg SG, Kuse AR (1978) Mental rotations, a group test of three-dimensional spatial visualization. Percept Motor Skills 47(2):599–604

Williford B, Runyon M, Malla AH, Li W, Linsey J, Hammond T (2017) Zensketch: a sketch-based game for improving line work. In: Extended abstracts publication of the annual symposium on computer-human interaction in play. ACM, pp 591–598

Williford B, Taele P, Nelligan T, Li W, Linsey J, Hammond T (2016) Persketchtivity: an intelligent pen-based educational application for design sketching instruction. In: Revolutionizing education with digital ink. Springer, pp 115–127

Yang MC (2009) Observations on concept generation and sketching in engineering design. Res Eng Des 20(1):1–11

Part VI
Creating Your Learning Environment with Sketching

Chapter 10
Personalizing Student Learning and Enhancing Peer-to-Peer Networks Through the Pen-Based MyEduDecks Application

Parv Shrivastava, Prateek Jukalkar and Aileen Owens

Abstract MyEduDecks is a pen-based flashcard application that has been in development at South Fayette High School since 2013. The project initially began as a South Fayette student project under the supervision of computer science professor Ananda Gunawardena of Carnegie Mellon University. The MyEduDecks team has extended the first iteration of the application to meet the user needs at South Fayette. This application intends to personalize student's learning and build collaborative networks in the classroom by leveraging pen-based technologies and their benefits. The application encourages the user to use a stylus to input questions and answers in an electronic flashcard format. MyEduDecks uses the Microsoft Ink API to integrate digital ink into the app. This research chapter highlights our application, its continued development, impact on a K-12 learning institution, and both qualitative and quantitative data analyzing the impact of an application reliant on pen and touch technology.

10.1 Introduction

The emergence of classroom technology has provided educators with the tools to facilitate personalized learning for students in K-12. Research has found a correlation between being successful and personalizing a student's learning (Cavanaugh et al. 2014). Additionally, digital learning in K-12 education has increased tremendously in traditional school settings with digital instruction models and techniques implemented more than ever before (Zheng et al. 2016). Digital pen-based technologies can assist in this process in five main ways: (1) offer the ability for students to personalize their learning experience, (2) provide teachers and students tools to

P. Shrivastava (✉) · P. Jukalkar · A. Owens
South Fayette School District, 3680 Old Oakdale Road, Mcdonald, PA 15057, USA
e-mail: parvshrivastava@gmail.com

P. Jukalkar
e-mail: psjukalkar@gmail.com

A. Owens
e-mail: aileen.owens@southfayette.org

T. Hammond et al. (eds.), *Inspiring Students with Digital Ink*, Human–Computer Interaction Series, https://doi.org/10.1007/978-3-030-17398-2_10

connect to further explore learning opportunities, (3) promote peer-to-peer networking to reap the benefits of collaborative learning, (4) explore the use of pen-based technology as an alternative to pen and paper, (5) and enhance knowledge retention.

10.1.1 Problem Statement

Educational institutions are inclining toward personalized learning to assess strengths and challenges at an individual level to tailor the curriculum and teaching models to be more effective. Furthermore, studies have indicated that peer-to-peer and student–teacher collaboration motivates the students to perform better (Roshan 2015). The challenge is to come up with the most effective way to achieve a personalized learning approach along with collaboration in the classroom.

Flashcards have long been an effective method for students to memorize and retain information. Paper-based flashcards have shown to be effective in helping people learn in discrete chunks of information (Kornell 2009). Electronic flashcards allow for more user interaction from the student and provide avenues to retain the same information. A key component of electronic flashcards is the opportunity for collaboration. However, beyond competing for scores, existing flashcard applications do not emphasize sharing and collaboration. Most electronic flashcard applications also have their main input through typing. This is problematic when trying to represent sketches or diagrams as answers. Additionally, students whose typing skills have not been fully developed find pen-based applications easier to use (Li and Fan 2015; Raymond et al. 2015; Solberg et al. 2012). Our application provides an easy to use interface for flexible input.

10.1.2 Context

Our context is K-12 learning institutions that stand to benefit from a study tool that utilizes a pen-based modality. The intent of our MyEduDecks research project is to personalize learning, increase collaboration, promote peer-to-peer, and student–teacher interaction, and explore benefits of a pen-based application. Through this chapter, we aim to reveal the changes the application has undergone, the results of a pilot being conducted at South Fayette School District, and the qualitative and quantitative data being collected (Fig. 10.1).

10.1.2.1 MyEduDecks Application

MyEduDecks is a pen-based electronic flashcards application built by South Fayette High School students. When the program development started in 2013, the MyEduDecks team was comprised of several high school students. When team members

Fig. 10.1 Students using the MyEduDecks application during the beta test

graduate from high school each year, new members are added to create a new channel of talent. This process provides invaluable software developmental skills that are transferable to the workplace. All of this happens while improving a product that has the potential to become a study tool for educational institutions across the country. The defining feature of the MyEduDecks application is its pen-based interface. The ability to write on the cards allows for more complex and unorthodox information, like mathematical equations and formulas, to be easily expressed. Students can create and play decks using the Microsoft Ink API. The current iteration of the app has added support for foreign languages, expanding the usability of the application to more classroom environments. Additionally, collaboration is becoming a vital skill in today's world, and the application now contains features for more interconnected experiences. Students can create and share decks with their peers across their class. This allows for the integration of healthy competition and motivates students to learn more through sharable decks. Each student now has a personal profile with basic information and the badge system. After procuring a certain amount of points, students earn various badges. Teachers have access to an Excel spreadsheet containing all the student's results, including accuracy and time of completion, for each student. Currently, we are working to incentivize students to use MyEduDecks through a virtual currency system which is now under development. Students will receive points for each deck completed based on accuracy.

10.2 Previous Work

MyEduDecks started five years ago as the Flashcards application (Kothuri et al. 2015, 2016). It was inspired by the Table Flashcard projects being explored at CMU (Jeong et al. 2010). The first working iteration of the app was built three years ago and was tested in grades K-2 at the district. Students had to solve basic math facts with the application in the beta test. The potential to personalize learning for students was evident, but bugs and design flaws persisted. The project was renamed to MyEduDecks to reflect the new functionality and direction of the product, which is to offer a more personalized approach to learning. The next year, the application was beta-tested with ten third grade students and received positive feedback. The team has since completely rebuilt the application, making it run more smoothly, and overhauling the outdated graphics. The interface was redesigned to make it more user-friendly and intuitive. The application has been tested at younger grade levels in the past, and educators found it to be beneficial in the classroom, expressing interest in incorporating the final version of MyEduDecks into their lesson plans. The feedback and suggestions of the educators and students have been invaluable and driven much of the change in the application since. This continued educational research has tracked the impact of personalized learning and student collaboration.

10.3 System Details

The MyEduDecks application contains three main modules which include creating, playing, and sharing decks. Each deck contains multiple electronic flashcards for students to answer. The app is programmed with an object-oriented programming language called C# using Visual Studio. The team focuses on making the app modular and separated into many components. This eases the process of debugging and allows for scalability in the future.

10.3.1 Student Interface

Currently in the application, there are two main interfaces which are comprised of the student and teacher interfaces. Students are navigated to the login screen when they launch the MyEduDecks application as shown in Fig. 10.2. The student can input their username and password through textboxes to progress to the dashboard. This year, we changed the login screen from ink panels to text boxes to allow more complex characters in usernames and passwords. When arriving at the dashboard, students will see decks they have completed, decks that have been shared with them, and decks that need to be completed. The three types of decks are denoted in specific colors. From the dashboard, students can create, play, or share decks. In the create deck screen, the student has three ways to create a deck: handwriting, importing a Word file, and the Automath feature. In the handwriting feature, students can write

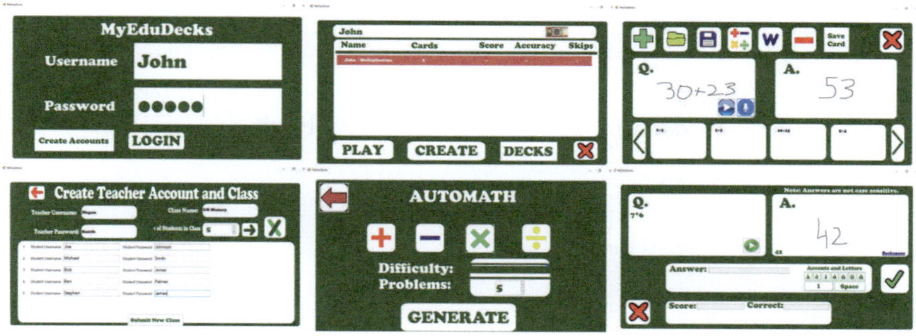

Fig. 10.2 Screenshots of the MyEduDecks application

the question and answer for each card in the electronic panels. This year, we have also added an audio feature which allows students to record audio and embed it into the cards. Furthermore, students can create decks using formatted Word documents. Students can import these Word documents into the application to automatically create decks. The last way to create decks is by the Automath feature which randomly generates math problems based on the parameters the user selects. Students can also play decks that they created or ones that were shared with them. Students use the digital ink interface to write the answers to the questions. The play deck screen tracks the percentage of questions the student got correct which is easily accessible by teachers. Students can share decks with other students in the MyEduDecks app. This allows for more peer-to-peer collaboration and helps build student networks.

10.3.2 Teacher Interface

From a teacher's perspective, the flow of the application is similar to the student interface. In addition to having all the features the students have teachers can assign decks to their class and view the class's scores in an Excel file. With the new MyEduDecks application, teachers can easily interact with students and see their progress. This allows for teachers to tailor to individual student needs by creating decks to help students build proficiency in areas where they need more assistance in meeting their learning goals. Teachers have the ability to personalize their instructional support to meet student needs.

10.3.3 Digital Ink Through Microsoft Ink API

The pen-based interface built into the app is only possible through the Microsoft Ink API. The Ink API had recently been updated with the release of Windows 10. This updated API allows for better recognition of the user's input. In the application, there are many ink panels where the user can utilize the pen-based input when interacting with the app. The ink recognizer built into the API translates the ink to text. There are text labels that update every time a user uses the ink which allows for instant feedback about what is written. There are errors with the ink recognizer sometimes, but the real-time feedback allows for users to fix these errors.

10.4 Method Employed

MyEduDecks was tested in a classroom setting by Mr. Miguel Hernandez, a Spanish teacher at South Fayette. Due to the nature of a language, vocabulary is an integral part of becoming proficient. The teacher felt MyEduDecks might be a way to incentivize learning vocabulary. He piloted the MyEduDecks program with sixty-three seventh-grade students to encourage them to practice Spanish vocabulary, grammar, and listening interpretation skills, and to give students the opportunity to personalize their learning. Mr. Hernandez felt that providing his students with a more interactive study tool could benefit their learning in the classroom. In addition, he felt that being able to easily and conveniently create and assign skill-building activities, and view student performance on the assignments, would provide him with a better understanding of the comfort level of each individual student. The MyEduDecks team trained Mr. Hernandez on how to use MyEduDecks prior to the start of beta testing.

In previous beta tests with the application, the tests only spanned for a few days. This year, we conducted the beta test for a month in Mr. Hernandez's Spanish classroom. This allowed us to pilot MyEduDecks for a longer duration and see how it benefits students. In the beta test, Mr. Hernandez assigned decks related to the material he was teaching to help reinforce and practice the concepts they learned in class. He was easily able to see the scores the students received on their practice decks. For students who struggled with the practice, Mr. Hernandez could easily identify students who were not grasping the material well and reassigned the practice decks to them. The students were given a total of three practice decks through the beta test and three assessments covering material on a specific deck. The three assessment scores in Mr. Hernandez's class were compared to another classroom's test scores studying the same curriculum without using MyEduDecks. In addition, a two-tailed Pearson correlation test with the statistical program SPSS was used to determine the effectiveness of MyEduDecks based on the assessment data. Also, students provided their feedback and input regarding MyEduDecks through a post-survey administered after completion of MyEduDecks.

10.5 Results

The 63 students participating in the pilot filled out a survey based on their thoughts and perception about MyEduDecks and general learning technologies. Table 10.1 shows the survey results that were collected from the students. In Fig. 10.3, the test scores

Table 10.1 Post-survey test results

	Responses	
Post-survey question	Agree (%)	Disagree (%)
Learning independently is important to me	90.6	9.4
Based on what I known about MyEduDecks, I think using MyEduDecks could enhance my ability to learn independently	74.6	25.4
Based on what I know about MyEduDecks, I think using MyEduDecks could enhance my ability to work collaboratively with teammates	60.3	39.7
I like to have the ability to pre-learn concepts before they are introduced in class	84.1	15.9
Based on what I know about MyEduDecks, I believe that using MyEduDecks could enhance my ability to pre-learn concepts before my teachers teach the material	73.0	27.0
I like to be in control of my own learning	85.7	14.3
Based on what I know about MyEduDecks, I believe that using MyEduDecks could enhance my ability to be in control of my own learning	69.8	30.2
I like to personalize my own learning	81.0	19.0
Based on what I know about using MyEduDecks, I believe I could personalize the way I learn by designing and creating unique cards or decks that align to the concepts that I most need and want to learn	73.0	27.0
Based on what I know about MyEduDecks, I believe I could create my own personalized assessments to help me learn concepts that I find difficult	74.6	25.4
I believe I would like answering questions on MyEduDecks using digital ink and a stylus rather than simply typing answers on the cards	40.0	60.0
I would like to be able to add my own graphics and pictures on the MyEduDecks digital flashcards system rather than using plain white paper-based flashcards with print	63.5	36.5
I can think of important reasons to include audio when creating MyEduDecks flashcard quizzes	58.7	41.3
I think using the MyEduDecks flashcards would help me learn things that were hard because I could test myself and practice what I do not know	81.0	19.0
I think being able to add pictures on the Flashcards would be very helpful	81.0	19.0
I think hearing a person's voice reading, or having sound on the Flashcards, would be very helpful	66.7	33.3
If I could make my own online flashcard deck using MyEduDecks I believe I could make my own questions and could help improve my learning.	69.8	30.2

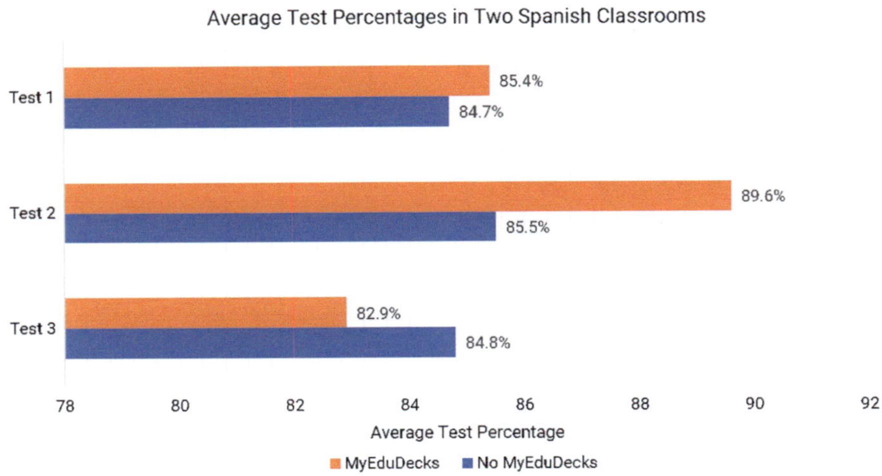

Fig. 10.3 Clustered bar graph depicting average test scores for both classes

Correlations

		MyEduDecks Test 1 Practice	Test 1
MyEduDecks Test 1 Practice	Pearson Correlation	1	.390**
	Sig. (2-tailed)		.004
	N	52	52
Test 1	Pearson Correlation	.390**	1
	Sig. (2-tailed)	.004	
	N	52	52

**. Correlation is significant at the 0.01 level (2-tailed).

		MyEduDecks Test 2 Practice	Test 2
MyEduDecks Test 2 Practice	Pearson Correlation	1	.300*
	Sig. (2-tailed)		.022
	N	58	58
Test 2	Pearson Correlation	.300*	1
	Sig. (2-tailed)	.022	
	N	58	58

*. Correlation is significant at the 0.05 level (2-tailed).

		MyEduDecks Test 3 Practice	Test 3
MyEduDecks Test 3 Practice	Pearson Correlation	1	.434**
	Sig. (2-tailed)		.003
	N	46	46
Test 3	Pearson Correlation	.434**	1
	Sig. (2-tailed)	.003	
	N	46	46

**. Correlation is significant at the 0.01 level (2-tailed).

Fig. 10.4 Two-tailed Pearson correlation test between practice decks and test scores

of two different classes are shown. The class with orange bars used MyEduDecks to study for tests, and the class with the blue bars did not use MyEduDecks to study for tests. For the first two assessments, the students who used MyEduDecks had a higher class average by 0.7 and 4.1%, respectively. In the last assessment, the students who did not use MyEduDecks had a higher class average by 1.9%.

We also did a two-tailed Pearson correlation test between the students' MyEduDecks practice scores and their assessment scores. For the AR quiz and the AR verb practice on MyEduDecks, the correlation coefficient was 0.39 and it was significant at the 0.01 level. Furthermore, the correlation coefficient for the preposition quiz and the preposition practice on MyEduDecks was 0.3 and it was significant at the 0.05 level. Finally, the correlation coefficient for the chapter test and the AR verb practice on MyEduDecks was 0.434 and it was significant at the 0.01 level. The correlation coefficients ranged from 0.3 to 0.434 and were all positively related (Fig. 10.4).

10.6 Discussion

The survey results indicate that most students found MyEduDecks to be a beneficial learning tool. The initial data collected gauges the interest of students and how they think MyEduDecks can be used to supplement their learning. The beta test results above indicate that a majority of students believe it can enhance their learning of concepts. The findings are discussed below.

Being able to take control of your own learning is an important skill to being successful, and one that can be enhanced by technology. Over ninety percent of respondents agreed that learning independently is important to them over the previous 2 years, proving its importance to students. Over seventy percent of these same students indicated that MyEduDecks helps them achieve this. The application does this by allowing students to create their own decks, attempt them multiple times, and clearly indicating their progress over time on their personal dashboard. Pre-learning concepts give students an opportunity to understand some of the material in advance so they can better understand what is being taught the first time. Nearly eighty-five percent of students agreed with this based on the survey results. MyEduDecks enables students to look ahead by allowing teachers to create decks with future material, giving students the chance to get familiar with the concepts in advance. Seventy-three percent agreed that MyEduDecks helped them do this. Being able to personalize learning has been important to students participating in beta tests, with over eighty percent indicating as such. Personalizing learning is also one of the goals of the MyEduDecks application. This is achieved by allowing students to create their own decks to master information they consider relevant. Additionally, each student has their own dashboard that displays the results of the decks attempted to track their progress. Furthermore, a student profile feature is currently being developed to be added to the application. This will give students access to some basic statistics regarding their performance and give each of them something unique. Seventy-three percent of the participating students agreed that MyEduDecks helps them personalize their learning.

Part of the team's focus this year was on encouraging collaboration between teachers and students as well as among students and their peers. Educators now receive an Excel spreadsheet with each student's statistics. This allows them to track their progress and identify high achieving and low achieving students. To increase peer-to-peer collaboration, students now have the option to create and share decks with peers. In addition, a virtual currency system is being developed to promote healthy competition and active learning for students. Reaching a certain amount of currency will unlock badges that can be viewed in the aforementioned student profile screen. These features will provide students with immediate gratification after completing a deck and encourage positive competition. The ultimate goal of any educational product is to improve student performance on assessments. Based on three student assessments, a positive correlation between using MyEduDecks and increased test scores exists.

One interesting data point from the survey was that 60% of students would rather type out their answers than use the digital ink to write the answers on the cards. Last year, we tested the app with seventh grade students, and more than half would have rather typed the answers. This is likely because most seventh graders are generally proficient in typing their answers, and it would be slower for them to write out their answers with the ink. This aversion to ink-based input was very different from the results we collected from the first two beta tests with students from grades K-3. They preferred the ink-based input rather than typing. Usually, students in younger grades have not developed proper typing skills, which makes writing a more attractive option. With results over the past 3 years consistently supporting this notion, the team will consider toggling the mode of input depending on the age group being tested to ensure that the students are most comfortable.

The students' assessment average scores were also compared between the class that used MyEduDecks and the class that did not use MyEduDecks. The first two assessments did show that MyEduDecks helped the students score better on the tests. However, in the third assessment, students who did not use MyEduDecks scored marginally higher than students who used MyEduDecks. Overall, MyEduDecks seems to have an impact on students getting higher scores on the tests.

In regard to the correlation test, the strength of the correlation between the scores of the practice decks and assessments is modest. The correlations ranged from 0.3 to 0.434 from a scale from -1 to 1. In addition, the correlations were significant at the 0.01 and 0.05 level. There is a clear positive correlation between both scores, and it does show that people who score well on the practice in MyEduDecks score well on the tests.

10.7 Future Work

With the results and feedback offered from students and through ongoing collaboration and support from Mr. Hernandez, we will continue to improve the application in the future. A few key features that will be added include the ability to view a student's profile from the teacher interface, the ability for students and teachers to add graphics to the cards, and the implementation of a leaderboard system. By allowing teachers to view student profiles through the review sets, the teacher can better determine each individual student's learning needs and how to address them. In the same way, students will be able to determine their own individual areas of improvement. Students will be able to take control of their learning by creating practice decks that are designed to improve areas of weakness. In the future, we hope to fulfill the great potential the MyEduDecks application possesses in helping students to improve their learning through increased collaboration with peers and with greater connections to the teacher. We plan to develop the features in MyEduDecks that will allow for more peer-to-peer network. For example, instead of completing tasks individually, students can compete in team challenges and collaborate with other students. Supporting a team approach to learning builds on the peer-to-peer networks these students have established through MyEduDecks. We will continue to gather input from students and work toward improving the user experience by making the app more responsive and easier to use.

10.8 Conclusion

Through another year of development and research, we have gained valuable insight on the current capabilities of MyEduDecks in addition to taking significant steps to address issues identified in past years. While developing the current iteration, we focused on expanding the boundaries of the application into foreign language by adding Spanish capabilities. This addition broadened potential user base while making the app more versatile. Furthermore, we have added another avenue for collaboration through the sharing of decks. This enables students to create their own decks and share them among their peers. The app has also undergone an overhaul from the teacher's perspective. Teachers and educators can quickly and easily assign decks to their students to be completed. The ability to incorporate sound and audio recordings has also been added to decks. This allows teachers to assess their students' listening comprehension skills in an efficient manner. The results of completed decks can then be downloaded as an Excel spreadsheet with statistics beneficial in gauging the progress of students. MyEduDecks have shown that it can be a useful tool in many classrooms through personalizing learning for students and promoting collaboration.

Acknowledgements We would like to give a special thanks to Mr. Miguel Hernandez who piloted the application in his classroom and to Dr. Ananda Gunawardena, professor of computer science at Princeton University, who began the project with us and continues to support and guide each new team. We would also like to thank Vinay Pedapati, Zoe Koutavas, and Priya Matreja for helping program the application and the support they provided to the middle school students during the pilot of this program. We would also like to thank former members of the team who have graduated and are pursuing their careers. Furthermore, we would like to thank the students taking part in the beta test and answering all of the survey questions. Finally, we would like to thank Superintendent Dr. Bille Rondinelli and the South Fayette School District Board of Education for their generous support for this project which has allowed us to present at conferences and to continue our ongoing research.

References

Cavanaugh C, Maor D, McCarthy A (2014) Handbook of research on k-12 online and blended learning. In: K-12 mobile learning. ETC Press, Pittsburgh, PA, USA, pp 391–413. http://dl.acm.org/citation.cfm?id=2811036.2811060

Jeong Y, Gunawardena A, Koedinger KR (2010) Designing a pen-based flashcard application to support classroom learning environment. In: Extended abstracts on human factors in computing systems, CHI EA'10. ACM, New York, NY, USA, pp 4695–4698. https://doi.org/10.1145/1753846.1754214

Kornell N (2009) Optimising learning using flashcards: spacing is more effective than cramming. Appl Cognit Psychol 23(9):1297–1317. https://doi.org/10.1002/acp.1537
Kothuri R, Cohen S, Wilke N, Owens A (2016) Personalizing student learning using the MyEduDecks application through teacher supervision and peer-to-peer networks. Springer International Publishing, Cham, pp 275–285. https://doi.org/10.1007/978-3-319-31193-7_18
Kothuri R, Kenawell B, Hertzler S, Babatunde M, Wilke N, Cohen S (2015) Analyzing trends in pen computing among K-2 students through flashcards application. Springer International Publishing, Cham, pp 259–265. https://doi.org/10.1007/978-3-319-15594-4_26
Li JT, Fan YN (2015) Using iPad to make E-flashcards and sharing the E-cards through Doceri. Springer International Publishing, Cham, pp 249–257. https://doi.org/10.1007/978-3-319-15594-4_25
Raymond D, Liew J, Hammond AT (2015) A vision for education: transforming how formal systems are taught within mass lectures by using pen technology to create a personalized learning environment. Springer International Publishing, Cham, pp 355–363. https://doi.org/10.1007/978-3-319-15594-4_37
Roshan S (2015) The flipped classroom: touch enabled, academically proven. In: The impact of pen and touch technology on education. Springer, pp 215–222
Solberg VS, Phelps LA, Haakenson KA, Durham JF, Timmons J (2012) The nature and use of individualized learning plans as a promising career intervention strategy. J Career Dev 39(6):500–514. https://doi.org/10.1177/0894845311414571
Zheng B, Warschauer M, Lin CH, Chang C (2016) Learning in one-to-one laptop environments: a meta-analysis and research synthesis. Rev Edu Res 86(4):1052–1084. https://doi.org/10.3102/0034654316628645

Chapter 11
iCanTrace: Avatar Personalization Through Selfie Sketches

Alexander Berman, Leela Krishna Chaitanya Gottumukkala, Zepeng Huo, Seth Polsley, Francis Quek and Tracy Hammond

Abstract This chapter introduces a novel system that allows users to generate customized cartoon avatars through a sketching interface. The rise of social media and personalized gaming has given a need for personalized virtual appearances. Avatars, self-curated and customized images to represent oneself, have become a common means of expressing oneself in these new media. Avatar creation platforms face the challenges of granting user significant control over the avatar creation and of encumbering the user with too many choices in their avatar customization. This chapter demonstrates a sketch-guided avatar customization system and its potential to simplify the avatar creation process.

A. Berman (✉) · L. K. C. Gottumukkala · Z. Huo
Department of Computer Science & Engineering, Texas A&M University,
College Station, TX, USA
e-mail: anberman@tamu.edu

L. K. C. Gottumukkala
e-mail: glk.c.93@tamu.edu

Z. Huo
e-mail: guangzhou92@tamu.edu

S. Polsley · T. Hammond
Sketch Recognition Lab, Department of Computer Science and Engineering,
Texas A&M University, College Station, TX, USA
e-mail: spolsley@tamu.edu

T. Hammond
e-mail: hammond@tamu.edu

F. Quek
Department of Visualization, Texas A&M University,
College Station, TX, USA
e-mail: quek@arch.tamu.edu

T. Hammond et al. (eds.), *Inspiring Students with Digital Ink*, Human–Computer Interaction Series, https://doi.org/10.1007/978-3-030-17398-2_11

11.1 Introduction

With the proliferation of social media and gaming, many questions have emerged about how people represent themselves online. A common way of representing the appearance of virtual selves is through avatars, images that are user customized and curated to help represent their appearance and assist others in distinguishing between virtual entities. Avatars have been shown to play important roles in representing individual identity and increasing loyalty within online communities (Lee and Saharia 2012).

11.1.1 Avatars in Social Media

In social media, avatars can serve as ways to enrich written and recorded media, and can help in distinguishing other users online. Mobile applications like Bitmoji and MyIdol encourage users to send messages to each other with personalized avatars with props and emotions similar to emojis. Avatar-augmented messages can facilitate more meaningful communication, and encourage more "fun" interpersonal interactions (Lee et al. 2009).

Bitmoji utilizes one common variety of avatar customization, where the user selects from a menu of static appearance components that concatenate into a more unique visual creation, as demonstrated in Fig. 11.1. These curations can easily be changed over time, and many users in social sites modify avatars frequently (Burke

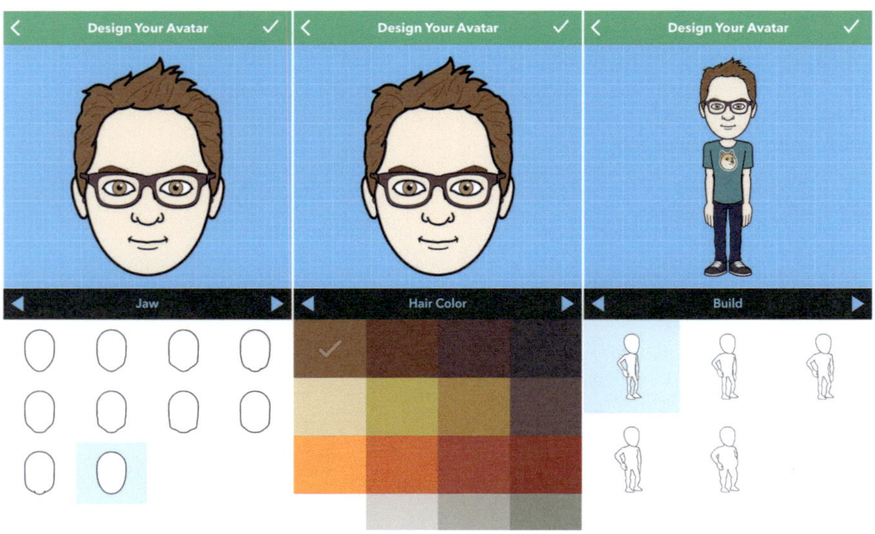

Fig. 11.1 Bitmoji menu-based avatar customization

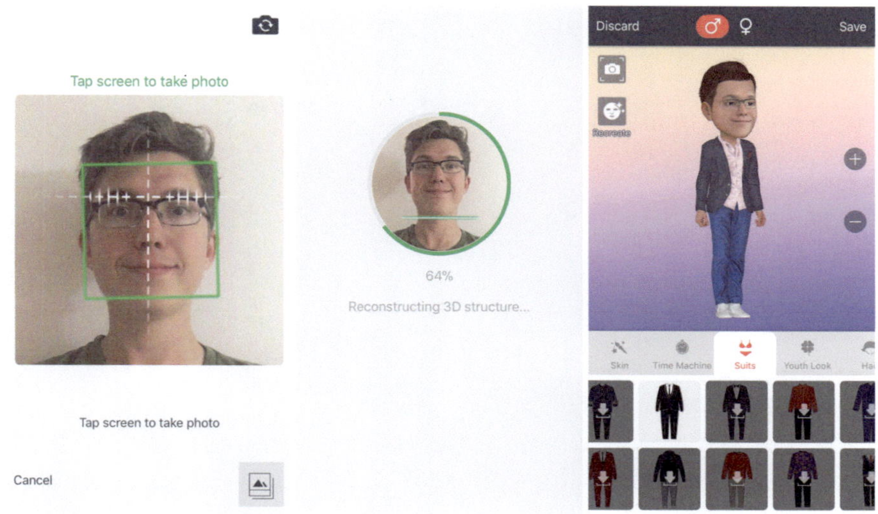

Fig. 11.2 MyIdol avatar creation via selfie

2013). Burke claims that recognition of identity and identity formation are fluid and change based on situated roles and actions. In this way, all elements of discourse shape identity, as we shift between different selves. She explains that, this is especially pertinent to children in learning settings, as they are still learning how to change their expressed identity in response to situated actions. This is further supported by Vasalou et al. (2008), who claims that people change avatars based on the context in which they will be utilizing them.

Social media applications like MyIdol feature a relatively hands-off approach to avatar customization. These applications assume users want lifelike avatars and will either generate or superimpose self-taken images of the user's face, which are often referred to as selfies, shown in Fig. 11.2. These selfie-driven avatar creations, while consistent with real-world appearances, often are off-putting to users as they may breach into the uncanny valley (Tinwell et al. 2011).

11.1.2 Avatars in Gaming

Gaming media often encourages users to customize characters or icons. In social online Massive Multiplayer Online Roleplaying Games (MMORPG) like Second Life, users can create several variations of themselves, making avatars that do not even resemble humans. See Fig. 11.3 as an example. Users of these social games still tend to make avatars to represent themselves (Conrad et al. 2011).

In exercise-oriented games, the a priori stimulus of creating personalized avatars has been shown to have significant effect on how users perceive their own immersion

Fig. 11.3 Second life in-game menu-based avatar customization

and quality of interactions in the game (Jin 2009). When users customize avatars, they experience increased perceived interaction, cooperation with others, and participation when playing Wii Sports (Dolgov et al. 2014). Overall, avatar customization plays a large role in increasing perceived participation in games.

11.1.3 The Paradox of Choice in Avatar Creation

Users become frustrated when an avatar customization system does not accommodate visual features with which they strongly identify (Conrad et al. 2011). Users, in particular children, often have difficulty with avatar creation and require significant social support to create self-satisfying avatars (Kafai et al. 2010). Vasalou et al. (2008) claim "when constructing one's self-presentation, lack of flexibility over one's options ultimately determine the avatar's final appearance and, thus, the degree of idealization the avatar owner expressed."

When presented with a large number of options for avatar components, we are faced with what Park et al. describes as a paradox of choice (Park et al. 2014). Users may not be able to fully imagine all potential combinations of component options, leading to user frustration. Recommendation systems for these component options can greatly aid the user in the avatar customization.

Avatar customization should give users enough control so that they can successfully curate identifiable avatars, but should not give too much control and encumber the user's ability to create the avatar. An ideal system would fulfill these requirements. The system presented in this chapter is an attempt at reaching a compromise in these needs to create an intuitive and expressive system for avatar customization. Our approach combines interface elements from previous avatar creation systems with tools facilitated by sketch recognition.

11.2 Relevant Work

There are many avatar generating systems that currently use a reference photo of the user to create an avatar. One approach employs hand-selected facial landmarks to identify individual facial components (Rhee and Lee 2013). Each selfie component in this system is compared to artist drawn components using graph similarity and Hausdorff distance. Matched templates of each individual facial component are collated into an avatar image of the user.

Park et al. (2014) utilize facial points provided by MultiPIE dataset to divide a face image into facial components, which are then matched to a game avatar. They provide different types of avatar images, but they do not provide user with the flexibility to select and modify attributes of the avatar.

Zhang et al. (2014) apply a facial alignment algorithm from Cao et al. (2014) to locate the facial landmarks and decompose the input face into separate components. Then for each component, the most similar component from the artist drawn stylized version of each representative realistic component (Zhang et al. 2017). Alpha bending has been adopted to compose all components into an avatar, which they then warp a cartoon face to better match the input face (Schaefer et al. 2006). Sepehri Nejad and Balafar (2016) employed a modified Active Shape Model (ASM) to create personalized avatars. Facial components are matched with avatar template components, drawn by artist, based solely on comparison of contours between the sketch and the selfie using a normalized Hausdorff distance variant.

Rosin and Lai (2015) described an image-based non-photorealistic rendering pipeline for creating portraits in two-styles—one somewhat "puppet" like rendering, and the other inspired by artist Julian Opie in which the human face is reduced to essentials. Diego-Mas and Alcaide-Marzal (2015) created a system to generate avatar by using genetic algorithms and artificial neural networks. Tang and Wang (2004) created the avatar images by transforming the real photos into sketch by morphing Eigenfaces.

Park et al. introduce an avatar recommendation system (Park et al. 2014) that uses semi-supervised learning algorithm to learn the facial attributes. Since facial attributes are diverse and subjective, human labeling might be biased.

All these systems provide avatars based on their picture, but they do not provide the user with much ability to modify avatars or be as expressive as an artist. The goal of this system is to facilitate a similar expressiveness to users by means of sketching, to allow users to experiment more with avatar components while not having to search through a menu at each step.

Fig. 11.4 Tracing over a selfie in formative study

11.3 Formative Study

To better inform how people sketch selfie portraits, we conducted a preliminary study to see how participants would trace over their face.

Five participants traced over the photos of themselves without other knowledge about our system, shown in Fig. 11.4. Researchers then wrote high-level notes describing common patterns across the traces. Most of the users prefer to give detailed sketching of some facial components, such as hair and eyelashes. Some components are less likely to be drawn in detail, such as the iris and pupil within an eyeball. Most of the participants just drew the contour of their eyes. Similarly most of the participants preferred to draw the face and chin shape first, then draw some smaller facial components later such as ears and mouth.

11.4 User Interface

Our system combines elements from existing selfie-driven and menu avatar customization platforms. The user initiates the system by capturing a selfie with the device's front-facing camera, shown in Fig. 11.5. While the system requires the taking of a selfie, it does not presently use any data from the image to aid in the avatar creation process. The photo is kept in the background to aid the user to sketch a decent portrait. This is similar to how someone could trace a complex object on an overlaid piece of paper by following significant features of a photo underneath. This

Fig. 11.5 Selfie capture and gender selection

is to help the user create portraits with decent proportions and spacing and to help guide users to create self-resembling avatars as is often desired (Conrad et al. 2011).

The system creates an avatar by matching template sketches, that are mapped to cartoon assets, to the user traces of individual facial components. Templates were created by having researchers trace over each of the cartoon facial components. Avatar facial component artwork was purchased from DeeThemes.[1] Convex hulls are extracted for each template sketch. All matching in our system is done to the hulls of all the facial components. The created template hulls are stored in a database, which is then compared to user sketches as they are drawn. Cao et al. (2011) employed a similar method for raw contour-based matching of sketches.

The user then selects a gender, shown in Fig. 11.5, which changes the potential avatar characteristics and components. This avatar is visible in all the subsequent steps and will change as the user progresses and traces each face component.

Over the captured image, the system will create a canvas that slightly blurs the underlying image. This may help the user trace high-level details of the face, ideally captured in the avatar, rather than fixating on tracing less significant details. The user will be prompted to facial components in a set order over their blurred selfie, including the jaw, nose, eyebrows, eyes, mouth, ears, hair, mustache, and beard. The user has a software black pen to facilitate sketching, which is always visible on the white transparent layer over the image. The user will only be prompted to draw one of these components at a time, clicking navigation buttons to switch between the component of focus. Components not in focus are still visible on the canvas but are grayed so the user does not confuse them with the black strokes of the component drawing that they are presently drawing.

[1]http://svgavatars.com.

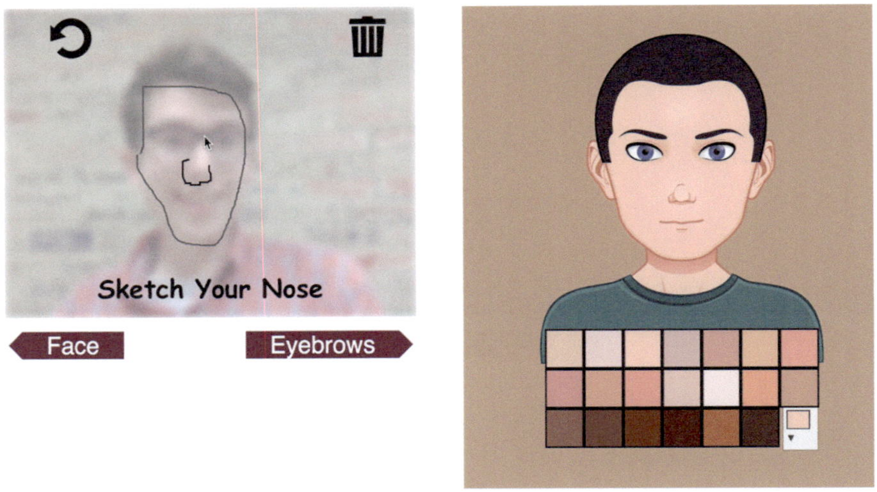

Fig. 11.6 User sketch (left) updating avatar (right)

The user has a couple of methods of reverting the focused component drawing. They are given two buttons on the canvas: an undo button and a clear button. Clear erases all of the sketch data for that component, while undo only erases the pen data since it was last lifted, i.e., the last pen stroke. The stack of pen strokes is saved per component, so as a user switches between components they can undo the last stroke in that component.

Whenever the user presses undo, presses clear, or the pen is lifted, the system will run a collection of sketch recognition algorithms to find the best matching cartoon component and transform it to be similar to the user-input sketch. This is explained in detail in the Sketch Recognition section but consists of fitting a convex hull to the component sketch and matching to hulls of templates via Hausdorff distance. Whenever the user performs these editing actions to the sketch, the system will provide live feedback by modifying the avatar with the updated cartoon component. This is shown in Figs. 11.6 and 11.7.

Underneath the updating avatar, the user is given a palette of many common color choices for each component. If they select any of these colors, the avatar component they are presently focused on will update to match this color. Components are grouped such that each change in color may change other components. For example, changing nose color will also change other skin tones. The border of components also changes color to be more visually appealing to the composition. There is also an option for the user to select any color of their choosing in the hue–saturation–value color space.

When completed with the sketches of facial components, the user can select accessories from a list, as shown in Fig. 11.8. This includes glasses, clothing, and the background behind the avatar. During this whole process of selection and sketching, the user can navigate between focused components to edit them to their liking.

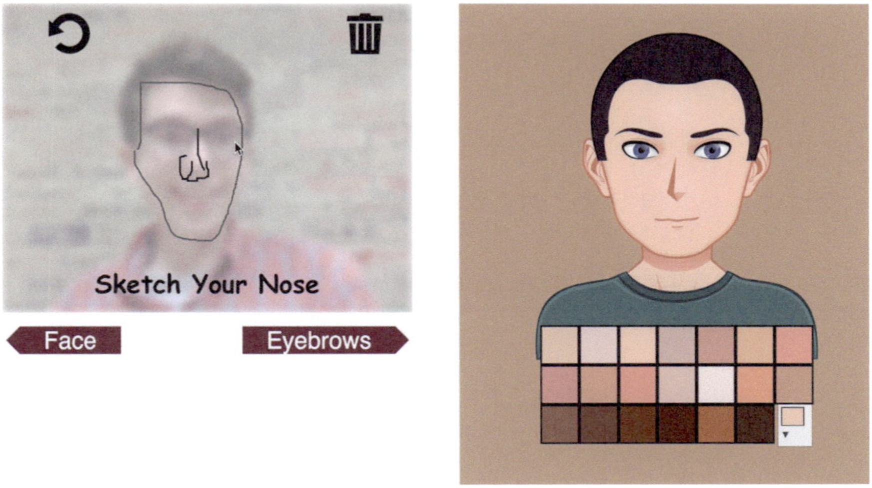

Fig. 11.7 Nose on avatar is updated after additional sketching

Fig. 11.8 Selecting accessories and final changes to avatar

After they are done editing, they click submit and the system generates a page with downloadable images of their selfie, their sketch, and their customized avatar.

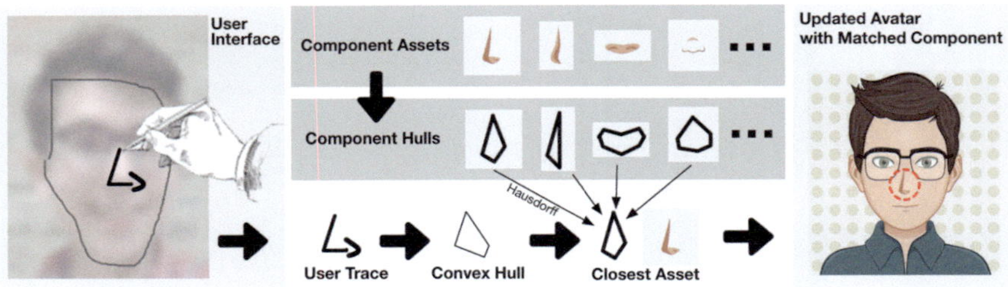

Fig. 11.9 Overview of how sketched components are matched to cartoon assets in the customized avatar

11.5 Sketch Recognition

Each avatar is generated by matching each face component sketch from a user to template sketches of the art assets individually. This involves generating a convex hull from both the user face component sketch and all the variations of sketched templates for each facial component. Hausdorff distance is then calculated between the convex hull of the user sketch and all the template convex hulls. The closest match is then chosen and updated in the avatar. Figure 11.9 illustrates this process.

11.5.1 Generating Convex Hulls

Extracting the contour of the facial components and discarding the details inside the contours can not only make the system less complex in terms of time and space complexity but also make it more robust. Bao et al. (2005) gave an enhanced edge detection method by performing scale multiplication. The points inside may give false matches if they look similar to a template even though this template is not the desired one. Li (2014) gave a contour extraction algorithm in bean-shaped sketch which is constructed by connected components of Canny edge points in scale space. Since we want to extract contours from a point cloud of a sketch, we have to employ different methods.

To match user sketches to the nearest template, we generate the convex hull of the templates and the user sketch. The convex hull algorithm first sorts all the points in ascending order in terms of x-coordinates and y-coordinates. Then the algorithm will compare three consecutive points at a time, and if one point is closer to the center of point cloud than the line formed by the other two points, then it will be discarded. All the remaining points can form a set of lines which represent the outer contour of all the points.

Convex hulls did not initially work as intended for facial components with two parts (eyes, ears, or eyebrows). If the contour of these facial components is extracted, such as eyes, the system will give a big contour which contains both of the eyes, which is not desirable. The left and right elements are separated before generating the convex hull to lessen this issue.

Some components, like eyes and ears, have two instances per typical human face. The system assumes that the nose is always in between these two elements. This is true when users take pictures where the head is at most a slight angle. Each stroke is kept whole, and strokes are sorted into left and right depending on the majority of points that reside on that side of the nose x-coordinate centroid.

11.5.2 Hausdorff Distance Template Matching

The system compares hulls of our researcher generated template sketches to hulls of user sketches by their Hausdorff distance. Zou et al. (2013) compare 12 Hausdorff distance variations for template matching, claiming that arctangent variation of Hausdorff distances is more precise than the other 11 variations of Hausdorff distance (Field et al. 2011; Kara and Stahovich 2005). The arctangent variation of Hausdorff distance was chosen for the system to match template hulls to hulls of user drawn sketches.

We also observed that some variations of Hausdorff distance tend to choose a particular template over others more often, even though there is a variation in the sketch. Arctangent variation measures the extent to which each point of user's sketch lies near some points of each template and vice versa. It is more tolerant of perturbations in the location of points because it measures proximity rather than exact superposition. It calculates the max of the average of arctangent of the minimum distance between a point from one to all points in another. $H(A, B) = \max(h(A, B), h(B, A))$ where $h(A, B) = \text{avg}(\arctan(\min(a, b)))$.

11.5.3 Line Smoothing

Many users may have difficulty in tracing lines perfectly. To aid these users, a line smoothing functionality was added. This functionality is only turned on for face components where it is easier to predict if the user will draw smoother lines. When outlining their head shape smoothing will be used, but not when drawing hair where they will often draw many lines with sharp corners.

Line smoothing is performed by a moving average algorithm. The aim of smoothing is to capture the relatively slow changes in the line's user created. Therefore, drastic changes are changed into smooth changes. The simplest implementation of moving average algorithm is "unweighted sliding-average smooth." The method replaces each point in the sketch with the average of m adjacent points, where "m" is a positive integer called the "smooth width." Usually "m" is an odd number. For our trial, when the number is 5, the system gives decent smoothing performance.

Fig. 11.10 Expressive eyebrows by their slope

When specific facial components get smoothed, it was guessed the matching result will be perceived better. This has yet to be evaluated, as can be done in future work.

11.5.4 Eyebrow Angles

In addition to matching the shape of the eyebrows like other face components, eyebrows can have different configurations based on the angle with which they are drawn. The points are separated by the proximity to the right and left of the nose, described above. A line of best fit is then generated for both of these groups with linear regression. The slopes are then extracted from these lines and are used to rotate the eyebrows individually. Doing this allows for an expressive range. For example, two steep eyebrows angled toward the nose can make the avatar look more deter-

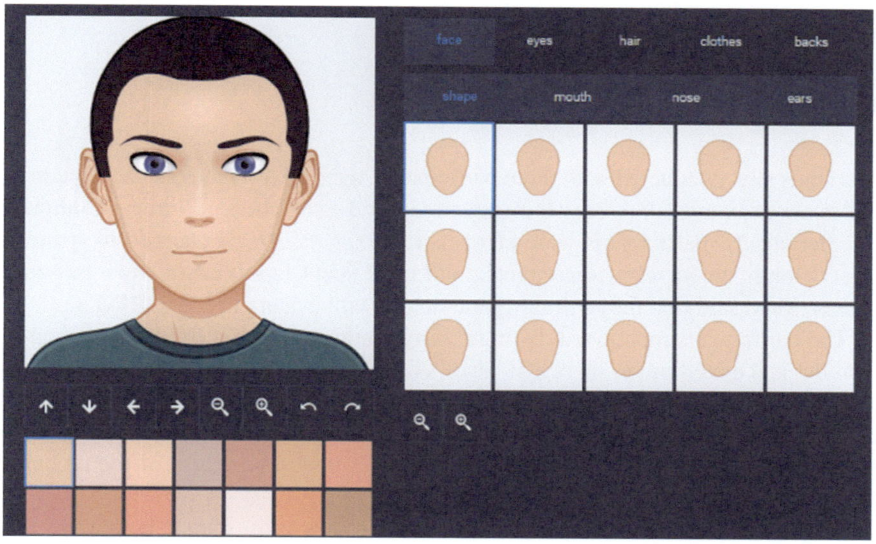

Fig. 11.11 Menu-based avatar creation system

mined or angry, while one angled and one flat eyebrow can make the avatar look like it is skeptical. Example avatars are shown in Fig. 11.10.

11.6 Methodology

A brief initial within-subjects study was conducted to compare the sketching system described in the chapter with a menu-based avatar creating software. The menu-based avatar customization system is shown in Fig. 11.11. Researchers gave the participants a small questionnaire at the beginning, asking about participant demographic information and their background in avatar creation media.

Researchers then randomly selected one of the systems and tasked the participants with customizing an avatar. Researchers did not provide a purpose for the avatar, nor did researchers ask the participant to make the avatar a direct resemblance of their appearance. After they were done with one system, researchers instructed them to complete the same task with the other system. During their interactions with both systems, users were encouraged to think aloud.

After completing these tasks, researchers performed a semi-structured interview, focusing on how users identify with their created avatars and with changes they desire to see in either system. Both systems had the same cartoon assets and similar systems for gender selection.

11.7 Results and Discussion

11.7.1 Results

The study was conducted with three participants, ages 20 though 30. Two were male and one was female, all computer programmers and researchers in Human–Computer Interaction. All participants were students at Texas A&M, all claimed to spend at least 7 hours on social media a week, and most spent few hours a week on video games. Most said that they primarily interacted with avatars in MMORPG's.

The participants mentioned distinguishing features of avatar to be customizable, cartoon, and a medium to represent "another person's personality." They mentioned avatars as ways to "present myself to other people" and in detail customization of face and clothes. They all expressed that gaming avatars were their favorite ones to create and to interact within their games. This may be because of the common demographics and small number of participants.

All participants felt that the menu avatar system represented them better, like that they could see all the options. A couple mentioned that the sketch system seemed faster and was more fun, without prompting from the interviewer. With the menu interface, they liked the feeling of control.

One mentioned the sketch system was "smooth," and selected components "pretty well." The same person did not like the blur on the photo, claiming that he wanted to see their face details more clear. Multiple users liked emphasizing features with sketches and emphasized liking eyebrow details.

All participants did not like the hierarchical ordering of components and options in the menu, as well as the rotating and sizing buttons. One said it "was not intuitive." One wanted a reference selfie image to use alongside the menu avatar creation.

One participant wanted to adjust the pen width in the sketch interface. One wanted to have the system automatically reflect the sketch of the symmetrical features like eyes and ears.

11.7.2 Limitations

These limited results hint that better template matching is needed, or the system should potentially allow users to receive more control over how the system decides which component options to draw on the avatar. More customization of canvas and pen features could give this feeling of control.

It seems users would like an opacity slider to allow themselves to just adjust how blurred their selfie would be when sketching, however, giving users freedom to see a completely clear selfie that may be detrimental to their creativity when drawing, as users may just copy the small details shown on the image rather than including their own mental model of their own visage. Our participants mainly interacted with avatars in games so it would be worthwhile to gain feedback from participants with a large background working with social media avatars.

As participants mentioned personality being a large factor in avatar presentation, those types of features should be emphasized in future design iterations. More ways to accessorize or sketch on avatars and backgrounds could be added, so that there is more than just a generic face for each avatar. More studies with larger sample sizes need to be done to gain more insight into the potential of sketch avatar customization systems.

11.8 Future Work

Dixon et al. (2010) created the iCanDraw system that provides visual aid to the user in sketching. We plan to implement something similar which will help user better create avatars that meet their expectations. Constraints on the arrangement of components on the human face can aid the sketch recognition algorithms and avatar-drawing. It may be possible to employ methods to evaluate the user's tracings as in Wang et al. (2016) to return feedback. Similar methods could be done to create better templates.

A large issue with the present system is that the matching is not always very consistent and does not always match user expectations. To improve this, several aspects of matching need to be improved. Using concave hulls could improve the Hausdorff distance matching, but Hausdorff distance may not always capture the needed information that the user conveys when sketching. For components like hair, where the user often draws individual hairs rather than a contour, it could be useful to look into matching methods that look for shapes and patterns in strokes in addition to the shape of the entire composition. Another way to better match user expectations is to warp the cartoon assets based on sketch attributes, similar to how the eyebrows are warped in the present system to change characteristics such as orientation and size. More visual features besides the hull and stroke shapes may be employed to give better matches.

Better templates could also help the matching process. Having more participants generate templates could give us better matches. Similarly, running a larger study similar to this chapter could give us more sketches, which could show us different variations in user sketches. We could then ask users to match facial components on their own and others' drawings to different cartoon assets, which would allow us to build better classification methods in the future. We would have to experiment on whether to optimize matches to the individual's perceived features or to their peer's perception of the users' features. A study could be run looking at recognizably and self-identification of avatars generated with match classifiers from peer or self-identified labels for facial components. Similar studies have been done with the familiarity of human subjects in morphed photographs (Chu et al. 2013).

Facial landmarks can be found as in Saragih et al. (2011) to identify the part of the face being sketched, instead of asking the user to draw individual components serially on one singular canvas. This will also allow users more flexibility to draw and edit in any way they see fit. Everything in this type of system would be on one canvas. This may reduce frustration of the user switching between different facial component canvases, trying to get combinations they like.

Feedback given by the system can be improved. Currently, the system gives a match for any random scribble. This can be avoided by introducing geometric features for each component and check confidence of the sketch belonging to that particular component before proceeding for the match.

Allowing the user to free-form draw on top of a completed avatar could grant them more freedom of expression of their identity. Users could then add jewelry, tattoos, and other real-life customizations not presently offered by this system. Accessory recognition from sketches could aid the user in this part of the customization process.

Only one side of eyes, eyebrows, and ears are used to get a match. The system could inspect the two sides and show the two closest matches each based on each part and ask user to select from them.

The system displays a random avatar at the beginning of the avatar creation process, but it is possible to extract facial components from the selfie to get a guess initialization avatar. The system can then ask the user to sketch desired features to change any specific component. This system could grant similar simplicity as MyIdol, while giving similar freedom of expression as menu-based systems like Bitmoji.

The system presently mandates that the users capture a blurred selfie to trace, but the system can provide an option to allow free sketching without the selfie and provide varying levels of selfie blur intensity. This could lead to a user study comparing avatars created by free sketches, tracing over blurred selfies, and tracing over non-blurred selfies. This can approach the question of whether the reference image during avatar creation helps users identify more with their avatar.

For social media applications and multiplayer games, it becomes important for others to be able to match avatars to familiar people. Another user study could look to rank user-generated avatars from the different avatar personalization systems to see if people familiar with the avatar's owners can better recognize the person from an avatar. Similarly, it would be interesting to see if strangers could match avatars to several selfie images. Their ability to do so would reveal a stranger's ability to dox online individuals based on their avatar. Comparing strangers' ability to match avatars customized from different methods could prove valuable to many online communities, especially when protecting the identities of more vulnerable populations like children.

11.9 Conclusion

When designing avatars, users often want the ability to pick from a large variety of facial components but are often encumbered if forced to pick all those options from a menu. Selfie-driven avatar customization helps quickly to make an avatar that resembles the user but can limit the user's creative expression when customizing an avatar. Participants claimed the selfie sketching system was fun and intuitive, although in its present state it did not create an avatar that the participants would consistently perceive as satisfying to their own self-images. There are many questions about virtual user identity, ease of use, and the ability of sketch recognition algorithms that can be explored in future iterations. More investigation is needed to provide any significant observations about how humans will generally perceive and interact with these systems, however, there is potential for future systems to successfully combine positive aspects of selfie-driven and menu-driven avatar creation platforms.

References

Bao P, Zhang L, Wu X (2005) Canny edge detection enhancement by scale multiplication. IEEE Trans Pattern Anal Mach Intell 27(9):1485–1490

Burke A (2013) Children's construction of identity in virtual play worlds-a classroom perspective. Lang Lit 15(1):58

Cao X, Wei Y, Wen F, Sun J (2014) Face alignment by explicit shape regression. Int J Comput Vis 107(2):177–190

Cao Y, Wang C, Zhang L, Zhang L (2011) Edgel index for large-scale sketch-based image search. In: 2011 IEEE conference on computer vision and pattern recognition (CVPR). IEEE, pp 761–768

Chu SL, Fedorovskaya E, Quek F, Snyder J (2013) The effect of familiarity on perceived interestingness of images. In: Human vision and electronic imaging XVIII, vol 8651. International society for optics and photonics, p 86511C

Conrad M, Charles A, Neale J (2011) What is my avatar? Who is my avatar? The avatar as a device to achieve a goal: perceptions and implications. In: Reinventing ourselves: contemporary concepts of identity in virtual worlds. Springer, pp 253–273

Diego-Mas JA, Alcaide-Marzal J (2015) A computer based system to design expressive avatars. Comput Human Behav 44:1–11

Dixon D, Prasad M, Hammond T (2010) iCanDraw: using sketch recognition and corrective feedback to assist a user in drawing human faces. In: Proceedings of the SIGCHI conference on human factors in computing systems. ACM, pp 897–906

Dolgov I, Graves WJ, Nearents MR, Schwark JD, Volkman CB (2014) Effects of cooperative gaming and avatar customization on subsequent spontaneous helping behavior. Comput Human Behav 33:49–55

Field M, Valentine S, Linsey J, Hammond T (2011) Sketch recognition algorithms for comparing complex and unpredictable shapes. In: Proceedings of the Twenty-Second International Joint Conference on Artificial Intelligence, pp 2436–2441

Jin SAA (2009) Avatars mirroring the actual self versus projecting the ideal self: the effects of self-priming on interactivity and immersion in an exergame, Wii Fit. CyberPsychol Behav 12(6):761–765

Kafai YB, Fields DA, Cook MS (2010) Your second selves: player-designed avatars. Games Cult 5(1):23–42

Kara L, Stahovich T (2005) An image-based, trainable symbol recognizer for hand-drawn sketches. Computers & Graphics, 29(4):501–517

Lee Y, Kozar KA, Larsen KR (2009) Avatar e-mail versus traditional e-mail: perceptual difference and media selection difference. Decis Support Syst 46(2):451–467

Lee YE, Saharia AN (2012) The influence of self-concept improvement on member loyalty to online communities: an empirical comparison between social networks and virtual worlds. In: 2012 45th Hawaii international conference on system science (HICSS). IEEE, pp 3550–3559

Li Q (2014) A primal sketch based framework for bean-shape contour extraction. Neurocomputing 142:508–519

Park Y, Choi Y, Yang HS (2014) Avatar recommendation method based on facial attributes. In: 2014 international conference on virtual systems & multimedia (VSMM). IEEE, pp 267–272
Rhee CH, Lee C (2013) Cartoon-like avatar generation using facial component matching. Int J Multimed Ubiquitous Eng 8(4):69–78
Rosin PL, Lai YK (2015) Non-photorealistic rendering of portraits. In: Proceedings of the workshop on computational aesthetics. Eurographics Association, pp 159–170
Saragih JM, Lucey S, Cohn JF (2011) Deformable model fitting by regularized landmark mean-shift. Int J Comput Vis 91(2):200–215
Schaefer S, McPhail T, Warren J (2006) Image deformation using moving least squares. In: ACM transactions on graphics (TOG), vol 25-3. ACM, pp 533–540
Sepehri Nejad S, Balafar MA (2016) Component-based cartoon face generation. Electronics 5(4):76
Tang X, Wang X (2004) Face sketch recognition. IEEE Trans Circuits Syst Video Technol 14(1):50–57
Tinwell A, Grimshaw M, Nabi DA, Williams A (2011) Facial expression of emotion and perception of the uncanny valley in virtual characters. Comput Human Behav 27(2):741–749
Vasalou A, Joinson A, Bänziger T, Goldie P, Pitt J (2008) Avatars in social media: balancing accuracy, playfulness and embodied messages. Int J Human-Comput Stud 66(11):801–811
Wang N, Gao X, Li J, Song B, Li Z (2016) Evaluation on synthesized face sketches. Neurocomputing 214:991–1000
Zhang Y, Dong W, Deussen O, Huang F, Li K, Hu BG (2014) Data-driven face cartoon stylization. ACM
Zhang Y, Dong W, Ma C, Mei X, Li K, Huang F, Hu BG, Deussen O (2017) Data-driven synthesis of cartoon faces using different styles. IEEE Trans Image Process 26(1):464–478
Zou Y, Dong F, Lei B, Fang L, Sun S (2013) Image thresholding based on template matching with arctangent hausdorff distance measure. Opt Lasers Eng 51(5):600–609

Part VII
Forward Directions with Haptics

Chapter 12
Touching with Feeling

J. Edward Colgate

Abstract Dr. Edward Colgate gave a keynote on morning of the second day of the conference. He spoke about haptics and their vital role in everyday life. He showed that, on contrary, haptics are decidedly less important when interfacing to the digital world. Our touch screens treat the finger as a pointer and more or less ignore the thousands of mechanoreceptors within, not to mention the somatosensory cortex. This is an odd state of affairs. Dr. Colgate explained that part of the reason is technological: how do you go beyond simple vibrations and create versatile, programmable haptic experiences? Research in his lab has focused on solving this question for better than a decade now. In his talk, he explained the rapidly expanding capabilities of "surface haptic" technologies. Dr. Colgate also showed how limited are the data on haptics used to create great experiences, be they for education, entertainment, or elsewhere. That turns out to be a much more difficult problem. He described some incipient efforts and offered some thoughts for the future. This chapter provides a lightly edited transcription of that keynote.

12.1 Keynote Transcript

Dr. Edward Colgate: I'm going to talk to you today about the topic of getting information out of a computer and into the brain via touch, and in particular doing so via interactive surfaces, which has been a big passion of mine for about the last decade.

I'm going to guess that this audience knows more than most, but this word "haptic," which maybe five years ago very few people ever heard, is now often heard and associated, in pretty limited context, with the idea of something vibrating a little

Electronic supplementary material The online version of this chapter (https://doi.org/10.1007/978-3-030-17398-2_12) contains supplementary material, which is available to authorized users.

J. E. Colgate (✉)
Northwestern University, Evanston, IL 60208, USA
e-mail: colgate@northwestern.edu

T. Hammond et al. (eds.), *Inspiring Students with Digital Ink*, Human–Computer Interaction Series, https://doi.org/10.1007/978-3-030-17398-2_12

bit on a screen when you push it. The word "haptic" is one that engineers and psychologists have been using for quite a long time to refer to the entire perceptual system associated with touch and movement, and involves both the cutaneous sense—sensing via the skin—and the kinesthetic sense—sensing via the muscles and joints. These work together and enable us to get information from the world through physical interaction.

I love to show things like this Youtube video (Amazing Contact Juggling 2019). This is a contact juggler. What this guy is doing with his hands and his eyes is really quite extraordinary. His ability to do this depends on vision, but also on haptic information that he perceives through his skin. Whether you have that level of dexterity or not, it turns out that touch sensation is an important thing for all of us. Prof. Roland Johansson is one of the leaders in the field of haptic neuroscience, and he put together an amazing demonstration. First, he asked a woman to strike a match, which she did easily, but then he anesthetized her thumb, index finger, and middle finger. Anyone who's ever been to the dentist and been numbed up should understand: it's that type of sensation or a lack of sensation, but on your fingers. Then he asked her to repeat that same task. Her vision was unimpaired and she was able to move her fingers just fine. The only thing that she lacked was the ability to feel what she was doing. She struggled mightily to light the match, unable to keep it from falling from her fingers. Finally, she succeeded in about six times longer than normal.

It turns out that that ability to sense the world via touch is critical in almost every moment of your life. You could not strike a match, hold a fork, type on a keyboard, shave, button a button, tie your shoes, hold your coffee cup or sign your name, without it.

My career has been primarily about haptic interface: building devices that let us use the sense of touch to interface to the digital world.

Back in the day, I used to work in devices like the one shown here, which is called a force-feedback device, where you grasp on to the end effector, and we can simulate different types of virtual worlds you can feel and interact with. This type of technology is used on things like surgical simulation. When many people in my field say "haptic interface," this is the sort of device that comes to mind (Fig. 12.1). But there are other devices that are really more about interfacing directly to the skin, so electronic Braille would be an example of a programmable interface, very specific purpose interface for interfacing with the skin (Fig. 12.2).

I'll stop my discussion of the breadth of haptic interface here, because we're going to focus on surfaces. It's really when touch screen interfaces, about a decade ago, began to become a very prominent part of all of our life that I began to ask the question, "how can we do the sorts of things that we had been doing when we had the luxury of grasping on to a device now that we don't have that luxury anymore: when we need to interface through the bare fingers." I refer to this as surface haptics, the idea of providing programmable haptic effects on physical surfaces. The question that I've been occupied with for quite some time is: how do you do that?

There are various approaches that are out there in the literature. One of the really fun ones is electrical stimulation (Kajimoto et al. 1999). The idea here is to deliver sufficient current through some patch of skin to cause nerves to fire. It's unfortunately

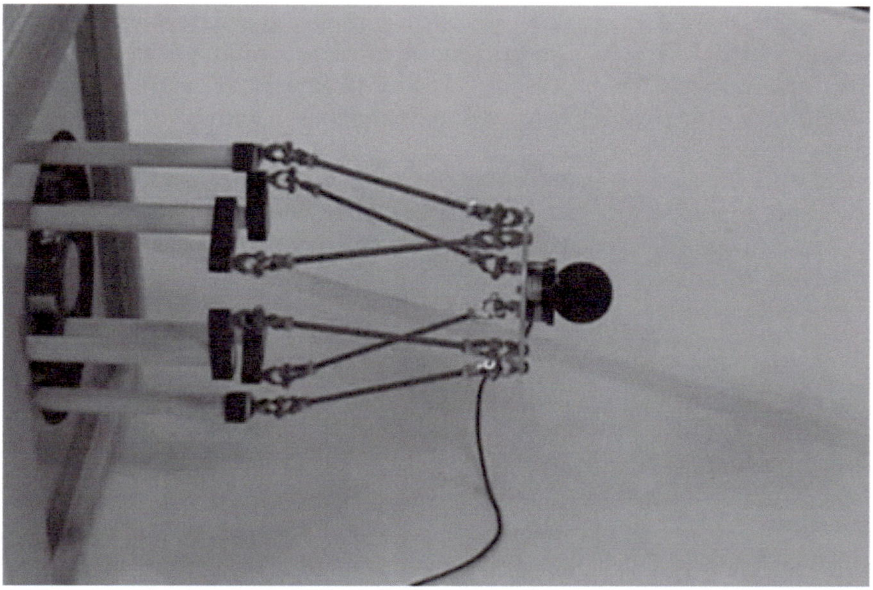

Fig. 12.1 A haptic interface developed in the author's lab at Northwestern University

Fig. 12.2 Brailliant BI 40 (NEW generation) braille display [http://humanware.com/en-usa/home]

very difficult to get the mechanical receptors like this so-called Pacinian Corpuscle, which is a specialized nerve ending for sensing vibration to fire, and not get the bare nerve endings, which are responsible for pain. My usual experience with electrical stimulation is primarily that of pain, but nonetheless there continues to be a lot of research in this area.

Probably the most common sort of thing that we see is simply making things vibrate. It is common in the commercial world today. There are lots of variations on the theme, but the fundamental thing here is that when we do think about our skin as an interface to the world, there are both situations like I've been talking about so far where we are manipulating the world—us reaching out and touching the world—and there are lots of situations where the world comes and touches us: when a mosquito lands on your arm, when you brush against a thorn. You need to know that, and you need know it quickly. So our skin acts as an alert system. Those Pacinian Corpuscles I just mentioned which are vibration sensors are incredibly sensitive. They tell us when the world's touching us.

As a consequence, it's relatively straightforward to engineer devices that by vibrating into the proper frequency range, which would be around 200–300 Hz, deliver information. Most of the technology you'll find out there in the world for haptics today is based on this idea. I find it a rather limiting, narrow window in the haptics, but nonetheless, it's proven to be important. Another approach is to actually modify the shape of a surface (Harrison and Hudson 2009). I think a lot of people view this as the holy grail in haptics. It is extremely challenging, however, to build a surface that is deformable under computer control. Practical devices of this nature may be many years away.

Having looked at those options, I wasn't too satisfied. I took inspiration from some very early work done in our field, actually by Margret Minsky, the daughter of the famous Marvin. In my late days as a graduate student at MIT, she was working there in the Media Lab and building one the very early force-feedback haptic devices. It was a two-axis joystick with force feedback. She had the notion of simulating virtual environments using in-plane forces. This thing only moved in the plane, but the forces applied in the plane were used to simulate roughness—a sort of out of plane shape. She created this pattern of forces and found that if she moved the device, it felt as if you were moving over something that had, essentially, rough 3D geometry (Minsky et al. 1990).

This idea was then formalized in a really beautiful study by one of the titans in our field Vincent Hayward and his student Gabriel Robles-de-la-Torre (Robles-De-La-Torre and Hayward 2001). They initially had people who move a handheld device over a bump and asked, "What do you feel?" People said, "I feel a bump." Then they had to move over a completely flat surface, but they hooked it up to a haptic device to play a pattern of forces. They played the pattern of forces that one would encounter going over a bump. Think about it, you have to initially push your way up the hill, and then there is no force at the top, and then it pushes you down the other side. You could play that same pattern of forces, even though you're not going up and down, and ask people, "What do you feel," and what do they say? They say "I feel a bump." In fact, it's a very compelling illusion. So compelling, that you can have them physically going down into a dip, but play that pattern of forces, they'll still experience the bump. It's exciting: the ability to perceive a three-dimensional shape in a system, which is moving on a flat surface.

I thought that was pretty cool. And so the work that I've done in surface haptics is based upon the question: how can you do that for a bare fingertip? If I've got a bare fingertip on a surface, how can I control the shear force design in order to convey to you things like a three-dimensional shape or textures?

How do you control the shear forces on the bare fingertip? One of the earliest things I've seen out there, 15 years ago, was the idea of putting an overlay over a display, and then just moving that overlay, have some motors that would tug it side to side (Wang et al. 2004).

Another idea is some strings that go to a little pad you put your finger on, and then have motors pull the strings (Saga and Deguchi 2012). Another idea is the use of asymmetric vibrations to push the finger along (Kaye 2012). In our group, what we came to was the idea of modulating friction. When you're moving your finger against a surface the in-plane forces that exist are principally due to friction. The magnitude of friction depends upon a frictional coefficient, typically, and upon a normal force. According to Coulomb, the friction force is the product of the friction coefficient and the normal force, which is an approximate empirical relationship. The main point I'm making here is to say, "If we come up with technology for either modulating coefficient of friction or modulating normal force, then we might be able to influence friction." Friction is the force that you're experiencing as you slide around, so that might be useful.

Let me talk about technologies that we've developed for doing both of those things, and I'll start with the idea of modulating coefficient of friction. Well, it turns out that we didn't have to invent this. Back in the mid-'90s, Japanese researchers discovered that if you take the surface that you're touching, and you vibrate it out of plane at ultrasonic frequencies with sufficient amplitude, then the surface feels slippery (Watanabe and Fukui 1995). These are surfaces that are vibrating at high frequency but low amplitude so you can't see this motion and you can't feel it either because you can feel vibrations up to only a few hundred Hertz.

What's the point of something you can't see or feel or hear? The point is that these vibrations make the surface go from its native coefficient of friction, to something much less, so we can make the surfaces very slippery. Here are some data taken in our lab (Fig. 12.3). The vertical axis shows friction force, and then the horizontal axis is vibration amplitude, from very small to larger vibrations. Even the largest vibration amplitude shown here is three microns or three millionths of an inch. You can see that the friction force varies by approximately in an order of magnitude, so this is not a small effect. You can take a surface like glass, which is kind of sticky, and make it very, very slippery, simply by vibrating the surface.

We learned how to take this effect and make it work over a piece of glass large enough to cover a useful display. Here I am showing a greatly exaggerated oscillation mode on a glass plate that is, say, the size of a phone screen (Fig. 12.4). To build this, you glue a piezoelectric actuator to one end of it, and then use it to excite a particular resonance. The particular resonance is typically one that has a corrugated shape. The

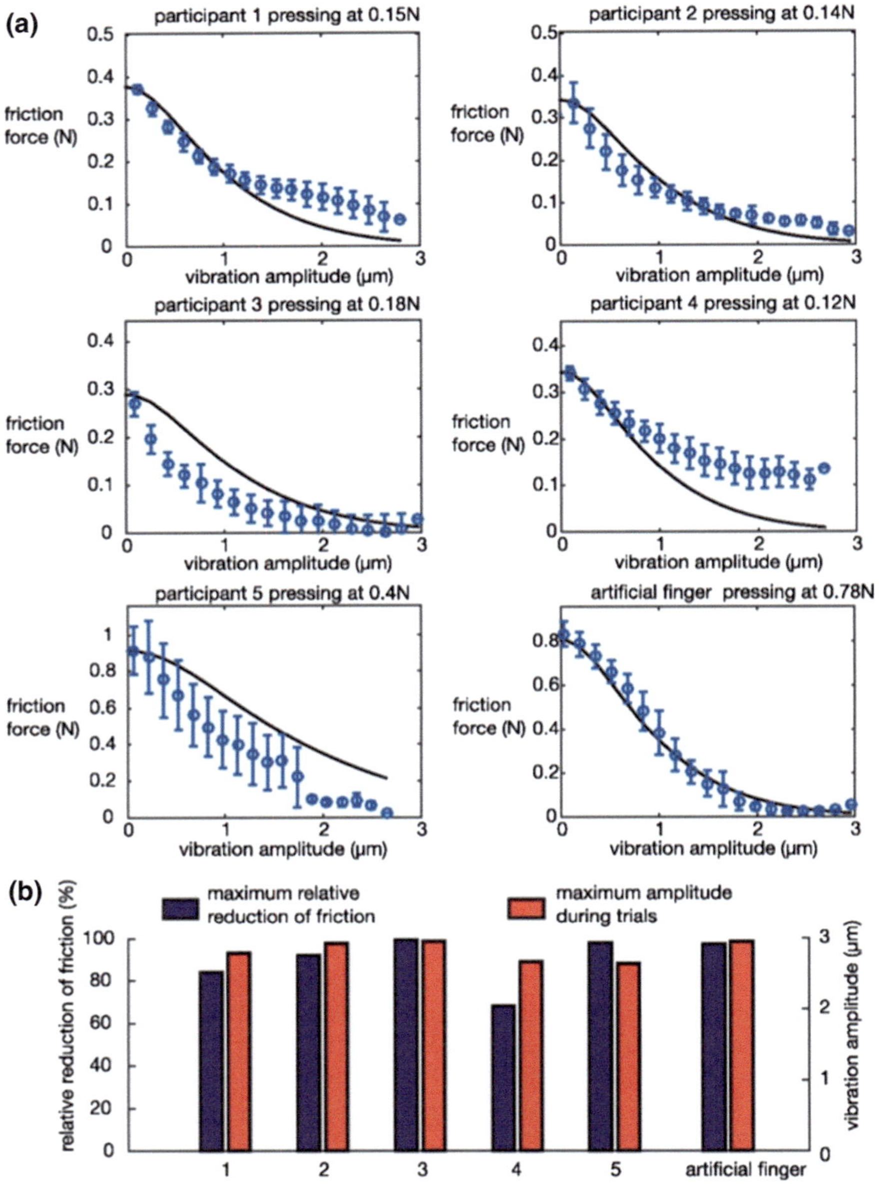

Fig. 12.3 **a** Friction measurement for each participant compared with the prediction from the model. **b** Summary of the effectiveness of the friction reduction at the maximum vibration amplitude tested (Wiertlewski et al. 2016)

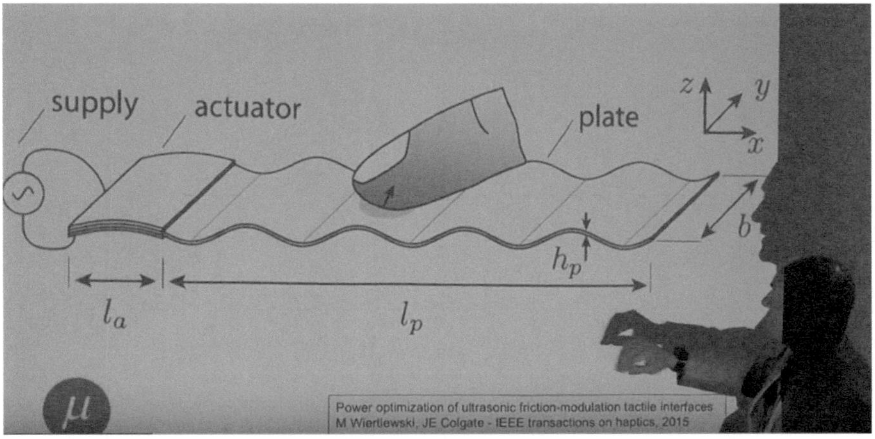

Fig. 12.4 Oscillation mode on a glass plate (Wiertlewski et al. 2014)

vibration of this glass is out of plane. This image is just a freeze-frame of a vibrating piece of glass, but actually every point on it is moving up and down at an ultrasonic frequency.

My former student, Joe Mullenbach, developed what he called the TPaD phone (Fig. 12.5) (Mullenbach et al. 2013). TPaD was our named for this technology, short for Tactile Pattern Display. He took a piece of glass like I just showed you and he put it on top of an Android SmartPhone and put it in a nice case, and developed all the software. He did this with another student, Craig Shultz, and quite a few of our undergraduates, and made this available to researchers in haptics. So there are quite a few of these things out there in the world today.

This is a video that Joe took of a finger moving across the TPaD (Slide21.mov). Now he's going to slow it down. Do you see the finger getting stuck on those black lines? Well, it's not really that they're getting stuck on anything that's black. It's getting stuck on those things because that's where you turned down the vibration amplitude, and the finger encounters the native stickiness of glass. In between, in the white areas, we're making it vibrate. The black and white lines are images for your benefit, but in fact, what's really happening has nothing to do with the color. It has to do with the pattern of vibration amplitude. That's one technology that we developed.

You might be curious about how it works. There have been a lot of different theories. One of them is that the friction is reduced because of something called squeeze film levitation. Another is that the finger's somehow bouncing and there are some nonlinear areas. Another one is that it's bouncing, but your finger has a finite lateral mechanical impedance or stretchiness, so when it's touching for a very short period of time, there's not enough time for the lateral forces to build up.

The squeeze film theory may be understood as follows. When two plates that are vibrating out of plane are brought close together and there's some air in between, then due to both the compressibility, shown by the C, and the viscosity, shown by

Fig. 12.5 TPaD phone (Mullenbach et al. 2013)

the R, a levitation force occurs. When the plates are moving toward one another, they're compressing that air which acts as a spring. But, at the same time, the gap between them is getting small, which means it's hard for the air to escape due to its own viscosity. The air is trying to escape from the edges, but it can't, because the gap is so small. As they move apart from one another, the pressure drops. Now the gap is getting big, it's easy for air to flow in. It's easier for the air to flow in than out, so it gets captured and creates an air bearing. This theory has been validated for steel plates, but what about fingertips?

We used a laser doppler vibrometer, which is a beautiful instrument for measuring vibrations, to look at what the finger was doing on a TPaD (Fig. 12.6) (Dai et al. 2012). These data show that the out of plane velocity of the vibrating plate is a beautiful sinusoidal curve but the velocity of the finger is quite different. What appears to be happening is that the finger reaches a peak velocity, then quickly drops back close to zero, and then is similar to the velocity of the plate for a while. This cycle repeats itself. Those data suggest that there is a collision where the finger is hit by the plate causing its velocity to change suddenly after which it is stuck to the plate for a while, then it flies off, then it gets hit again, and the cycle repeats.

The velocity data can be integrated, giving position. With position data, there's an arbitrary constant. You don't know what it is, but we took the two velocity traces and integrated them, and then we slid the curves together and sure enough they just

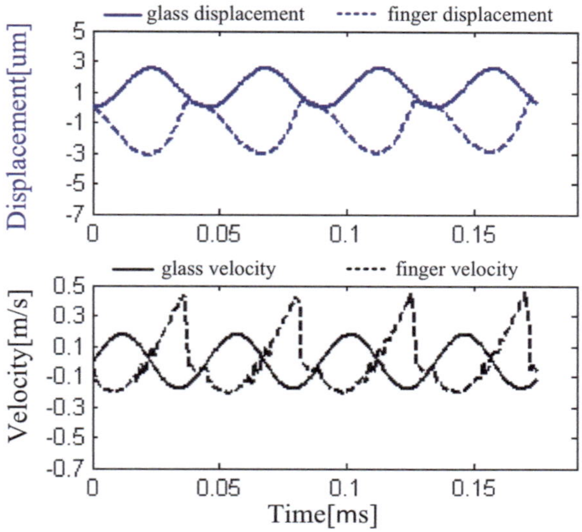

Fig. 12.6 Out of plane motion of a finger on a TPaD, apparently showing "bouncing" (Dai et al. 2012)

fit beautifully. The upshot is that these data suggest that the finger is bouncing off the plate, as opposed to levitating.

A postdoc of mine, Michael Wiertlewski, built a lovely apparatus in order to get to settle the levitation versus bouncing debate (Fig. 12.7) (Wiertlewski et al. 2016). He used frustrated total internal reflection. The idea is that you send light in from the edge of the glass, and due to total internal reflection, the light stays inside glass. But where your skin comes into intimate contact with the surface, some light is absorbed and you can imagine that, this gives a way to image the gap itself by measuring how much light is reflected versus absorbed.

The data showed here have a beautiful linear correlation between the amount of absorbed light and the measured friction of a finger against a TPaD (Fig. 12.8). What's going on here is that you get a nice bright image when the finger is intimately against the glass. High brightness correlates to high friction. As you increase the amplitude of vibration, the image gets less bright and friction decreases. These data and some other data that he took led us to conclude that all of the previous theories were correct! In other words, the finger bounces, but the air is incredibly important. If there were no air, then the finger might bounce, but it would bounce hard causing periods of high friction. We don't see this. The air does get captured, but at the same time, there's a bouncing effect. The ultimate conclusion is that the finger bounces off of the air.

Recall that friction depends on both coefficient of friction, and also normal force. So we must ask, is there some way you can modulate the normal force? It turns out there is, and it involves the use of electrical fields. If you apply a potential between the finger and the surface that it is touching, you can create a normal force.

I'd like to explain how these things actually work. What we typically do is start with a conductive layer to which we can apply a potential, and then cover it over

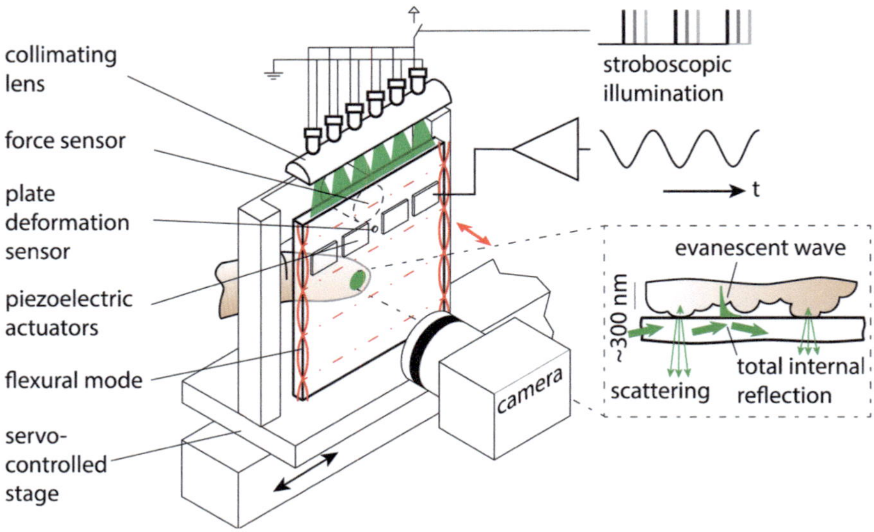

Fig. 12.7 Apparatus developed in order to settle the levitation versus bouncing debate. The TPaD is mounted on a servo-controlled stage equipped with a six-axis force sensor. Illumination from the side of the plate provides a uniform illumination of the true contact area through frustrated total internal reflection (Wiertlewski et al. 2016)

with an insulator. The outermost layer of skin, called the stratum corneum, is dead dehydrated skin cells. All that is left is the outer part of the cell, which is mainly keratin, same stuff as hair. These things get brick-and-mortared together. That's what the outer layer of your skin is a whole bunch of dead skin cells that are stacked up. It's fairly insulating, but not, by any means, perfectly insulating. It also has a very high dielectric constant. Skin is also rough. When you put your skin down against the surface, there's a thin air gap that occurs.

An electric model of this system looks like three series impedances: the insulator, the air gap, and then the skin (Fig. 12.9) (Shultz et al. 2018). It turns out that the air gap, that part in the middle, is critical. We can compute the force that develops across the air gap using the electrostatics of parallel plate capacitors. Note that force develops across the plates of any parallel plate capacitor, pulling them toward one another. Since the finger and surface are in partial contact with air in between, they get pulled together which increases the actual contact area, and thereby, friction.

Craig Shultz developed a device with an electroadhesive surface (Shultz et al. 2015). He measured friction, and friction depends upon normal force and the lateral force with and without the electric field. The lower cluster is his data without an extra electric field, and what you see is classic Coulombic friction (Fig. 12.10). The harder you press, the greater the friction force.

Now, he does the same thing again, having turned on electric field, and he sees a lot more friction force (upper cluster). You can infer how much additional normal force there was by how much you would have to slide the top curve horizontally in

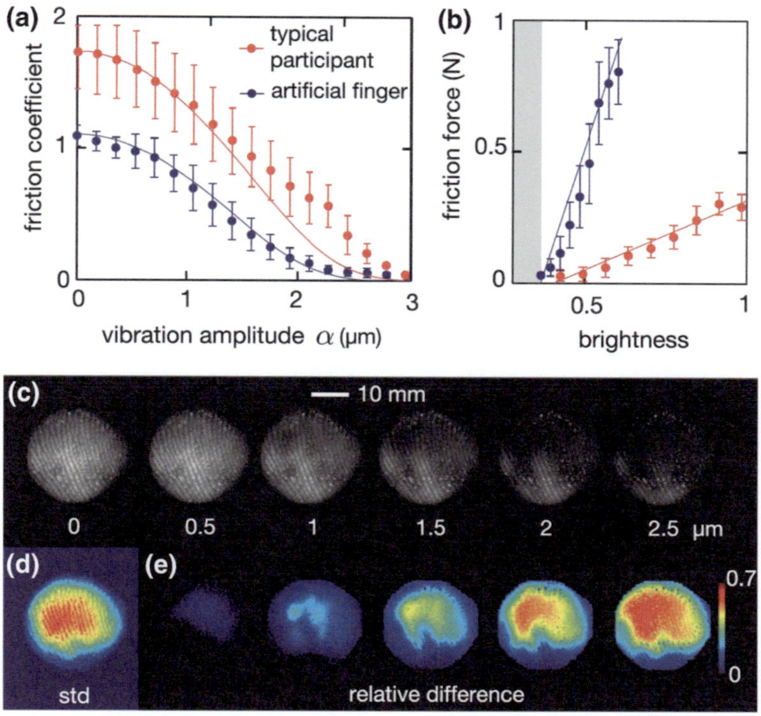

Fig. 12.8 **a** The sliding friction force gradually decreases with increasing vibration amplitude. The line represents the (**b**) brightness and friction force correlation. The illumination technique reveals those asperities that are within a few hundred nanometers of the plate; therefore, the spatial average of the brightness received by the camera is linearly correlated with the friction force and under the adhesive theory of friction, linearly correlated with the true area of contact. **c** Images of the contact area under ultrasonic vibration amplitudes of 0–2.5 μM. **d** Spatial distribution of the variation of brightness over a cycle where the amplitude of stimulation is slowly varying. The center of the contact experiences the most variation, whereas the edge remains unaffected. **e** The difference between the brightness at selected amplitudes and the brightness at rest highlight those areas that are more or less affected by vibration (Wiertlewski et al. 2016)

order to match the lower one. It's a lot in this particular case, about seven Newtons. Just for a reference, people almost always press on touch screens with less than one Newton of normal force. This is an extreme case, but it shows that it is possible to generate a lot of normal forces.

One thing I haven't mentioned yet is that you can turn this effect on and off very, very fast. I'm going to play audio in this video (Slide33.mp4). In the beginning, you are watching slowly changing friction. You can see how the finger bounces along. Now we turn the added friction on and off 1,000 times per second. You hear sound! Now we're playing music. Where's the sound coming from? It is actually coming from the finger. Friction is being modulated so rapidly that the vibrations in the skin are in the audible range.

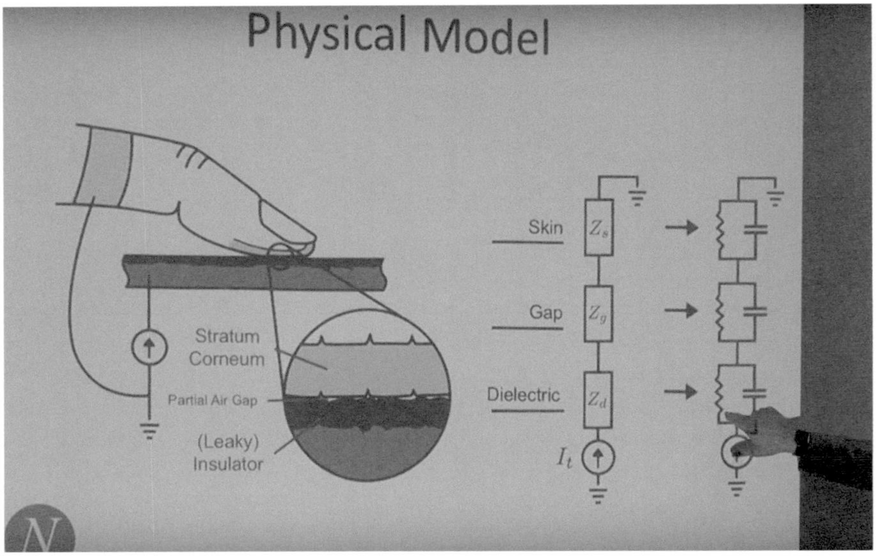

Fig. 12.9 Physical model of electroadhesion (Shultz et al. 2018)

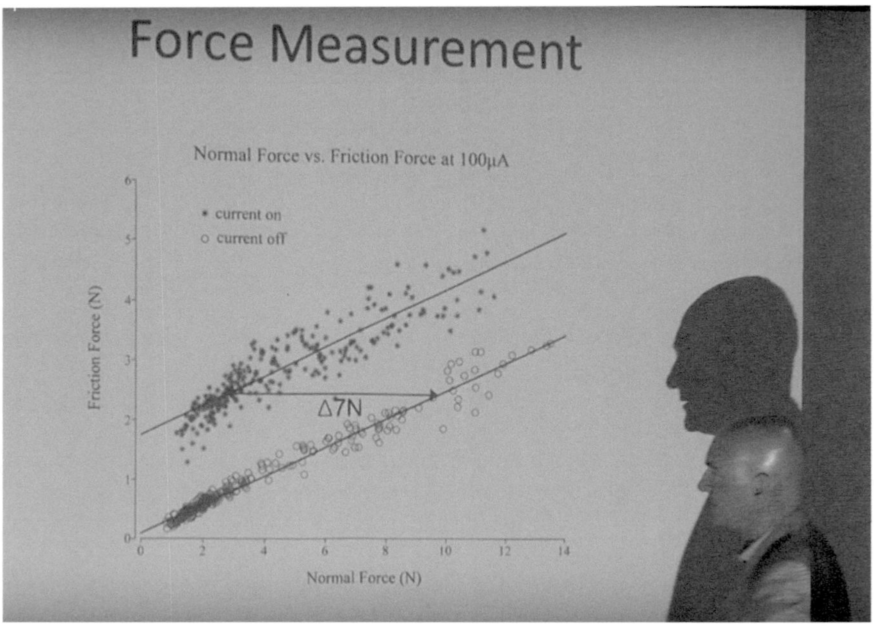

Fig. 12.10 Force measurement

Something to note about this technology is that it is entirely solid state. The only thing that moves is the skin, and not by very much. That lead my colleague Michael Peshkin and myself to think that it should be a commercializable technology for touch screens. Over the years, Michael and I have done several start-up companies together. In this case, we started a company named Tanvas with the goal of taking that core technology and putting it into commercial devices. To accomplish this, our team had to solve some challenging problems like reengineering the touch panel itself and integrating touch sensing with electrostatic haptic output.

At this point, a reasonable question to ask is why we are interested in this at all. What is the value of surface haptics? I will share with you my thoughts. I've broken these up into three categories. The first is skeuomorphism, the second is physics assist, and the third is adding one more channel for information to get into your brain.

Let me go through some ideas and work that we've done in each of these areas. If you're not familiar with the word skeuomorphism, it's when your interface design tries to take cues from and mimic the physical world. This is an example from Craig Shultz using electroadhesion to create the feel of sandpaper (Slide36.mov). It is easy to create a rough feeling, and with the ability to play sound he can create that characteristic sandpaper sound as well. He did that by taking a recording of sandpaper and playing that recording back to the device. It feels and sounds quite natural.

Unfortunately, there is quite a bit of lag in the graphics. Another way that you can do this type of experiment is to play a video of someone sanding wood. If you as a research participant move your finger back and forth on an electroadhesive surface programmed to feel like sandpaper, and you sync your motion to what you see in the video, something really cool happens. Because sight and sound and feel all sync up very nicely, you get drawn into the virtual world at a pretty deep level. Things begin to feel very realistic.

Here's another example from Craig's work: toggle switches. What he's doing is taking impulse response functions of the sound from things like wood or ceramic and convolving those with a very simple haptic model of a toggle switch (Slide37.mov). He's able to make toggle switches that you can feel and that sound as though they are made of various materials such as metal or ceramic.

While Joe Mullenbach was a student in our lab, he worked closely with Prof. Anne Marie Piper of our School of Communications to study social aspects of surface haptics, including interfaces for young children. They were particularly interested in the way that haptics might influence the type of discussions that children and their parents would have when reading e-books. The team took Clifford, the Big Red Dog, a storybook, and then put that storybook on a tablet and integrated it with haptics (Mullenbach et al. 2014).

Think about this problem: how do you decide what Clifford's nose should feel like, or the grass, the leaves or the fur? To facilitate texture design, Joe developed a simple tool based on grayscale bitmaps. Using it, Photoshop and your creativity, you can come up with different patterns that might feel approximately right. Quite frankly, even to this day, that tool remains the state of the art.

There is ongoing work in our lab that I won't talk about, but is that is geared toward understanding the perceptual determinants of texture: what makes one texture feel different from another. It is not enough to identify determinants, but one also wants to express them mathematically and then give the designer the proper tools so that he or she may design textures for specific purposes (Meyer et al. 2016).

The second idea I want to talk about is physics assist. Earlier I showed you that the finger motion is physically influenced by haptics. We want to see whether we could exploit that physicality. A team of colleagues at the University of British Columbia, led by Prof. Karon MacLean, did this really nice experiment a number of years ago in which they used a notion of Fitts law (Levesque et al. 2011). Fitts law provides a relationship between how far you have to move to a target, the size of the target, and how difficult it is to hit that target. In their experiment, subjects moved to different sized targets that, in some cases, had enhanced friction. You would expect that to have an impact on one's ability to hit the target, and sure enough, it does. Indeed, by a variety of metrics, variable friction makes it much easier to acquire a target on a touch screen. In the same study, the team demonstrated benefits in a number of other tasks, including using time pickers and selecting items in a drop-down list.

The final idea I'll discuss is simply that of providing you with additional channels of information. One example of this is using touch screens while driving. Touch screens simply cannot be used without constant visual attention. Haptic feedback offers the possibility of reducing eyes-off-road time. Joe Mullenbach, whom I've mentioned frequently, worked with a team at Ford Motor Company, using their full-size vehicle driving simulator, to study the impact of haptics in a couple of basic touch screen tasks: finding a button on a screen, and adjusting a slider (Mullenbach et al. 2013).

Their data demonstrated significant reductions in eyes-off-road time for both tasks (Fig. 12.11). There were also benefits views through a number of other measures as

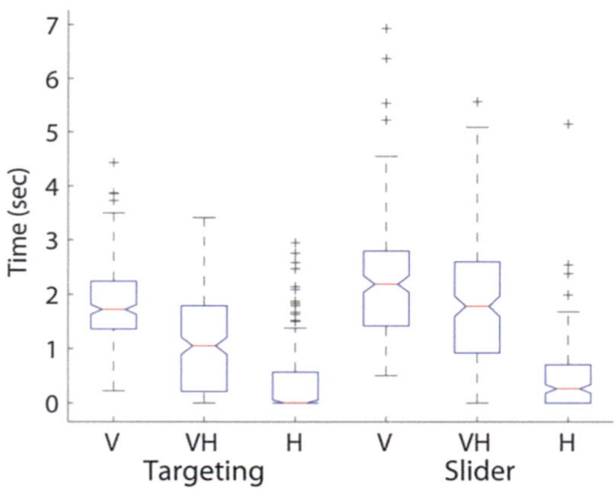

Total Glance Duration (sec)/task	Lower Quartile	Median	Upper Quartile
Targeting V	1.36	1.72	2.24
Targeting VH	0.21	1.05	1.79
Targeting H	0.0	0.0	0.57
Slider V	1.42	2.19	2.79
Slider VH	0.92	1.78	2.59
Slider H	0.0	0.26	0.70

Fig. 12.11 Significant reductions in total eyes-off-road time for visual/haptic and haptic cases (Mullenbach et al. 2013)

well, including number of glances and maximum glance duration. Although there's some physicality involved in this work, it's mainly about getting information into your brain through your skin allowing you to make decisions, for instance by counting the number of clicks.

I would like to return now to the talking about technology for providing haptic feedback. In particular, I want to talk about the idea of providing full control of the force vector acting on the fingertip. To understand why, let's think about friction for a moment. Friction always acts opposite to the direction of relative motion between two surfaces. So if I'm sliding to the right, then friction is acting to the left, and so on. It would be useful to have forces acting on the finger in other directions. For instance, if I'm sliding along the edge of this table, the force keeps me up against the edge that is mainly perpendicular to my direction of motion. That would be really useful if I want to actually guide the finger along an edge.

Also, as I've emphasized, variable friction devices cannot be experienced unless the finger is moving. It would be valuable to be able to apply forces to a finger, which is not moving. For instance, you might want to have an area of the screen such as the center of a button that draws the finger toward it. If the finger touches a little bit off to the side of that spot, the forces should push the fingers back toward it. This would make it much easier to get your fingers onto touch screen buttons.

How, then, can we go about applying forces in an arbitrary in-plane direction to a stationary finger? It turns out that we can do this with friction. The key is to move the surface. If the surface does move, then it can use friction to drag the finger in a desired direction.

Of course, it is not very realistic to have touch screens making large side to side movements. Touch screens need to be essentially solid state. The technique that we've been developing in our lab is one in which we vibrate the surface side to side, and to synchronize those vibrations to changes in friction. If I want to push a finger to the right, then I'll vibrate left and right and every time the surface is moving to the right, I'll increase the friction, so that the screen drags the finger along, and every time the screen moves back to the left, I'll make it low friction so that the screen slips under the finger. It's like a series of little impulses acting on the finger. That may seem like it would feel awful, but if you do it fast enough, you won't feel the impulse. It's kind of like old-style cathode ray tubes that would scan 60 times a second, which is fast enough that your eyes can't keep up and the image looks continuous.

The ability to measure where your finger is located, coupled with the ability to apply lateral forces to it allows for the creation of force fields. Earlier I mentioned the idea of a spot on the touch surface that would "attract" the finger: any movement away from that spot would cause the finger to be pushed back toward it. We think of that as a potential well.

If you line up a potential well, a potential hill, and another potential well, you have something that behaves like a toggle switch. The finger tends to "pop" from one well to the other as if flipping a light switch (Slide52.mp4). We were able to demonstrate this with one of the earliest lateral forcing devices, the ShiverPad. The ShiverPad was developed by Chubb et al. (2010). It vibrated side to side at about 850 Hz, which is fast enough so that a person cannot feel the vibrations, but still in the audible range. In that device, we were limited by the ability to turn friction up and down rapidly. We were using ultrasonic friction modulation which is limited by the ring-down, ring-up resonance of the vibrating glass plate.

More recently, we have begun to use electroadhesion for modulating friction. As I've mentioned, it has extremely high bandwidth. The ubiquitous Joe Mullenbach demonstrated that lateral vibrations and electroadhesion could be combined to generate substantial forces on a fingertip (Mullenbach et al. 2017), but his devices still vibrated at audible frequencies. More recently, Heng Xu has created the UltraShiver that combines electroadhesion with 30 kHz lateral vibrations to produce large lateral forces and silent operation (Slide56.mp4) (Xu et al. 2018). As a result, we now have a nearly solid-state solution for applying in-plane forces to the finger. With a tool like the UltraShiver, we can begin to investigate a variety of physics-based applications including virtual inertia, damping, and springiness, as well as novel user interactions. The future is full of possibilities.

Acknowledgements The author is grateful to the students and colleagues mentioned in this article as well as collaborators Michael Peshkin, Roberta Klatzky, Tom Royston, and Sliman Bensmaia. Much of the material presented here is based upon work supported by the National Science Foundation grants number IIS-1302422 and IIS-1518602. Thank you to David Hoeft for videotaping the sessions.

References

Amazing contact juggling: Object manipulation. https://www.youtube.com/watch?v=w5MqvtiHpOw. Accessed 4 April 2019

Chubb EC, Colgate JE, Peshkin MA (2010) Shiverpad: a glass haptic surface that produces shear force on a bare finger. IEEE Trans Haptics 3(3):189–198

Dai X, Colgate JE, Peshkin MA (2012) Lateralpad: a surface-haptic device that produces lateral forces on a bare finger. In: 2012 IEEE haptics symposium (HAPTICS). IEEE, pp 7–14

Harrison C, Hudson SE (2009) Providing dynamically changeable physical buttons on a visual display. In: Proceedings of the SIGCHI conference on human factors in computing systems. ACM, pp 299–308

Kajimoto H, Kawakami N, Maeda T, Tachi S (1999) Tactile feeling display using functional electrical stimulation. In: Proceedings of the ICAT 1999, p 133

Kaye J (2012) Sawtooth planar waves for haptic feedback. In: Adjunct proceedings of the 25th annual ACM symposium on user interface software and technology. ACM, pp 5–6

Levesque V, Oram L, MacLean K, Cockburn A, Marchuk ND, Johnson D, Colgate JE, Peshkin MA (2011) Enhancing physicality in touch interaction with programmable friction. In: Proceedings of the SIGCHI conference on human factors in computing systems. ACM, pp 2481–2490

Meyer DJ, Peshkin MA, Colgate JE (2016) Tactile paintbrush: a procedural method for generating spatial haptic texture. In: 2016 IEEE haptics symposium (HAPTICS). IEEE, pp 259–264

Minsky M, Ming OY, Steele O, Brooks Jr, FP, Behensky M (1990) Feeling and seeing: issues in force display. In: ACM SIGGRAPH computer graphics, vol 24. ACM, pp 235–241

Mullenbach J, Blommer M, Colgate JE, Peshkin MA (2013) Reducing driver distraction with touchpad physics. PhD thesis, Thesis, Master of Mechanical Engineer, Evanston, Northwestern University, IL

Mullenbach J, Peshkin M, Colgate JE (2017) eShiver: lateral force feedback on fingertips through oscillatory motion of an electroadhesive surface. IEEE Trans Haptics 10(3):358–370

Mullenbach J, Shultz C, Colgate JE, Piper AM (2014) Exploring affective communication through variable-friction surface haptics. In: Proceedings of the SIGCHI conference on human factors in computing systems. ACM, pp 3963–3972
Mullenbach J, Shultz C, Piper AM, Peshkin M, Colgate JE (2013) Surface haptic interactions with a TPad tablet. In: Proceedings of the adjunct publication of the 26th annual ACM symposium on user interface software and technology. ACM, pp 7–8
Robles-De-La-Torre G, Hayward V (2001) Force can overcome object geometry in the perception of shape through active touch. Nature 412(6845):445
Saga S, Deguchi K (2012) Lateral-force-based 2.5-dimensional tactile display for touch screen. In: 2012 IEEE haptics symposium (HAPTICS). IEEE, pp 15–22
Shultz C, Colgate E, Peshkin MA (2018) The application of tactile, audible, and ultrasonic forces to human fingertips using broadband electroadhesion. IEEE Trans Haptics
Shultz CD, Peshkin MA, Colgate JE (2015) Surface haptics via electroadhesion: expanding electrovibration with Johnsen and Rahbek. In: 2015 IEEE world haptics conference (WHC). IEEE, pp 57–62
Wang D, Tuer K, Rossi M, Shu J (2004) Haptic overlay device for flat panel touch displays. In: 2004 12th international symposium on haptic interfaces for virtual environment and teleoperator systems, HAPTICS'04. Proceedings. IEEE, p 290
Watanabe T, Fukui S (1995) A method for controlling tactile sensation of surface roughness using ultrasonic vibration. In: 1995 IEEE international conference on robotics and automation, 1995. Proceedings, vol 1. IEEE, pp 1134–1139
Wiertlewski M, Friesen RF, Colgate JE (2016) Partial squeeze film levitation modulates fingertip friction. Proc Natl Acad Sci 113(33):9210–9215
Wiertlewski M, Leonardis D, Meyer DJ, Peshkin MA, Colgate JE (2014) A high-fidelity surface-haptic device for texture rendering on bare finger. In: International conference on human haptic sensing and touch enabled computer applications. Springer, pp 241–248
Xu H, Peshkin MA, Colgate JE (2018) Ultrashiver: lateral force feedback on a bare fingertip via ultrasonic oscillation and electroadhesion. In: 2018 IEEE haptics symposium (HAPTICS). IEEE, pp 198–203

Author Biography

J. Edward Colgate received the Ph.D. degree in mechanical engineering in 1988 from M.I.T. He subsequently joined Northwestern University in Evanston, Illinois, where he is currently a professor in the Department of Mechanical Engineering. Dr. Colgate's principal research interest is human–robot interaction. He has worked extensively in the areas of haptic. The sliding friction force gradually interface and teleoperation, and he, along with collaborator Michael Peshkin is the inventor of a class of collaborative robots known as "cobots." He has served as an associate editor of the Journal of Dynamic Systems, Measurement and Control and the IEEE Transactions on Robotics and Automation, and he is the founding Editor-in-Chief of the IEEE Transactions on Haptics. In addition to his academic pursuits, Dr. Colgate is a founder of Stanley Cobotics, the leading supplier of intelligent ergonomic assist devices to the industrial marketplace and of Kinea Design, a start-up devoted to rehabilitation robotics and advanced mechatronics. Dr. Colgate is currently the co-director (with Don Norman) of the Segal Design Institute at Northwestern University. In this capacity, he directs the Master of Science in Engineering Design and Innovation, which combines graduate-level engineering courses with a broad exposure to human-centered design.

MIX
Papier aus verantwortungsvollen Quellen
Paper from responsible sources
FSC® C105338

If you have any concerns about our products,
you can contact us on
ProductSafety@springernature.com

In case Publisher is established outside the EU,
the EU authorized representative is:
Springer Nature Customer Service Center GmbH
Europaplatz 3, 69115 Heidelberg, Germany

Printed by Libri Plureos GmbH
in Hamburg, Germany